The Fashion Designer's Textile Directory

The Fashion Designer's Textile Directory

Gail Baugh

BARRON'S

A QUARTO BOOK

First edition for North America published in 2011
by Barron's Educational Series, Inc.

All inquiries should be addressed to:
Barron's Educational Series, Inc.
250 Wireless Boulevard
Hauppauge, New York 11788
www.barronseduc.com

Library of Congress Control No.:
2010940124

ISBN-13: 978-0-7641-4628-2

QUAR.TXD

Conceived, designed, and produced by
Quarto Publishing plc
The Old Brewery
6 Blundell Street
London N7 9BH

Senior editor: Lindsay Kaubi
Art editor: Susi Martin
Designers: Susi Martin, Joanna Bettles
Picture researchers: Sarah Bell, Susi Martin
Copy editor: Diana Chambers
Photographer: Philip Wilkins
Illustrator: Chris Taylor
Art director: Caroline Guest

Creative director: Moira Clinch
Publisher: Paul Carslake

Color separation by Pica Digital Pte Ltd, Singapore

Printed by 1010 Printing International Ltd in China

9 8 7 6 5 4 3 2 1

Contents

Continued ▶

Author's foreword

I can't remember a time when fabric wasn't important to me. Working in Chicago-based Marshall Field & Company's enormous fabric department inspired me to complete my bachelor's degree in Textiles and Clothing, specializing in the chemistry of textiles, with an emphasis on apparel design.

My education was immediately useful when I became a womenswear and menswear buyer for Macy's. Later, as a sales agent representing a Japanese trading company, N.I.-Teijin Shoji (USA), Inc., I visited textile mills throughout Asia and Europe and saw firsthand how their behavior impacted local labor conditions and the environment. In 2010, my master's degree work focused on learning how consumers' behavior influenced the current selling and discarding of clothing and how their practices affected local economies and the environment.

I now teach the next generation of fashion designers and retailers and find that my students are eager to learn how to create a cleaner, less exploitative fashion industry. Further, the challenge of climate change is motivating the industry to explore new manufacturing and production methods throughout the traditional textile and garment supply chain.

This book represents my commitment to an ever-changing fashion industry that demands new information to implement new concepts. It is my aim that this book inspires designers and retailers whose decisions will truly express social and environmental values in the fashion industry.

The Fashion Designer's Textile Directory is a visual guide to fabric, focused on the way designers are trained to create apparel, rather than on how fabric is produced. This book simultaneously instructs in fabric, while also developing skills for the design room. Unlike many textile books, this text speaks to how a fabric will look on the body. And, for the first time, this directory acknowledges the environmental consequences of a designer's fabric choice.

Gail Baugh

About this book

This comprehensive guide to fashion textiles comprises four sections: an introduction to the role of the designer; an examination of the textile industry; an exhaustive directory of the textiles available to the designer, and a series of at-a-glance charts: it is a go-to reference for the designer.

Section one: Responsible design (pages 14–19)

This section is an introduction to the ecological and social responsibilities of the designer, and it includes in-depth discussion of how fashion designers can work toward a sustainable textile industry.

Section two: The language of textiles (pages 20–47)

This section discusses the role of designers in the fashion and textile industries and explains everything you need to know in order to understand and communicate with fabric producers and suppliers: it includes information on everything from fiber, yarn, and fabric production to finishing processes such as dyeing and printing.

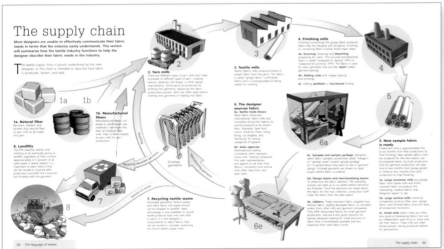

Section three: The textile directory (pages 48–287)

This comprehensive directory of textiles features everything from natural-fiber textiles such as linen and cotton to the latest technological manmade fabrics. It is organized into five color-coded chapters intended to lead the designer quickly to the right fabric.

The icons (see page 13)

Enlargement
Where relevant, an enlarged photo of the fabric is provided.

Fashion photography
Many of the textiles in the directory are illustrated with full-color photographs straight from the catwalk; demonstrating how fabrics are used in garments.

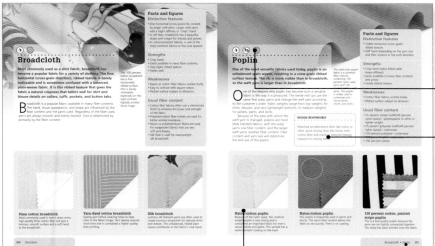

Textile swatches
Each textile featured includes swatches of some of the many different ways the textile can appear as a fabric.

Color coding
Each chapter of the directory is color coded.

Design responsibly
Throughout the directory, where relevant, the author raises any ecological concerns, good or bad, to maintain awareness of the designer's responsibility to consider the environmental and sociological impact of using certain textiles.

Chapter one:
Structure: form that stands away from the body, line created through shaping and seam detail.

Chapter two:
Fluidity: fabrics that flow over the body, following the human form.

Chapter three:
Ornamentation: creating details that will enhance the design.

Chapter four:
Expansion: exaggerating shapes away from the body.

Chapter five:
Compression: compacting the body, following the exact shape of the body.

Within these five categories the fabric entries are organized by weight, working progressively from top weight to bottom weight. Each textile entry includes a discussion of the textile's qualities; a list of distinctive features; strengths and weaknesses; and usual fiber content. The information is accompanied by a series of photographs of fabric samples showing the breadth of textiles available within each category, as well as relevant and inspiring images of the particular textile used for a fashion garment.

The icons
Graphic icons appear on each textile entry and indicate fabric weight and structure at a glance. They also illustrate any special features of the textile, such as water resistance or a wicking action. The icons allow the designer to understand the basic qualities of a fabric without the need for a lot of reading.

Continued ▶

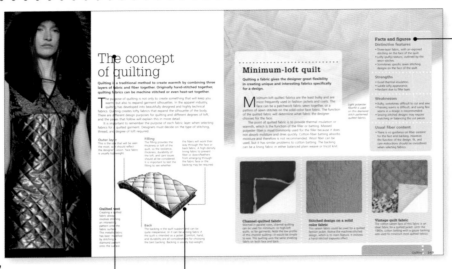

Facts and figures

For each fabric entry, there is a listing of facts and figures including distinctive features, strengths and weaknesses, and usual fiber content.

Textile "concepts"

Throughout the directory, key textile and garment construction concepts, such as quilting, pleating, and interlining are explained, with photographs and diagrams illustrating the idea.

Diagrams

Where a fabric has a specific technical quality, clear graphic diagrams explain how the textile is structured and how it functions.

Section four: The charts (pages 288–311)

The guides are a series of informative charts, which condense and present a lot of the information at the heart of the directory into highly functional tables. Organized by fabric structure—weave, knit, or massed fiber—they give information on fiber content, yarn type, fabric names, fabric weight, advantages and disadvantages, any finishes, and end use. The charts include the icons, cross refer to directory page numbers, and are color-coded so that you can easily find the relevant chapter in the directory.

Glossary, resources, and fold-out flap

At the end of the book you'll find a glossary of essential terms used in the book and listings of resources, including further reading, useful Websites, and relevant organizations. Opposite page 319 there is a fold-out flap that features a handy instant reference to the icons; you can leave it open while you look at the book so that you won't need to keep referring back to the icon explanation.

Color coding

Each fabric listed in the charts is color-coded to correspond with the chapters in the directory.

The icons

The icons illustrate the qualities and structure of a textile at a glance. They indicate the weight of the fabric and whether it's woven, knitted, or massed fiber, and any particular qualities, such as pile, water resistance, or wicking. Below is a key to all of the icons. This list also appears on the fold-out flap opposite page 319. For convenience you can keep the flap open while you use the book.

Fabric weight

 Top weight or lightweight fabrics (below 4 oz/113 g)
Blouses, shirts, tops, soft skirts, and dresses.

 Medium-weight fabrics (4 oz/113 g–below 6 oz/170 g)
Soft tops and bottoms with little structure. Dresses, tailored shirts, and lightweight jackets.

 Bottom-weight fabrics (above 6 oz/170 g)
Tailored jackets, skirts, and pants. Outerwear, coats, jeans, casual pants, and skirts.

Fabric production method
Knits

Weft knits

 Single knit

 Double knit

 Loop pile

Warp knits

 Raschel knit

 Tricot knit

 Loop pile

Fiber to fabric

 Fiber to fabric (massed fiber)

Fabric production method
Weaves

 Balanced (square) plain weave

 Unbalanced plain weave

 Basketweave

 Twill weave

 Satin weave

 Jacquard weave

 Dobby weave

 Loop pile

 Velvet weave

Finishes

 Brushed/sanded

 Cut (sheared) pile

 Coated finish

 Laminated

 Water-resistant

Responsible design

In this chapter, the designer's role in garment production will be explored, with a focus on responsible design and materials selection, awareness of the life cycle of a garment, and the sustainability of fabric production for the future.

The future of fabric production

Clothing consumption in the future can only be sustained when resources are conserved and workers in the clothing industry are respected.

Sustaining fiber and fabric production for the future of the apparel industry requires the designer to fully understand the components that support the fiber and fabric industries:

Land: arable land used for raw material and fiber production.
Chemicals: quantity and type of chemicals used.
Water: high water use.
Energy: high energy use.
Waste: fiber and fabric thrown away; chemicals and wastewater discarded.

An increasing global population demands more apparel. Therefore, the designer must choose fiber and fabrics that are more efficient in production and that reduce environmental impact. For many designers and consumers alike, organic fiber is the solution to the complex environmental issues that surround fiber and fabric production. In the future, the choice between natural fiber, and manufactured fiber, and how the fabrics are produced must be carefully considered.

Natural fiber
Occurring in nature, natural fiber is perceived as the best option when considering the impact on the environment of fiber and fabric

Soaking cocoons in water is an important step when separating silk fiber from the cocoon. The energy and water used to process the silk fiber involves a labor-intensive process and has yet to be measured in terms of its environmental impact.

production. Originating in the 1960s "hippie" movement, that rejected manufactured fiber in favor of natural fibers such as cotton or wool, this thinking continues today among designers. However, innovations in fiber, driven by the demand for high performance fabrics, and the need to find additional raw material supplies, have complicated fiber choices.

Natural fiber: Positives and negatives
Positives: renewable; feels good against the body; perceived luxury.
Negatives: excessive use of chemicals and water; chemicals and wastewater drained from cropland; too much land devoted to fiber production that is needed to grow food; large quantities of fiber and fabric discarded before garment production.

Manufactured fiber
Manufactured fiber is produced using a variety of raw materials. Fibers produced from oil (polyester, nylon, spandex, acrylic, and olefin) were developed between the 1950s and the 1970s. Fibers produced from plant raw materials (rayon and acetate) were developed over a century ago, and since the late 1990s they are becoming more popular again, with the introduction of PLA (corn) fiber, bamboo rayon, and others. Manufactured fiber consumes large amounts of energy and produces chemical emissions and chemical waste. Many innovations have now made some fiber production methods more efficient and produce less emissions and waste than ever before.

Manufactured fiber: Positives and negatives

Positives: Oil-based fibers (polyester and nylon) can now be recycled into new, high-quality fiber and can be manipulated for high-function fabrics. Plant-based manufactured fibers generally feel good against the skin. New fibers have been developed that nearly eliminate chemical pollution. There is often less fiber waste before fabric production than with natural fiber production.

Negatives: Both types of manufactured fiber produce chemical emissions and chemical waste that is expensive to neutralize and that is bad for the environment. Oil-based fibers use a nonrenewable raw material. Generally, these fibers don't feel good against the skin unless they are manipulated to address moisture control. Large quantities of fiber and fabric are discarded before garment production.

Considering sustainability

Regardless of the designer's point of view about the fiber selected, always consider its future sustainability. Assumptions regarding traditional fiber choices must be challenged, and it is the designer's role to forge new paths to show how emerging fiber and fabric innovations can be adopted rather than resisted.

Land, water, and energy resources

Designers need to understand the consequences of creating garments that require large amounts of land, water, and energy to make the fabrics and produce the garments. The designer must also inform the target market about how they can conserve water and energy during the care of the product.

Land

Renewable fibers and renewable raw materials for fiber can occupy arable land that could be used for food or energy production. Traditional natural fibers require large land areas for production. New renewable raw materials for manufactured fiber, such as corn, soy, and bamboo are competing with biomass energy-production resources. Therefore, the efficient use of land for fiber production must be considered.

Water

Water is the new gold, as the global population expands and the uncertainties of climate change make traditional water resources unpredictable. Designers must consider water use in fabric selection and garment finishing. For example, cotton fiber, produced in large quantities and accounting for nearly half of global fiber production, requires 1,400–2,100 gallons (5,300–7,950 liters) of water per pound (454 grams) of fiber, whether conventionally or organically grown.

In addition, garment producers now regularly garment-wash finished products for a softer, worn look that the consumer expects. Denim garment washing uses large quantities of water mixed with chemicals to achieve the desired color, softness, and appearance.

Top: Removing washed garments from large washing machines. The wet garments are extremely heavy, requiring manual strength to load into dryers. Bottom: Settling tanks to remove solid waste (dye, resins, and other chemicals) from wastewater after denim washing. Designers should consider how their designs use water, particularly in developing nations, where safe drinking water is not always available to the local population.

Denim jean producers are often located in developing countries, where clean drinking water is at a premium. The vast amount of wastewater from denim jean washing is not always cleaned before it is returned to the water system, making safe drinking water less available to the local population. Designers must consider how water is being used to create their designs. You should also be aware of innovations in fiber, fabric, and garment washing that will reduce water consumption.

In addition to the water used for clothing production, 80 percent of water used in the lifetime of a garment is devoted to consumer care. Designers can inspire consumers to conserve water in the care of their clothing through creative care labels and marketing.

Energy

Greenhouse gas emissions, usually in the form of carbon dioxide created during the generation of energy, are a major concern for global warming. Designers need to be aware of innovations in the textile field that will reduce energy use. Recycling fiber, particularly polyester and nylon fibers, can greatly reduce the energy required in production and create a new "closed loop" supply chain. Designers can now create products that, at the end of their lives, can be recycled into new, high-quality fiber, using substantially less energy than in the production of virgin fiber. It is your responsibility to know about these energy-saving innovations and translate them into your designs.

Passive solar air-drying (or "line-drying") should be encouraged by the designer to reduce energy used during consumer care. Avoiding the dryer not only conserves energy but extends the wearing life of a garment.

Lead by example

Conserving basic resources for sustaining fiber, fabric, and garment production for the future requires the designer to lead by example, selecting raw materials and

Line-drying fabric is common in developing countries, using very little energy to dry the fabric. This method may cause the dye to dry unevenly. Therefore, to prevent uneven color distribution in the fabric or garments, most drying in production is accomplished by tumble-action dryers, consuming significant amounts of energy in heat generation.

creating designs that use land, water, and energy efficiently and reduce chemical use. Awareness of conservation is a part of the designer's role, providing leadership by experimenting with production innovations as a part of the creative process.

Society and the environment respected

Designers have the opportunity to influence the fashion industry's social and environmental responsibility through "smart" design. Good labor practices and clean waste and wastewater disposal practices must be discussed in the design room. Insisting that all parts of the fashion industry treat workers and their communities fairly and do no harm to the environment as a part of the design process will bring more awareness of the designer's influence.

Smart design

Integrating innovation into new products is the role of the designer. Designing products that have "zero cutting waste," using sewing labor efficiently and, choosing materials that are sustainable and have multiple lives is not included in the majority of clothing design educational programs. It will be up to the designer to see for themselves how to implement design innovations that:

- Use sewing labor efficiently.
- Choose materials that can be sustained easily and be recycled.
- Reduce cutting waste to zero.
- Design products that have more than one life.

Social responsibility

Treating sewing factory workers fairly is one of the fashion industry's biggest challenges. Seeking low-cost labor to produce complicated designs quickly can encourage suppliers to exploit labor in developing countries. Designers must engage in discussions about creating designs that can be produced using fair labor practices. Their designs should take into account how much waste is being generated in production, both fabric-cutting waste and wastewater containing dyes, bleach, and other chemicals. Designers must understand the impact on local society of these waste products generated in the production of their designs.

Environmental responsibility

According to the United States Environmental Protection Agency, all clothing will go to a landfill, even donations that are given to charity. All clothing, whether organic cotton or polyester, will eventually be thrown away unless it is recycled into new fiber, so it is the designer's responsibility to design products that can have multiple lives. The concept of reuse has been limited to those who are unable to afford new. Today, reuse means diverting products from landfill and continuously using them in varying forms. Therefore, in addition to the waste products mentioned, designers must consider what happens to their product when the consumer has finished using it. Selecting materials that can be reused or recycled is one way to begin avoiding landfill use.

Top: A worker applying chemicals to individual jeans for a particular "worn" appearance. Bottom: Sewers in a garment factory's sewing line. Protecting the health and safety of garment workers must be part of the designer's responsibility.

The language of textiles

The ability to communicate easily, using terms that the textile industry understands, is a skill successful designers need to master. This chapter will help the designer understand what questions he or she must be prepared to ask when visiting textile suppliers: What is the function of the design? What is the fabric construction? Does fiber content matter? What fabric weight is required? When is fabric needed?

The supply chain

Most designers are unable to effectively communicate their fabric needs in terms that the industry easily understands. This section will summarize how the textile industry functions to help the designer describe their fabric needs in the industry.

The textile supply chain is poorly understood by the new designer, so this chart is intended to describe how fabric is produced, shown, and sold.

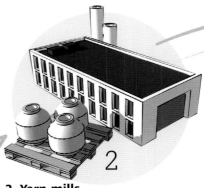

2. Yarn mills

There are different types of yarn mills that make hundreds of different types of yarn, creating texture, elasticity, soft drape, or other design requirements. Some yarns are produced for knitting into garments, bypassing the fabric production process. Yarns are often dyed before knitting into garments or making into fabric.

1a   1b

1a. Natural fiber

Ranchers, herders, and farmers ship natural fiber to yarn mills to be made into yarn.

1b. Manufactured fibers

Manufactured fibers—oil-based or plant-based raw materials—are made into fiber at chemical fiber mills. Fiber is then shipped to yarn mills for yarn production.

8. Landfills

The EPA classifies textiles and clothing as all eventually going to landfill, regardless of fiber content. Approximately 4–5 percent of all solid waste is textile related. It is important to select fabrics that can be reused or recycled after production and after the consumer has finished with the garment.

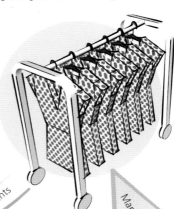

Recycling

Recycling discarded garments

Manufacturing garments

Finished garments

Factory cut waste

7. Recycling textile waste

Discarded garments, factory waste, and other fabric mill waste should not be shipped to landfills. New technology is now available to recycle textile products back into new fiber or yarns. It is the designer's responsibility to select fabrics that can be reused or recycled, sustaining the future textile supply chain.

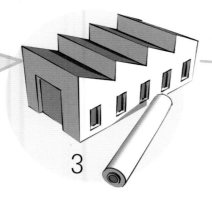

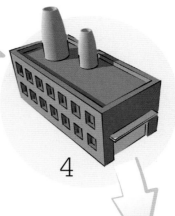

3. Textile mills
Textile (fabric) mills produce knitted or woven fabric from the yarns. This fabric is called "greige fabric" (unfinished fabric) and is unrecognizable as being usable for clothing.

4. Finishing mills
Finishing (converting) the greige fabric produces fabric that the designer will recognize. Finishing or converting fabric involves three major steps:

4a. Scouring (cleaning) and **bleaching** (preparing for color). This scoured and bleached fabric is called "prepared for dyeing" (PFD) or "prepared for printing" (PFP). The fabric is used for sewn garments that are later **dyed** (called garment-dyeing).

4b. Adding color and images (dyeing and printing).

4c. Adding **aesthetic** or **functional** finishes.

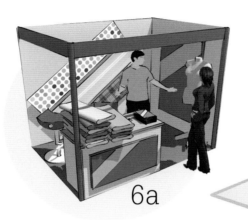

6. The designer sources fabric
6a. Textile trade shows: Most fabric shows are international. Fabric mills and converters bring their fabrics to central locations to be shown: Paris, Shanghai, New York, Como, Florence, Prato, Hong Kong, Los Angeles, and Hamburg, for various categories of apparel.

6b. Sales agencies: Multinational trading companies often represent many mills. Trading companies hire sales representatives and agents to sell their mills' fabrics. Converters and vertical mills often have their own sales team.

6c. Samples and sample yardage: Designers select fabric samples (sometimes called "hangers" or "sample cards") and/or sample yardage (3–15 yards/meters) they want to test in garment design. Finished garments are shown to retail buyers before fabric is ordered.

6d. Design teams and merchandising teams: To determine the fabric selection. The sampling process can take up to six weeks before decisions are finalized. Once the decisions are made about the fabric for the new collection, production staff order the fabric from the sales agent.

6e. Jobbers: These important fabric suppliers buy leftover fabric, slightly damaged fabric, or canceled orders from other mills and garment companies. They offer discounted fabrics for small garment production, and are a very good resource for startup designers looking for small amounts of fabric that is immediately available and less expensive than retail fabric stores.

5. New sample fabric is ready
Production time is approximately five to six months from fiber production to final finishing. New sample fabrics that are prepared for the new season can be prepared faster, but bulk production time for garment production will take one to two months from greige goods, or three to four months from yarn production to final finishing.

5a. Large converter mills buy greige fabric from textile mills and finish (convert) fabric to produce the interesting, creative fabrics that designers expect to see.

5b. Large vertical mills (chemical companies) produce fiber, yarn, greige fabric, and finished fabric (one mill does all production functions).

5c. Small mills (fabric mills) are often very good at developing fabrics but use an independent sales force to show and sell their fabrics. These mills are often family-owned, having produced textiles for generations.

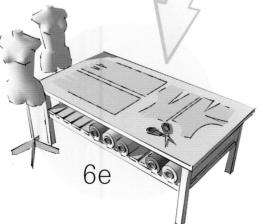

Fabric orientation

Like reading a map, planning a garment design requires the designer to describe the fabric in terms of direction and placement. Grain line direction greatly influences the performance of the fabric in the garment silhouette. Placement will influence fabric texture, color, and pattern matching.

I t is essential to understand basic fabric terminology. This diagram provides a visual landscape of how any fabric is described during the designing, fitting, cutting, and sewing process.

The fabric side intended for the outside of the garment is called the "face." The designer can choose and clearly mark for the "face" side. The textile mill should be informed of the designer's intention so the fabric face can be well inspected. The side intended for the inside of the garment is called the "back."

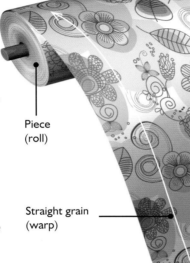

Top

Bias (45-degree angle across the fabric)

Piece (roll)

Straight grain (warp)

Cross-grain (weft or filling)

Face

Selvage

Top and bottom

Knowing the top and bottom of a fabric will assist in determining the orientation of the garment pieces being cut.

- You should know the nap direction of a brushed or cut-pile fabric (nap-up and nap-down): the up and down directions are determined from the "top" of the fabric.

- A one-way image on a fabric must have pattern pieces cut in the same direction. Determining the "top" of the fabric will direct the fabric cutters as to how to lay down the pattern pieces on the fabric.

Velvet (bottom: nap-up and top: nap-down)

One-way image

Terms to know

Grain lines on the fabric guide the designer as to how to use the fabric's characteristics to the design's best advantage. Both woven and knitted fabrics have grain lines—straight grain, cross-grain, and bias grain.

Straight grain

Straight grain is the strongest direction of the fabric, which is best at resisting pulling and tearing. Designers use the straight grain for strength and to keep the fabric close to the body. In woven fabrics, straight grain is also called the "warp" direction. In knitted fabrics, it is called "straight grain."

Cross-grain

The direction of cross-grain wovens will provide a little "give" or slight expansion of the fabric, which can accommodate normal body expansions such as sitting or breathing. The fabric will tend to fall away from the body, not stay close, in the cross-grain direction. In woven fabrics, it is also called the "weft" or "filling" direction. In knitted fabrics, it is called "cross-grain."

Bias grain

Bias is a very creative grain line because it can cause the fabric to become stretchable as well as flexible or drapey. A bias grain line is always at a 45-degree angle from the straight grain line and is the only diagonal grain line used in pattern-making. Bias grain lines cause the fabric to flare away from the body in very interesting ways. Both woven and knitted fabrics use bias grain.

Other terms

"Selvage" is the finished edge of woven fabric. In knitted fabric, the edge of the fabric can be the cut edge or similar to the woven fabric edge. In both fabrics, the selvage helps to stabilize the edges of the fabric for accurate cutting. In red selvage denim, red yarns are woven into the selvage, and the selvage becomes a visible part of the design.

"Piece" refers to a roll of fabric. Mass-produced fabric is rolled onto cardboard tubes, usually in 50- or 100-yard (50- or 100-meter) quantities. It is common to ask for one "piece" of fabric for design sampling. Only the terms "roll" or "piece" are used to refer to fabric for shipment.

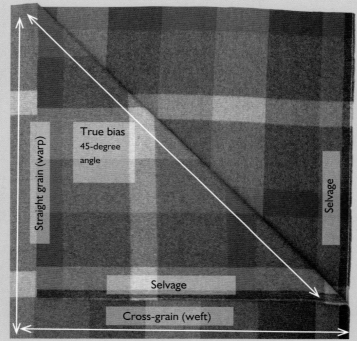

Straight grain (warp)

True bias
45-degree angle

Selvage

Selvage

Cross-grain (weft)

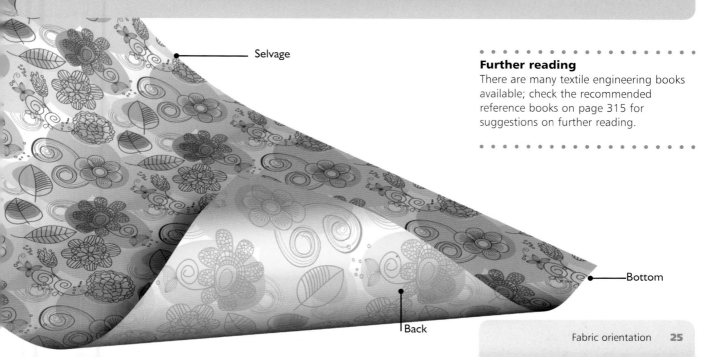

Selvage

Back

Bottom

Further reading

There are many textile engineering books available; check the recommended reference books on page 315 for suggestions on further reading.

Fiber

Fiber is the basic building block of textiles. Fibers are tiny, hairlike strands that are combined to create yarn and fabric.

There are two different types of fiber that go into the manufacture of yarn for fabric:

Staple: Short strands. Cotton is up to 2½ in (6 cm) long and stem (flax) fiber is longer. High-quality staple fiber is finer and longer, and low-quality staple fiber is coarser and shorter.

Filament: Continuous strands. High-quality filament fiber is usually finer and stronger, but quality is mostly determined by the end use of the fiber.

The fiber supply chain for fabric is complex, including the resources needed for natural fiber and for manufactured fiber. This complexity makes the transparency of the textile industry for social and environmental concerns difficult to maintain. There are several issues of concern in fiber production.

Social and environmental impact

Water use: Cotton accounts for nearly half of global fiber production and uses large amounts of water compared to other natural fibers. In addition, approximately one-third of the cotton harvest is usable. Hemp, bamboo, and flax (linen) use less water and have a higher yield than cotton.

Energy use: Manufactured fiber consumes large amounts of energy in production, but little water. Fiber production is very efficient, however.

Emissions generated: Crop chemicals and manufactured fiber production generate emissions that are unhealthy to breathe. Crop emissions are unregulated by clean air monitors, while manufactured fiber mill emissions are controlled.

Conservation of fiber supply

Innovations in fiber are especially concerned with how to conserve the fiber already produced. Designers must stay aware of these innovations to integrate them into their work.

Fiber reuse: Cut cotton fabric waste is now collected and made into new yarns and fabric. Wool fabrics have been recycled into new products for generations.

Recycling into new, high-quality fiber: All polyester and certain nylon fibers can be recycled. Designers should produce garments that can be easily recycled into new fiber.

Here, cotton waste has been bagged for landfill. Methods now exist to collect fiber and fabric waste at the mills and to use it for further yarn and fabric production.

The image at the top is texturized polyester fiber. Texturizing is one way to imitate natural fiber like cotton or wool. The other three images are of natural fiber sources: hemp, silk, and nettle.

This microscopic image of two different fibers, wool (light brown) and synthetic (red), shows differences in fiber surface texture and shape. These and other distinguishing features create the different fiber characteristics described in the fiber charts over the page

Staple fiber

Staple fiber can be either natural fiber or manufactured fiber. Characterized as short fiber, usually no longer than about 2½ in (6.4 cm), each fiber source provides certain characteristics to the fiber. This chart summarizes these characteristics for the designer.

Both plants and animals are primarily staple fiber resources. From top to bottom: flax (linen); sisal; Angora goat (mohair).

Natural staple fiber

Fiber characteristics

Fiber name	Positive	Negative
Plant (cellulose) fiber **Seed fiber (from seed pod)** Cotton Kapok	**Characteristics of all plant seed fiber** Absorbent Strong when wet Conducts heat well Good abrasion resistance No static buildup Dyes well Matte appearance	Not colorfast in dark tones Shrinks Heavy fiber when wet Not fast-drying Poor resilience Can be attacked by mildew/pests Flammable No elasticity Fair resistance to sun
Bast (stem) fiber Flax (linen) Hemp Ramie Bamboo Kenaf Nettle Jute	**Characteristics of all plant bast fiber** Very absorbent Very strong when wet Excellent abrasion resistance No static buildup Accepts dye moderately well Doesn't shrink much Dyes well Somewhat lustrous appearance No elasticity Some are mildew-resistant Some are anti-microbial Faster drying than cotton	Not colorfast in dark tones Brittle on folded edges Poor resilience Fair resistance to sun Flammable
Leaf fiber Sisal Pina Abaca	Varies by leaf origin	Stiff, coarse hand Poor dyeability
Animal (protein) fiber Fleece (sheared from sheep) Wool Merino wool	**Characteristics of all animal fiber** Matte appearance Good abrasion resistance Good elastic recovery Excellent resilience Excellent absorbency Wicks moisture Dyes well Good colorfastness Retains heat well	Poor strength Elongates easily Shrinks easily Very heavy when wet Dries slowly Can be attacked by insects Mulesing in shearing Sheep-dip chemicals
Specialty fleece Mohair (sheared from Angora goat)	Lustrous appearance Extremely resilient Very fine fiber Resists pilling Same as for wool	Expensive Same as for wool
Specialty hair Cashmere (usually combed from animal) Camel hair Alpaca/Vicuna	Very soft hand Retains heat without weight Dyes well Good colorfastness Excellent resilience	Expensive Poor abrasion resistance Poor strength Shrinks easily Can be attacked by insects

Manufactured staple fibers

Fiber created in a chemical plant can be produced as staple fiber, too. Several common staple fibers are manufactured and, when they are spun into yarn and fabrics, it is often difficult to distinguish them from natural staple fiber. It is important to compare fiber characteristics when choosing fabric fiber content.

Fiber blending

Combining two or more different fibers into a single yarn or fabric blends the fibers' characteristics. Blending cotton with small amounts of wool can create a wrinkle-resistant fabric without chemical finishing. However, when washed, the garment may shrink unexpectedly. Blending polyester with cotton also creates a wrinkle-resistant fabric without shrinkage concerns. Fiber blending can be accomplished in the following ways:

Intimate blending: mixing staple fibers together before spinning yarn. Staple polyester and cotton fibers are mixed, and then spun into yarn.

Complex yarn blending: combining different fiber content yarns together into one yarn. For example, one polyester yarn, one spandex yarn, and one cotton yarn are combined into a single complex yarn.

Fabric blending: combining several one-fiber content yarns together into one fabric.

Manufactured staple fiber   Fiber characteristics

Fiber name	Positive	Negative
Regenerated cellulosic staple fiber (plant material + chemicals) **Viscose rayon** **Note:** Other regenerated cellulose fibers, such as PLA, may also be used as staple fiber.	**Characteristics of both rayon fibers** Matte appearance Very soft, cool hand Excellent dyeability Fair colorfastness, especially black/deep tones Good abrasion resistance Very absorbent No static buildup Moderate cost Poor resilience	Poor resilience Polluting emissions Hazardous chemical waste Weakens when wet Not machine washable Can be attacked by mildew
Lyocell rayon	All of the above Machine washable Higher cost than viscose	Moderate resilience Fair colorfastness
Synthetic staple fiber (oil-based material + chemicals) **Polyester** Virgin (new fiber) Recycled polyester (recycled from polyester fiber/fabric/garments)	**Characteristics of both polyester fibers** Can be heat-set yet remain soft Excellent resilience Dries fast Excellent abrasion resistance Strong Manipulated for many functions Easily washed/no shrinkage Easily blended with other fibers Recyclable into high-quality fiber Sunlight-resistant Resists mildew/insects	Static buildup Nonabsorbent Absorbs oil easily Pills easily Melts in high heat
PET polyester (produced from plastic bottles) **Note:** A new generic fiber, "triexta" (USA) is partially plant-derived polyester and is recyclable, reducing the need for oil-based raw materials and lowering energy consumption and CO_2 emissions.	Fast-drying Excellent resilience Easily washed/no shrinkage Blended for strength Easily blended with other fibers Recyclable into same fiber	Same as above Irregular weak fiber Must be blended with virgin fiber for strength
Nylon Virgin (new fiber) Recycled (from nylon fiber, fabric, and garments)	**Characteristics of both nylon fibers** Excellent strength Excellent abrasion resistance Easily washed/no shrinkage Excellent resilience Recyclable Resists mildew/pests	Somewhat stiff Nonabsorbent Weakens on long exposure to sunlight Poor to fair colorfastness in sunlight
Acrylic and modacrylic (polluting emissions and chemical waste)	**Characteristics of both fibers** Imitates wool/hair Moderate resilience Easily washed Fair abrasion resistance	Nonabsorbent Pills easily Very heat-sensitive Not recyclable May shrink Acrylonitrile fiber chemical emissions linked to cancer

Filament fiber

Filament fibers are continuous, hairlike strands. Filament fiber occurs as natural fiber and is the initial phase in producing all manufactured fiber.

Spiders and silkworms produce continuous, smooth fiber from which to make webs and cocoons. Manufactured fiber imitates this natural method of extruding fiber from a liquid.

Manufactured filament fibers

Manufactured filament fibers are produced when a chemical fiber compound is passed through a spinneret to form filament fibers. Manufactured fiber was developed over 100 years ago to dramatically increase fiber supply for the new mass production of garments. The new clothing factories were expanding and in need of consistent fabric production. Imitating silk fiber was the original goal of manufactured fiber research. Rayon was the new "silk" and created low-cost fabrics for mass consumption.

Manufactured fiber process

The diameter and shape of the filament fiber often determines the hand, weight, and function of the fabric. There are four main fiber shapes:

Round: smooth/lustrous.
Lobed: bright sheen.
Serrated: textured/dull.
Hollow: very lightweight.

Microfiber is one filament fiber split into many new fibers for extremely fine, very flexible fiber. Microfibers are now produced in polyester, nylon, and acrylic fibers. Polyester is the most commonly used microfiber, manipulated to function in athletic apparel for wicking moisture and moisture resistance. Some microfibers are used for extremely soft, drapey fabrics that are also very lightweight.

Closed loop: definition

Manufactured fiber production creates waste products that must be neutralized/treated before they are released from the mill. In closed loop production nearly all unused products are recycled into new production. Minimal wastewater is generated, although emissions may be released.

Recyclable: definition

Fiber, fabric, and garments can be re-formed into the same or higher-quality fiber. A chemical process is required to break down the textile product and re-form it into fiber.

Manufactured filament fibers are produced by passing a chemical fiber compound through a nozzle with very fine holes called a spinneret.

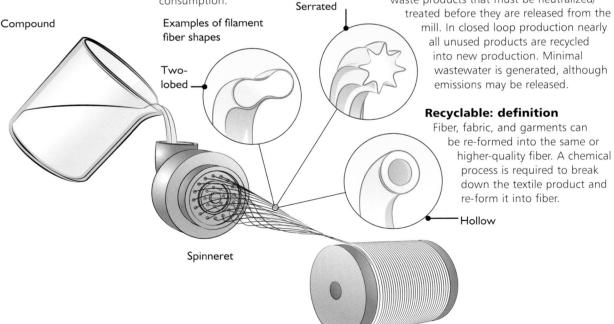

Compound

Examples of filament fiber shapes

Two-lobed

Serrated

Hollow

Spinneret

Regenerated cellulose filament fiber — Fiber characteristics

Fiber name	Positive	Negative
Cellulosic filament fiber (plant material + chemicals) **Acetate**	**Regenerated fiber characteristics** Very lustrous/shiny, silk-like appearance	Fair to poor absorbency Low heat resistance Not washable Not recyclable Polluting emissions
Viscose rayon	Lustrous/shiny appearance Very soft, cool hand Excellent dyeability, especially black/deep tones Good abrasion resistance Very absorbent No static buildup Moderate cost	Poor resilience Polluting emissions Hazardous chemical waste Fair colorfastness Weakens when wet Not machine washable Can be attacked by mildew Not recyclable
Lyocell rayon (Closed-loop fiber production; chemicals are recycled into new fiber production)	All of the above Machine washable	Fair resilience Fair colorfastness Can be attacked by mildew Not recyclable Higher cost than viscose
Bamboo rayon (If using closed-loop fiber production, this is a very sustainable fiber) **Note:** If a manufactured fiber, bamboo must include rayon in its name.	All of the above Antimicrobial/no mildew Easily renewable raw material Fair resilience	Always filament fiber If viscose method, not machine washable Not recyclable
PLA (From plant sugars, especially corn; closed-loop fiber production)	Similar to lyocell rayon Blends well with cotton fiber	PLA is very heat-sensitive (new research is addressing this problem)
Soy (Plant protein from tofu waste products; closed-loop fiber production)	Very soft/good drape Moderate strength Very absorbent Dyes wells/good colorfastness	Not easily available Fair abrasion resistance Weakens when wet Not recyclable

Note: New raw materials are being introduced for new fiber production. Stay alert for new developments. The list above includes fibers in use now.

These manufactured filament fibers can look very different from each other due to their fiber shape and the method of cooling the fibers after extrusion from the spinneret. Top: soy. Bottom: bamboo rayon.

Nylon filament fiber can be produced as microfiber and manipulated to resemble cotton fiber. Its quick-drying characteristic has made nylon a favorite fiber to blend with cotton for lightweight outdoor clothing.

Synthetic filament fiber

Fiber characteristics

Fiber name

	Positive	Negative
Polyester Virgin (new fiber) Recycled (from polyester fiber/fabric/garments) **Note:** "Triexta," formerly "ptt," is a new generic fiber, which is partially made from plant-derived polyester and which is also recyclable, thereby reducing oil-based raw materials and energy consumption needed for fiber production, and CO_2 emissions.	**Characteristics of both polyester fibers** Can be heat-set yet remain soft Excellent resilience Fast-drying Excellent abrasion resistance Strong Manipulated for many functions Easily washed/no shrinkage Easily blended with other fibers Recyclable into high-quality fiber Sunlight-resistant Resists mildew/insects	Static buildup Nonabsorbent Absorbs oil easily Pills easily Melts in high heat
Nylon Virgin (new fiber) Recycled (from nylon fiber/fabric/garments)	**Characteristics of both nylon fibers** Excellent strength Excellent abrasion resistance Easily washed/no shrinkage Excellent resilience Resists mildew/pests Recyclable into high-quality fiber	Somewhat stiff Nonabsorbent Static buildup Not sunlight-resistant
Elastic fibers (also monofilament yarns) Spandex Elastoester, triexta, and elasterell-p*	**Characteristics of both elastic fibers** Excellent elasticity Excellent resilience	Fair to poor abrasion resistance Fair to poor strength
Metallic (also monofilament yarns)	Shiny, metallic appearance Very lightweight	Weak fiber Poor heat resistance
Carbon fiber (nanotubes are of interest in fiber development) * Some polyester-based elastic fibers may be recyclable.	Extremely lightweight Extremely strong Conducts electricity	Very expensive

Silk fiber, while produced under varying cocoon circumstances, will always produce fiber that dyes beautifully.

Natural filament fiber

Fiber characteristics

Fiber name

	Positive	Negative
Silk (All silk fiber begins as filament, but may become staple fiber as fiber waste)	Lustrous Soft hand/drape Very good absorbency Moderate resilience Easily dyed	Expensive Fair colorfastness Fair elasticity
Spider silk (Working on genetically modified spider silk—not yet commercially available)	Extremely elastic Extremely strong Very lightweight Conducts electricity	In research now

Yarn

Recycled fiber

Certain types of nylon and all polyester fibers, which are oil-based, can be recycled into new, high-quality fiber. Polyester fiber represents more than 40 percent of global fiber production, yet supplies of its basic raw material, oil, will decrease in the future. All types of polyester fiber, yarns, fabric, and even garments can be recycled. Even PET fiber, from plastic bottles, can be recycled into new PET fiber.

Natural fiber is difficult to recycle. Efforts are being made to capture cotton fabric cutting waste and reuse it; however, the yarns are weak and virgin fiber must be added to strengthen the yarn. Wool has been recycled for generations, but the tradition is not widely used today.

A key point to understand is the need to select materials that are not blends but are 100 percent one fiber, and to select sewing thread that can also be recycled in the same manner as the fabric.

Manipulating manufactured filament fiber

Texture: After filament fiber is formed, the fiber is "crimped" or kinked to imitate cotton or wool texture. Texture is one way to create elasticity in a nonelastic fiber.

Bi-component: During extrusion (see page 30), two different fiber solutions are combined, forming one filament that contains two separate fibers. When heat is applied, the fiber will respond unevenly to create texture. There are other reasons to produce bi-component fiber, which should be explored by the designer with suppliers.

Performance: fibers can be modified to enhance moisture management, such as moisture wicking and absorption, water resistance, antibacterial qualities, shrinkage, stain resistance, anti-static qualities, thermal insulation, and decreased water and air resistance.

Yarn is a continuous strand produced from the various staple or filament fibers, or other materials. Yarns must be strong enough to be interlaced, looped together, or otherwise used to create two-dimensional, flexible fabric surfaces.

Yarns were invented by twisting staple fibers together (in a process known as spinning) to create a continuous strand. Creating yarns from long filament fibers is basically the same process, though less twisting (spinning) is necessary. The amount of yarn twist will determine the strength of the yarn (the higher the twist, the stronger the yarn) and the direction of the twist will influence the texture.

The three basic yarns are:

Spun yarn: uses staple fibers twisted together. Long staple fibers will produce a smooth, lustrous yarn (such as high-quality cotton or merino wool). Short staple fibers will produce coarse, dull yarn (such as low-quality cotton or PET polyester staple fibers). Some 20 percent of staple fibers for spun yarn becomes waste fiber. In most cases, this waste fiber is disposed of, whether it is organic cotton fiber or cheap polyester staple fiber. However, this "fiber dust" is now being captured and made into low-quality spun yarn. Remember that staple fibers can be natural or manufactured.

In general, high-quality spun yarns are finer in diameter and more lustrous than low-quality yarns because long staple fibers are spun together. Spun yarns are measured by a yarn count system, for example, a large cotton yarn size 12 is used for heavy denim and a fine yarn size 60 is used for fine shirting.

The importance of yarn in fabric

The yarn used greatly influences the hand, drape, and appearance of the fabric. It is important for the designer, especially a knitwear designer, to closely observe which yarns are used because yarn is one of the most important factors in fabric cost. There are two main categories of yarn—simple and complex—which include both spun and multifilament yarns.

Simple yarn
(One consistent fiber content)

Single yarn: one yarn

Plied yarn
(Two or more yarns combined)
2-ply (Contains two yarns of the same fiber content)

Complex yarns
(Multiple combinations of fibers and yarns)

Single yarn: one yarn
Tweed yarn (multiple fibers/colors)
Slub yarn (uneven yarn size)

Plied yarn
(Two or more yarns combined)
Bouclé
Chenille

Elastic plied yarn
(Contains elastic monofilament yarn covered by another yarn)
Core spun (plied with spun yarn)
Core wrapped (covered by bulky-textured multifilament yarn)

Monofilament yarn: uses only one filament (mono) fiber as a yarn, such as spandex or metallic fiber.

Multifilament yarn: uses filament fiber only, such as filament silk, polyester, or rayon. There is almost no fiber waste in multifilament yarn production. Two main types of multifilament yarns are used:
1. Texturized multifilament yarns that create elastic, spunlike, or bulk or loft yarns.
2. Smooth multifilament yarns that create lustrous, sometimes shiny yarns.

High-quality multifilament yarns are generally judged by the fineness of the diameter and the perceived value of the fiber used. Most new designers perceive silk filament yarns to be higher quality than polyester filament yarns. However, to an athletic apparel designer, the nuances of performance polyester fiber are highly valued. A yarn count denier (D) system is used to measure yarn size. A size 15D yarn is used for lightweight lingerie and a 100D yarn is used for backpacks.

Yarn categories

Simple yarns (one fiber content)

Single yarn

Plied yarn

Complex yarns (multiple fiber content), plied yarns

Tweed yarn

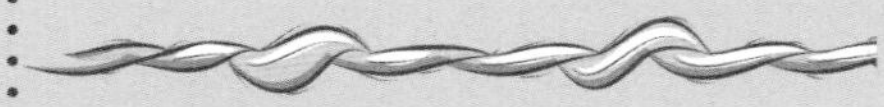

Slubbed yarn

Specialty yarns for special effect

Boucle yarn

Chenille yarn

Elastic plied yarns (monofilament elastic core)

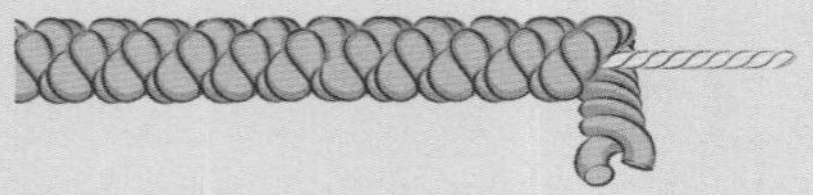

Core-spun: Spun yarn coiled around an elastic core.

Core-wrapped: Bulk textured mutifilament yarn wrapped around an elastic core.

Fabrics

Fabric is the medium of the garment designer. It is a two-dimensional, flexible surface that is transformed into a three-dimensional form through the vision of the designer.

Knowledge of why and how a fabric behaves in the design process is often rooted in understanding the construction of the fabric. While fiber and yarn will help determine hand and drape, the overall performance of a fabric depends on how the fiber or yarn is used during construction and finishing. Fabric is produced using one of three methods:

1. Massing fiber together creates fabric directly from fiber, without the need for first producing yarns. This requires an understanding of a fiber's characteristics and what will hold fibers together to form a two-dimensional surface. The fibers can be shrunk, melted, or tangled together.

2. Weaving requires yarn production first. The strength of the yarns and their texture are important determining features for the woven fabric.

3. Knitting also requires yarn production. Yarns can be less strong than for weaving, allowing for wide variety in yarn type for greater texture in knitted fabric.

Environmental impact
It is important to understand the environmental impact of fabric and fiber production. Spun yarn production generates 20 percent fiber waste. Fabric production requires machinery, technical expertise, access to yarn mills, and efficient use of labor. Both fiber and fabric production impact the available clean water, air emissions, chemical waste, and use of energy.

Mill waste
Weaving creates more waste than knitting, both as yarn released from the loom and as selvage trim waste, and it is nearly all considered unrecoverable waste. Considering the amount of denim produced each year, the designer should ask how the denim mills manage waste.

Energy use
The power used to run textile mills is significant. It is important to understand how the energy consumed is generated, especially as a large amount of fabric production takes place in developing countries. The use of regional energy sources, such as solar, wind, water, and others should be encouraged, especially in the production of sustainable fiber sources, such as organic cotton or recycled polyester.

Recycling textile products
Methods for recycling discarded textiles include shredding fabric and garments into fiber and using the fiber in felted or fiberweb fabrics. This process is a newly emerging area; designers should stay alert to new developments.

Fabric method 1: Massing (fiber to fabric) characteristics

Fiber is massed together on a flat surface (similar to paper-making) to create fabric. Yarn is not used. There is ongoing research to create more apparel fabric using fiber instead of yarn.

Method	Positive	Negative
Felt (Mostly wool fiber, sometimes blended with rayon or polyester)	Thick fabric to hold form Can be shaped with steam and pressure	Shrinks Poor strength
Fiberweb (Bonded together by various methods)		
Needle-punch fabric (Dry-laid process; staple fibers used)	Uses spinning mill waste and recycled staple fibers	Fair to poor strength No water in fabric production
Wet-laid fabric (Staple fibers used)	Uses spinning mill waste and other low-quality fibers Water is reclaimed and reused	Little use in apparel
Spunbonded fabric (Filament fibers are melted)	No water used Used as interlining for apparel	Uses oil-based fibers

Fabric method 2: Weaving

Weaving fabric is accomplished on a loom by interlacing two or more yarns at right angles. It is this angular construction, with yarns at 90-degree angles—warp yarns parallel to the selvage and weft yarns perpendicular to the selvage—that distinguishes weaving from other fabric construction methods. Most woven fabrics are rigid, with little stretch.

There are four main weave structures that are commonly used: plain weave, basketweave, twill weave, and satin weave. There are also a variety of other special-interest weaves, such as jacquard and dobby. Weaving requires strong warp yarns, and production is slower than for knitted fabric.

Fabric density, or yarn count, combined with yarn size, determines the weight of the fabric:

- **Higher density fabric:** more yarns in a square inch/cm = more opaque.
- **Lower density fabric:** fewer yarns in a square inch/cm = more sheer.

Weaving is now an automated process, using a variety of loom machinery to produce fabric at high speed. All looms require strong warp yarns to be set up first before weaving can begin.

Plain weave

In plain weave, each yarn is interlaced with every other yarn. There are no floating yarns and the surface has subtle texture. Ribbed weaves have a cross-grain (horizontal) ribbed texture.

Balanced plain weave			Unbalanced plain weave
(Also called square weave)			(Also called ribbed weave)
Batiste	Flannel	Muslin	Broadcloth
Buckram	Flannelette	Organdy	Crêpe de Chine
Burlap	Gauze	Organza	Faille
Challis	Georgette	Ripstop	Ottoman
Chambray	Gingham	Sheeting	Poplin
Chiffon	Homespun/crash	Voile	Shantung
China silk	Lawn		Taffeta
Crepon	Madras		
Crinoline			

Basketweave

Some basketweave fabrics are slightly different but use the same fabric name.

Balanced basketweave
(2 warp x 2 weft)
Canvas
Duck
Hopsacking

Unbalanced basketweave
(1 warp x 2 weft)
Canvas
Duck
Oxford/pinpoint Oxford
Oxford
Sailcloth

Twill weave

Twill weave is recognized by the diagonal line texture on the fabric surface, which is created by floating over two or more yarns at regular intervals. There are balanced and unbalanced twill constructions, but all are referred to simply as twill fabrics.

Cavalry twill
Chino twill
Drill
Gabardine
Herringbone
Houndstooth
Serge
Surah

More about twills

Because of the diagonal surface texture, fabrics are softer and more drapey than plain, basket, or satin weaves.

All denim fabric is a twill weave, but yarn size and quality will influence the final product.

Due to the floating yarns over two to four yarns, twill fabrics are considered the most durable construction, especially when using cotton, hemp, flax, polyester, or nylon yarn.

Satin weave

Satin weave is made up of randomly floating yarns over five or more yarns and is recognized by its smooth, shiny, or lustrous surface. Satin weaves tend to be stiff, except when fine, very flexible yarns are used.

Bridal satin
Charmeuse
Satin

All satin fabrics use lustrous multifilament yarns.

Sateen

All sateen fabrics use spun yarn, relying on the shiny, floating yarns to create the lustrous, smooth surface.

Other weaves

Weaving includes a variety of other weaves for other effects:

- Momie crêpe produces a tightly woven "pebbly" surface.

- Jacquard produces a woven-in curved design.

- Dobby produces woven-in small geometric designs.

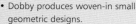
- Loop pile (terry cloth) produces loops on the face and back of the fabric.

- Cut pile (corduroy, velveteen, velvet) produces a luxurious soft surface.

From top to bottom: duck; cotton gabardine; bridal satin.

Fabric method 3: Knitting

Unlike weaving, knitting can be done with one or more yarns, creating stitches that are looped together to create fabric. There is a tremendous variety in knitted fabrics because a greater variety of yarns can be used; the strong warp yarns used in weaving are not needed in knitting. There are two methods of producing knits: weft knitting and warp knitting.

Positive issues about knits:
- Faster fabric production compared to weaving.
- Innovations in machinery make knitting very efficient, even in high-labor-cost countries.
- The looped stitch construction makes knits softer, more drapey, and easier to fit on and move with the body.
- Great variety in surface texture and pattern.
- Flexibility in producing fabric or garments, even seamless garments.

Negative issues about knits:
- Not wind-resistant due to looped structure.
- Loop stitches snag easily.
- Can stretch out of shape easily, depending on the yarn used and the density of the knit stitch construction.

From top to bottom: jersey wool-like polyester; doubleknit ponte di roma; fine-gauge ribbed knit rayon.

Weft knitting characteristics

Looping stitches in the cross-grain (weft) direction across the fabric. Most commonly used in sweater production, casual and dressy knits, and hand-knitting. Weft knitting uses only two stitches: knit stitch and purl stitch. The arrangement of knit and purl stitches will determine the name and properties of the fabric.

Knit type	Positive	Negative
Single knit (Can be produced as a tube of fabric or flat yardage)		
Jersey (Usually fine and medium gauge)	Lightweight, Inexpensive, Easily available	Shrinks easily, Rolls at cut edges, Easily stretched out of shape
Sweater knits (Fine, medium, and big gauge)	Great variety	Easily stretched out of shape
Double knit (Fabric is stable even at cut edges; can be produced as a tube of fabric or flat yardage)		
Interlock knits (Rigid knit)	Very stable fabric	Bulky for weight
Ribbed knits (Alternating knit and purl stitches to form various ribbed wales)	Elastic	More expensive than jersey
Bottom-weight double knits (Two knit fabrics knitted together)	Stable heavyweight, Suitable for tailoring	Less available than jersey, Expensive

Warp knitting characteristics

Looping stitches in the straight-grain (warp) direction, parallel to the selvage edge. Most commonly used in lingerie, athletic apparel, and interior design. Knit and purl stitches are not used in warp knitting, and the fabric is very rigid in the straight-grain direction. It is high-speed knitting, using multifilament yarns only. There are two main groups of warp knits: tricot knit and raschel knit.

Knit type	Positive	Negative
Tricot knit (Face stitches are 90 degrees to back stitches)	Smooth surface Usually fine gauge Dense stitches Very fast production	Snags very easily
Raschel knit (Openwork fabric, sometimes lacy, meshlike, or waffle texture; face and back appearance less important for identification) **Raschel knit:** open-space knit fabric. **Raschel lace knit:** imitates handmade lace. **Netting:** lightweight, open-surface fabric forming geometric shapes with yarn. **Mesh:** knit fabric with many holes knitted in. **Powernet:** elastic mesh. **Thermal knit:** imitates other waffle textures.	Great variety	Snags very easily

From top to bottom: tricot with metallic yarn; raschel lace; lace and power mesh used in a corset.

Describing knit fabrics

Designers are often concerned about the fineness or coarseness of a knit fabric, which is defined as gauge. Counting stitches across vertical rows (wales) determines the gauge. The higher the gauge, the finer the fabric. The lower the gauge, the coarser the fabric.

Other knits for both weft and warp knits

Knitting is generally more efficient in production compared to weaving, and the knitted fabric surfaces are very similar to comparable woven fabrics, so many fabrics can be more easily produced by knitting.

 Looped pile knits (terry): extra set of yarns added for looped textured appearance.

Cut-pile knits (velour, faux fur): same as above, but cut (sheared) for luxurious appearance.

Jacquard knits: any knitted design, curved or geometric.

Note: Designers specialize in creating new knit fabrics and work with knitwear designers who are specialists in their field. It's an exciting part of the fashion industry that requires understanding of knit fabric production.

Adding color

Adding color to fabric is an art in itself. Designers often reach their market through the creative use of color, either by immersing in dye (dyeing) or by adding images onto the fabric surface (printing). This section will acquaint the designer with the methods of adding color to develop a basic understanding of the coloration process.

After the fiber or fabric is prepared for dyeing (PFD) or printing (PFP), color is ready to be added. The selection of coloring agents will depend on the expected result, type of fibers used, fabric construction, required colorfastness (ability of color to remain), cost, and water/energy consumption issues.

Colorfastness is described in three different ways:
Fading: color loss into the atmosphere, often from dry-cleaning fumes, called gas or fume fading.
Bleeding: color loss in water.
Crocking (wet and dry): color loss due to abrasion (rubbing).

Color can be applied at all stages in the production of textiles and garments, depending on the desired results. There are three main types of coloring agents:
Dyes (chemical bond with fiber): require water or chemicals for dye solution, fixing agent, and rinsing off excess dye. Different fibers require different classes of dyes. Not all dyes color all fibers. Colorfastness is dependent on the fiber, color, heat, and chemicals used.
Disperse dyes (chemical bond with fiber): require heat and pressure to be activated. No water, fixing agent, or rinsing is necessary. Specific and practical on polyester fiber only. Used on fabrics or garments only. Excellent colorfastness.

Pigments (no chemical bond): require binding agent plus heat to bind the color. Pigment is used on fabric or garments only and has moderate to poor colorfastness. Water is necessary only in dyeing to suspend the pigment particles during the coloring process. Printing with pigment color does not require water.

Note: There are many books available on dyeing and printing textiles; see the resources at the back of the book (page 315) for suggestions on further reading.

Environmental impact of adding color to fabric

Color in apparel design is a key factor when appealing to the target market. However, after controlling fiber and greige fabric production to be socially and environmentally responsible, entering the color finishing process can undo all the good. Adding color can pollute drinking-water systems with dyes and fixing agents, including concentrations of heavy metals and salts. Energy conservation is also difficult because of the heat required to

dissolve the dye and support its chemical binding to the fabric. The issues are the same whether dyeing or printing.

Dyes: natural vs synthetic
The controversy around using naturally occurring dyes from plants and minerals instead of synthetic chemical dyes that use a variety of components, including heavy metals, to achieve bright, intense colors means that there are few answers for the designer when selecting color. Here are several points to consider when discussing the use of natural or synthetic dyes. At the moment, natural dyes tend to be used in developing countries, where there is little opportunity to clean the wastewater. Therefore, the wastewater, heavy in fixing agents and dye, is poured directly onto fields and into open-water systems. Synthetic dyes are used in large-volume dyeing mills, and there is often more opportunity to treat the wastewater before it is put back into the local water supply.

For denim washing, most jeans are garment-washed to achieve the required soft hand. Cotton colorfastness to dark colors is fair to moderate, so excessive washing will bleed large amounts of dye into the wastewater. With the large quantities of denim produced globally, it is particularly important for designers to ask how denim-washing facilities manage their wastewater.

Designers can guide merchandisers and production teams to consider either natural or synthetic dyeing processes that:
• avoid dyes that use heavy metals.
• use dyeing processes that absorb 80 percent or more of dyes so wastewater is cleaner (an electric current in dye baths is one low-cost idea).
• insist on dyers managing a clean dyeing mill for the safety of workers and the community, conserving water and energy.

Dyes: natural vs synthetic		
	Natural	**Synthetic**
Large quantity available?	Sometimes	Yes
Fixing agents required?	Yes	Yes
Wastewater	Yes	Yes

Dyeing: Immersion in dye solution

There are five methods of dyeing fabric.

Dyeing method	Colorfastness	Quantity required	Coloring agents	Accessibility for garment production
Pre-fiber dyeing (also called solution dyeing, before the fiber is extruded). Dye is added to the manufactured fiber chemical solution before passing through the spinneret. The manufactured fiber emerges already colored.	Excellent	Large quantity/color	Dyes only	Poor; color must be added before fiber production
Fiber dyeing (also called top dyeing). Fiber is colored before being made into yarn.	Very good	Large quantity/color	Dyes only	Fair; fiber must be dyed before yarn is produced
Yarn dyeing (also called skein dyeing). Yarn is dyed before fabric/ garment production.	Very good	Moderate quantity/color	Dyes/pigments	Fair; color added to yarn before fabric production
Fabric dyeing (also called piece dyeing). Fabric is dyed before garment production.	Moderate to very good	Low quantity/color	All	Good; color added to fabric and available in 30 days
Garment dyeing (dyeing proceeds after garment is sewn).	Poor to fair	One garment/color	Low temperature	Excellent; colored garments available immediately

Dyeing blended yarns, fabrics, or garments

Fiber blending is very common, yet dyes are specific to a particular type of fiber. Therefore, dyeing mills have adapted dyeing techniques for multifiber blends to create a solid color or a multiple color yarn, fabric, or garment.

Dyeing method	Fiber content	Color agents	Color result
Cross-dyeing	Two or more different fibers	Dyes only	Two or more colors
Union dyeing	Two or more different fibers	Dyes only	One solid color

Printing: applying colored images to the fabric surface

Pigment printing is used on blended fabrics to avoid a cross-dyed effect. There are four mass production printing methods (hand-printing is not addressed here). Shiny or napped images can also be printed, but the chart below shows the basics in printing.

Printing method	Colorfastness	Coloring agents	Maximum number of colors	Quantity required for print production	Accessibility for production
Screen-printing (also known as automated flatbed screen printing and rotary screen printing). Requires color separation (each color to be printed separately).	Dependent on color agent	All	Up to 24	Moderate to high	Good; available in 30 days
Roller printing uses etched metal rollers; requires color separation.	Dependent on color agent	All	Up to six	High	Good; available in 10–30 days
Inkjet/digital printing Printing directly (like a computer printer) onto fabric, garment, or heat-transfer paper. No color separation. Requires little or no water (steam or minor rinsing) and little heat. Entirely new type of images can be applied.	Dependent on color agent	All	Unlimited	Low to high Can print 1yd/1m	Good; available in 30 days
Heat-transfer printing (also includes sublimation printing). Requires only heat and pressure. Can use color separation printing or digital inkjet printing method. Images are printed on special paper and transferred to fabric or garment using heat and pressure. Use polyester fiber fabrics/garments only.	Excellent	Disperse dyes only	Dependent on printing method	Low (existing design) or high (custom design)	Good; available in 30 days

Finishing

All finishing of fabric after the application of color is to further improve the marketability of the final fabric. Some finishes enhance how fabrics look and feel, while other finishes improve their function.

The durability of finishes should be understood by designers. You will need to understand the following four degrees of durability:

Temporary finishes are removed after one cleaning/laundering.

Semi-durable finishes remain after several cleanings and may be renewed.

Durable finishes remain for the life of the product, although they may be diminished.

Permanent finishes always remain without diminishing.

Finishing is undergoing major technological advances, using new materials and procedures. It is in the designer's interest to stay up to date, in order to improve the ability to compete in the marketplace. Finishing today is often carried out to imitate a more expensive fabric and therefore brings to the market interesting fabrics at a lower cost than the original high-cost fabrics. It is important, though, to understand the social and environmental impact of these finishing advances.

Aesthetic finishes

Aesthetic finishes change the hand, appearance, or texture of the fabric. New ideas in aesthetic finishing are often created by designers searching for fresh ways to interpret their creative vision. Aesthetic finishes are grouped in the following charts.

Aesthetic mechanical finishes

Mechanical finishes are applied physically—sometimes with heat and pressure—without the use of water or chemicals. These are less polluting to the environment than chemical finishes.

Name of finish	Method of application	Result	Durability
Embossing	Heat and pressure	Luster or imprinted image	Variable
Chintz	Plus light resin (polish)	Lustrous	Temporary
Cire (polyester only)	Plus light resin (melted)	Wet look	Durable
Moiré	Heat and pressure	Wood-grain appearance	Durable
Pleating/puckering (mostly polyester)	Heat and pressure (heat-set)	Volume and texture	Durable
Plissé (mostly polyester)	As above	Puckered appearance	Durable
Embroidery	Sewing thread	Images in fabric	Durable
Napped	Brushed/sheared	Soft, raised surface	Durable
Velvet	Sanded		
Velveteen/corduroy			
Velour			
Sueded/peached			
Fulling (wool only)	Steam/heat	Compacting, softening	Durable
Beetling (mostly linen)	Heat/pressure	Lustrous, hammered look	Variable

Denim fabric can be laundered for a washed finish before the garments are produced. The soft hand of laundered denim is preferred for garments that will not be garment washed after sewing is completed.

Aesthetic chemical finishes

These are applied with chemicals, heat, and may include water. Waste chemicals and wastewater are produced, and the water must be cleaned before re-entering the local supply.

Name of finish	Method of application	Result	Durability
Mercerizing	Chemicals/heat/water	Smooth and improved dyeability	Durable
Stiffness			
Sizing	As above	Crisp, crunchy, stiff	Variable
Anti-curling	As above	Prevents curling of cut fabric	Temporary
Pleating/puckering (in natural fibers)	As above	Pleats in natural fibers	Durable
Plissé	As above	Puckered appearance	Durable
Enzyme wash	Enzymes/heat/water	Softening	Durable
Stone/sand wash	Bleaches/heat/water	Softening/color loss	Durable
Coating	Chemicals/heat	New surface	Durable
Silicone	Silicone/heat/water	Smooth hand	Durable
Flocking	Fiber/adhesive/heat	Napped surface	Durable
Burnout	Chemicals printed	Fiber removed in patterns	Permanent

Functional finishes

Functional finishes are applied to fabric to enhance its performance. Finishing applications are undergoing technological advances that are changing fiber's usual characteristics to meet certain functional requirements. For example, absorbent cotton fiber can be transformed to resist water absorption. Nonabsorbent polyester can be changed to absorb water. Beginning with the athletic apparel industry, manufactured fibers enjoy nearly total acceptance by athletes for their superior performance in competition. Much of the superiority of performance is due to new finishing technology.

With the exception of napping, all functional finishes are chemically applied. For designers who create athletic apparel, functional finishes are especially important to explore and understand. The designer

Functional mechanical finishes

Mechanical finishes are applied physically—sometimes with heat and/or pressure—without the use of water. They are less polluting to the environment than chemical finishes.

Name of finish	Method of application	Result	Durability
Napping *Polar fleece (polyester)*	Brushed/sheared	Insulation/warmth	Durable

Functional chemical finishes

These are applied with chemicals, heat, and sometimes water. Waste chemicals and wastewater are produced, and the water must be cleaned before re-entering the local supply.

Name of finish	Method of application	Result	Durability
Wrinkle-resistant	Chemicals/heat	Improved resilience	Durable
Flame-retardant	As above	Reduced flammability	Durable
Stain/soil-resistant	As above	Reduced absorbency	Semi-durable or durable
Anti-pilling	As above	Reduced pilling	Durable
Anti-static	As above	Reduced static buildup	Durable
Anti-microbial	As above	Kills bacteria/limits odor	Variable
Silver particles	Silver/chemicals/heat	Kills bacteria on fabric	Permanent
Pest/mold/mildew resistant	Chemicals/heat	Resists pests/mold/mildew	Durable
Water absorbency	Chemicals/heat	Induces water absorption	Durable
UV protective	Chemicals/heat	Absorbs UV radiation	Durable
Microencapsulation	Chemicals/binder	Absorbs/radiates heat	Durable
Phase-change		Absorbs/radiates heat (temperature regulation)	Durable

must work closely with fabric and finishing suppliers to stay updated on new functional finishing applications.

Anti-shrinking finishes are important in a fabric's fit and long-term performance. Always ask your supplier what shrinkage control has been applied to a fabric. **Note:** Many applications of chemical finishes are found in fragrances, moth-proofing, insect repellent, lotions, medicine, vitamins, and odor control.

High-performance fabrics

Staying dry and warm is a key part of high performance in fabrics.

Staying warm

Keep heat close to the body by reducing air movement (thermal insulation). This can be accomplished by:

Quilting: two fabric layers with a thermal insulating middle layer, stitched together into a single thick fabric.
- Down/feather, fiberfill, wool, cotton, or kapok batting.

Layering garments:
- Polar fleece with outside layer windbreaker jacket.
- Add wicking underwear to the above.

Bonding/laminating fabrics together:
- Thermal side, water-resistant side.

Staying dry

Resist moisture next to the skin, which is life-threatening in cold, windy weather. There are three types of moisture management:

Moisture wicking: Moisture moves from a wet area to a dry area along a textured surface, such as a textured wicking fiber. Fabric dries quickly and remains lightweight. Skin chafing is minimized for athletes.

Moisture (water) resistance:
- Water-repellent: a semi-durable finish that allows moisture to "bead" on the surface and can be brushed off. However, moisture is absorbed easily if left on the fabric surface.
- Water-resistant/breathable (also known as waterproof/breathable): a durable microporous membrane that resists moisture yet allows water vapor and air to pass through and is bonded to a water-resistant outside (shell) fabric.
- Waterproof: a nonporous surface that permanently resists moisture.

Moisture absorption

Moisture soaks into fiber and fabric. Moisture evaporates, cooling the skin. This can cause lower body temperature, known as hypothermia. The cooling effect is a plus in hot weather, however. Heavy, wet fabric can cause skin chafing and add weight to competitive athletes.

The fabric used in this snowsuit is chemically finished to resist moisture yet allow water vapor to escape for the baby to remain dry and warm. A water-resistant coating or breathable microporous membrane is applied to the back of the fabric before cutting and sewing.

Environmental impact of aesthetic and functional finishing

Innovations in finishing have made fabric performance and care more convenient. Consumers have found their clothing easier to wear and launder, with minimum effort. It is unclear, however, what impact these new finishes will have on the wearer or on the environment over time. Here is why there should be discussion about these new finishing applications.

Safety of the wearer

Most clothing is worn next to the skin. The skin surface can easily absorb chemicals and other products into the body. Since clothing may be worn next to the skin for many hours, there should be answers to the impact of the following.

Bleaches/other finishing chemicals in denim washing

Denim jeans fabric holds the residue of the various finishing products. It is unknown how much of these finishing compounds is absorbed into the skin.

Anti-microbial finishing

By killing bacteria on the fabric, will these finishes also kill the "good" bacteria on the skin? What are the long-term effects of using silver in anti-microbial finishing?

Nano-finishing

Extremely small particles are applied to fabric to change its characteristics. Nano-finishes for wrinkle resistance and stain/soil resistance also have the potential for the skin to absorb these nano-particles. Smaller than usual molecules, nano-molecules can move into the body easily compared to other chemical molecules. The long-term effects of nano-finishing have not been studied.

Microencapsulates

This new area of fabric finishing shows great promise in medical, military, athletic, and consumer applications. The binders used and the long-term effects of the products contained in the microencapsulates have yet to be fully studied. With these encapsulates intended to be worn close to the skin, the impact of the various products contained inside needs to be fully understood.

Concern for the environment

Fabrics have been enhanced to perform as quality clothing and to meet marketing needs. However, the impact on the environment of the chemicals used in finishing as well as when the consumer discards the product have yet to be studied. For example, the life cycle of clothing has been extensively studied. However, these chemical finishes, particularly the nano-finishes and micro-encapsulates, have an unknown impact on the environment when they are eventually discarded. The lifespan of these finishes must be understood more fully.

Developments in fiber recycling will require analysis of the chemical finishes that have been added to fabrics, especially cotton fabrics. Research is ongoing to learn how to reuse cotton fiber more effectively. However, the finishing that was applied must also be considered while learning how to reuse and recycle cotton fiber products.

As a designer, you are in a position to ask important questions about how the latest finishes impact the environment. It is the responsibility of the designer to stay alert to the issues that can influence how the textile industry takes responsibility for its activities.

Garment care

Nearly every person who wears clothing has experienced washing and drying apparel. Some people also experience having their clothing dry-cleaned.

It has been estimated that nearly 80 percent of all energy and water used in the process of textiles and clothing production and consumption is used in the consumer's effort to clean their apparel. The designer has a responsibility to provide simple, efficient care instructions that consider the use of energy and water.

The environmental impact of consumer care

Consumer care instructions have remained unchanged since the 1980s in the U.S. Now is the time to reconsider how designers instruct their customers to care for their clothing to conserve water and energy, and to use cleaning products that minimize chemicals discarded into the water supply and environment.

The laundry
- Reduce energy use by using cool water.
- Reduce water use—don't launder unless absolutely necessary.
- Avoid unnecessary dyes and perfume ingredients in detergents and soaps that do nothing to enhance cleaning power. Dyes and perfumes may irritate the skin and trigger asthma. In particular, avoid scented soaps/detergents around infants and the elderly. Avoid chlorine bleach.

Drying the laundry
- Avoid the tumble dryer whenever possible, especially to dry denim.
- Use an extractor to remove moisture from wet laundry.
- Line dry or dry flat.

Alternatives in dry-cleaning

The dry-cleaning method can be hazardous to human health, so try to minimize its use. Developed to clean textile products that were damaged in wet laundry, the chemicals used are often harmful to workers and customers alike.

- Reduce dry-cleaning and use only environmentally safe dry-cleaning chemicals, such as CO_2 "cold" dry cleaning or other EPA-approved substances. Avoid PERC dry-cleaning chemicals.
- Encourage laundering instead of dry-cleaning wherever possible.
- Advise consumers to avoid storing dry-cleaned items in an enclosed space, such as closets or rooms without ventilation.
- Avoid dry-cleaning chemicals around infants and the elderly.

Note: care instructions are provided by the mill and are adjusted for the garment. Never assume that care information is fully investigated. Much care information is not analyzed regularly to determine if there are better alternatives.

Garment care labels should advise consumers to reduce water, chemicals, and energy use as they care for their new purchases. Perhaps CO_2 reduction, quantified in a new icon, would help consumers understand their contribution to reducing carbon emissions.

Environmental factors

There are two main ways to clean clothing; each has environmental factors that need to be considered when it comes to designing a garment.

1. Laundering (requires water and usually heat)

Cleansers:
- Soaps (natural ingredients, which are not as effective on polyester, nylon, spandex, acrylic, or olefin).
- Detergents (synthetic chemical cleansers that effectively remove dirt/stains on manufactured fibers and blended fabrics).

Color-removers:
- Chlorine bleach or non-chlorine bleach.
- Optical brighteners (mask stains).

Softeners: add soft hand and reduce static buildup in the dryer.

Drying wet laundry:
- Tumble-dry in mechanical dryer: uses energy.
- Line or flat dry: with energy use.
- May need to press to remove wrinkles.

2. Dry-cleaning (requires chemicals and heat)

Chemicals used to clean clothing must be reviewed:
- Perchloroethylene (PERC) (linked to cancer).
- Non-PERC chemicals.

Emissions released from chemicals are controlled at the dry-cleaner, but not in the home. Heat used to dry chemicals from clothing and pressing should be reviewed.

The textile directory

It is the job of apparel designers to create three-dimensional forms from a two-dimensional surface. They use fabric as a painter uses color on a canvas. Fabric is the color, and the human body is the canvas. Once this visual understanding is clear, the journey to select the best fabric to realize the design can begin.

Introduction to the directory

Designers describe their designs in emotive terms, and the fabric must reflect the designer's intention. And here lies the continuing dialogue between designers and the textile industry: "What do you mean by the term 'techno'?" "What is 'edgy'?" "Clarify 'new.'"

Designers are trained to develop a vision in terms of surface, silhouette, and "good" design; they are not trained to translate that vision into understandable terms for the textile industry. So, as the designer finishes the design concept and moves to the textile suppliers to find the fabric, communication often breaks down between the supplier and designer.

This portion of the book is designed to bridge this gap in communication, so that the designer can view the fabric as the medium from which the design can be achieved right from the concept stage. The purpose of this book is to teach designers about selecting fabric in the same way that they are trained in design, so that they can feel confident working with suppliers in sourcing their fabrics.

The designer will be guided through five fabric categories, introducing them to fabrics that will help them to achieve the appropriate surface and create the desired silhouette. The five categories, color-coded for ease of use, are briefly explained, right. The categories have been designed to fulfill the designer's quest to find fabrics that perform in a specific way. Within the five categories, the fabrics are organized by fabric weight, working progressively from top weight to bottom weight.

STRUCTURE
is about creating form that stands away from the body and can create line through shaping and seam detail.

Military jacket
This structured, tailored coat includes an exposed metal zipper closure as ornamentation, as well as for function.

FLUIDITY
is about fabrics flowing over the body, generally following the human form. It is the aqueous movement that is important.

Collaboration
The contrasting structured tailored coat, layered over an ornamented sequin vest, fluid jersey tunic, and flowing georgette skirt provide a dynamic collaboration of color and texture.

ORNAMENTATION
is about creating interesting details
that the designer finds attractive and
that will enhance the design.

EXPANSION
is about exaggerating shapes away
from the body. These shapes
transform the body by expanding
the design silhouette.

COMPRESSION
is about compacting the body,
following the exact shape of the
body. Contracting and expanding
with the body, like breathing, is
the designer's purpose.

Intricate detail
This black and red dress uses sheer,
elegant fabric, beautiful ornamentation,
and studded trim to create intricate detail.

Expanding the silhouette
This red dress uses fabric to both expand
the silhouette away from the body and
compress the body in the same design.

Ensemble
This ensemble combines a compressing
corset, slim structured skirt that features an
ornamented, cutout hemline, and contrasting
textures in a tailored jacket.

Structure

Whether you are a new designer or a designer who is reinventing a concept, fabrics providing structural support to the design are the most plentiful in the textile world. However, too many choices can be as difficult as too few options from which to choose.

Many fabrics can provide the necessary structure. Two key points for the designer to understand are the variety of surface textures and the finishing techniques that communicate the emotional connection between the design and the consumer. The global textile fairs confirm this connection by dividing these fabrics with structure into different areas. The Paris-based Premiere Vision® textile show has created Distinction® (tailored career wear) and Relax® (casual and weekend wear) sections to display the majority of structure fabrics. Fiber content plays an important role in determining how a structure fabric is used. For example, wool fiber content is generally viewed as tailored career wear, and cotton fiber content is usually viewed as casual wear. However, the main focus for the designer is on selecting a fabric with structure that will allow the apparel vision to emerge.

How fabrics with structure work
Structural fabrics provide the "body" for the apparel design. They provide shape by themselves, and require certain fabric characteristics to implement this "body" silhouette: drape and weight.

Drape: The fabric must stay in place, rather than collapse when released. This ability to stay in place allows the fabric to show or "hold" a seam, meaning seaming detail can be an element of design, as in the seams of a denim jacket. Woven fabrics tend to be better for structure, as they are generally stiffer or crisper than knitted fabrics. Knitted fabrics tend to be too drapey and don't stay in place. Creating less drape can be achieved in a variety of ways, as we will show in this guide.

Sculpted dress
The fabric used for this long, sculpted dress has a crisp hand that does not fall fluidly over the body. The skirt stands away as the model moves, and the sleeves remain full over the arms. The metallic appearance combined with the "gunmetal," gray color gives the dress a "hard" characteristic.

Weight: The fabric must be heavy enough to hold the shape of the design. Medium-weight to heavyweight fabrics are generally used. Therefore, lightweight, sheer fabrics are poor choices for structural fabrics. Weight can be added to a lightweight fabric, as seen in this section, providing the shape that is required of a structural fabric.

A structural fabric can have many forms

The key to selecting the right choice for structure in a design is to understand how fiber content, yarn, and finishing techniques alter how a fabric will perform. In addition to showing fabrics used for structure, this section introduces the designer to how a fabric can be changed into a structure fabric to achieve the design vision.

Innovation in fiber and finishing for structure

Technology is playing an increasingly important role in how a fabric is presented as a structural fabric. The increasing cost of producing fabrics has pushed textile mills to focus on fewer different fiber contents and fabrics, finishing them in ways that expand their function, especially structural fabrics. The designer can select one fiber content and fabric, and have that one fabric fulfill several structure functions in design.

Tailored coat
The epitome of a structured design, this smooth, lustrous fabric surface tailors extremely well to show stitched edges and seams. The front closure has a concealed fastening, highlighting the contrasting structured pattern shapes used for the coat.

Structure
This shiny, metallic-looking structured cuff, left, covers the forearm and is layered over a soft, sheer knitted fabric. The hard-edged midriff, right, and hip in terraced layers is a repetitive rhythm at the center of this design. The flattened structure is in contrast to the softer fabric selected for the sleeves and upper body.

Lawn

Lawn is sometimes known as batiste (if cotton) or handkerchief linen (if flax).

This lightweight, sheer fabric has a smooth surface. The fabric is loosely compacted so yarns remain separated from each other to allow light and air to flow through the fabric. Fine yarn size is a key point in producing this beautiful, airy cloth.

This fabric is a favorite for hot-weather uses because of its lightweight, cooling capability. Seams can be sewn easily, though seam puckering can result if sewing tension isn't monitored.

Fine cotton fiber in evenly twisted yarns is often used, creating a smooth surface; mercerization enhances luster and strength. Alternatively, fine linen yarns create a slubbed surface and a stiffer, crisper hand than cotton. Finely spun polyester yarns result in a fabric similar to mercerized cotton but very drapable. Blended polyester/cotton or polyester/flax yarns are used for lower cost and enhanced wrinkle resistance.

White lawn fabric is a favorite hot-weather fabric. The sheer fabric, loosely woven, is emphasized in a cool, white color.

Facts and figures

Distinctive features

- Lightweight, sheer fabric.
- Soft hand.
- If sheer, handkerchief linen will have a slightly lustrous surface.

Strengths

- Sheer and very lightweight.
- Comfortable fabric to wear in hot weather.
- Fabric holds its shape in unfitted styles.
- If using polyester blends, fabric will be more wrinkle-resistant than cotton or flax.

Weaknesses

- Weak fabric. Seams easily "slip" (fabric pulls away at the seams, leaving one set of yarns, which are easily broken or torn).
- Not suitable for tight-fitting garments.
- If using polyester fiber, fabric will pill and will not feel as cool when worn.
- If using cotton or flax fiber, fabrics will wrinkle easily.

Usual fiber content

- Mercerized cotton fiber.
- Linen yarns.
- Spun polyester.
- Blended polyester/cotton or polyester/flax.

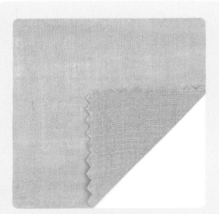

Handkerchief linen
Notice the slubbed surface, created by fine, slubbed (irregularly shaped) yarn. The irregular shape is a result of the stem fiber, which varies in thickness/thinness.

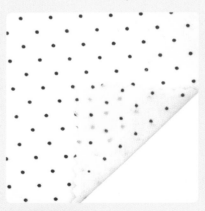

Printed lawn
A pin dot pattern is printed on this medium-quality cotton lawn.

Printed cotton
This finely detailed print shows up well on this high-quality cotton lawn fabric.

Calico

This lightweight, inexpensive fabric—sometimes referred to as sheeting—is most often used for low-cost printed textiles. Simple carded yarns (inexpensive cotton yarns) create a somewhat even surface. The fabric surface is slightly fuzzy and the fabric hand is stiff, due to the coarse, carded, low-quality yarns used to produce this fabric.

This fabric is a popular utility fabric for children's clothing, inexpensive shirts, and home-decorating projects. Its popularity continues due to its low cost.

This fabric is often made from 100 percent cotton but polyester and cotton blends are also used to lower cost and help with wrinkle resistance. However, if this fiber blend is used, pigment must be used in the printing, which may add additional stiffness to the hand of the fabric.

This printed calico fabric imitates the look of a yarn-dyed gingham check. The green pigment color adds a little stiffness to the fabric hand.

Facts and figures

Distinctive features
- Smooth, slightly fuzzy surface.
- Slightly stiff fabric hand.
- Nearly always printed, usually pigment printed.

Strengths
- Lightweight.
- Low-cost printed fabric.
- Holds shape easily.
- More wrinkle-resistant if using cotton/polyester blend.

Weaknesses
- Often shrinks and loses stiffness after one washing.
- Colors in prints may easily crock or bleed.
- If 100 percent cotton, will easily wrinkle.

Usual fiber content
- 100 percent cotton.
- Polyester and cotton blends.

Piece-dyed (fabric dyed) calico
Because calico is always cotton, the colors will not be very dyefast. Cotton doesn't hold dye well over time.

Wet-printed calico
An example of a wet-printed image with gold pigment printed on top of the print. The gold color may start to deteriorate after several wearings/washings.

Designer's tip: The pigment colors commonly used for blended cotton/polyester calico add binders that, when heated (cured), bind the pigment to the surface of the fabric. Surface-only pigment cannot withstand abrasion well, and the color will come off when wearing/washing. There are improved, more costly, pigment binders that will remain on the fabric longer and not noticeably stiffen the fabric.

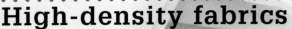

High-density fabrics

High-density fabrics, using polyester microfiber yarns invented in the 1980s, have been used in functional outdoor apparel for many years. These fabrics are comfortable to wear because air can pass through them yet they resist moisture in a light rain.

Fashion apparel has been using these fabrics more frequently recently as the cost of microfiber has been reduced. The fabrics function as follows:

- High numbers of very fine microfiber yarns are compactly woven together.
- Yarns are so tightly compacted together that water molecules are too big to pass easily through the spaces between the yarns, yet smaller air molecules can get through.
- No fabric finish is added to resist moisture.

The concept of a high-density fabric originated from down-proof fabrics that were produced to prevent the feathers from piercing the fabric that contains them, causing discomfort and loss of insulating feathers and down. Most down-proof fabrics today use

High-density fabrics always have a smooth surface when used for functional purposes, such as raincoats or windbreaker jackets. They are always lightweight fabrics, which can become medium-weight when laminates are applied to the back side of the fabric.

The yarns in a high-density fabric are so tightly compacted that water molecules are too big to get through, but water vapor can escape.

  Fabric

Skin

cotton or silk fiber, neither of which will resist moisture. Now, polyester microfiber, while originally intended to imitate silk fiber, has become the fiber choice in fabrics for the high-tech functional outdoor apparel industry. Microfiber fabrics are lightweight yet can resist inclement rain and wind conditions (characteristic of much heavier fabrics), while still keeping the wearer comfortable because the fabric "breathes" (allows heated body air to pass through).

High-density cotton
High-density cotton plain-weave fabric was produced to create a down-proof fabric (tiny feathers cannot poke through the fabric). It is still used in bedding and sometimes in down jackets.

High-density weave with ciré finish
A special ripstop fabric, also with a ciré finish on the back side. An example of a high-density recycled polyester microfiber fabric is ECO-CIRCLE™ fiber.

Ciré finish on high-density fine ripstop plain weave
This plain-weave polyester microfiber ECO-CIRCLE™ fabric is produced from post-consumer polyester garments. A ciré finish has been added to the back of the fabric.

Facts and figures

Distinctive features

- Nearly always balanced plain weave.
- Lightweight compared to other water-resistant fabrics using functional finishes.

Strengths

- Extremely lightweight as a functional fabric.
- Resists wrinkles.
- Lustrous, smooth hand.
- Sometimes very soft and drapable.

Weaknesses

- May pill.
- Very difficult to control thread tension when sewing.
- Puckering in seams is difficult to control.
- Can be expensive to sew because the sewing process is slower than usual to control tension.
- Will not resist moisture in heavy rain or snow conditions.

Usual fiber content

- Nylon and polyester microfibers.

Designer's tip: When importing apparel as "water-resistant" using high-density microfiber fabrics, some countries require evidence of a finish to qualify for a water-resistant import category. Therefore, a ciré finish on the back side of the fabric may be needed for it to qualify as water-resistant.

Cycling windbreaker
Cycling jackets use very lightweight, high-density fabrics that keep the cyclist comfortable and dry.

Broadcloth

Most commonly used as a shirt fabric, broadcloth has become a popular fabric for a variety of clothing. The fine, horizontal (cross-grain direction), ribbed texture is barely noticeable and is sometimes confused with a balanced, plain-weave fabric. It is this ribbed texture that gives the fabric a natural crispness that tailors well for shirt and blouse details on collars, cuffs, pockets, and button tabs.

Broadcloth is a popular fabric available in many fiber contents. The hand, visual appearance, and drape are influenced by the fiber content and the yarns used. Regardless of the fiber used, yarns are always smooth and evenly twisted. Cost is determined primarily by the fiber content.

This 100 percent cotton broadcloth has a fine horizontally ribbed surface that is barely noticeable, especially on this high-contrast, digitally printed floral image.

Facts and figures

Distinctive features
- Fine horizontal (cross-grain) ribs created by larger weft yarns. Larger weft yarns add a slight stiffness or "crisp" hand.
- In silk fiber, broadcloth has a beautiful drape and weight for dresses and jackets.
- In cotton/polyester blends, is one of the most common fabrics in low-cost apparel.

Strengths
- Crisp hand.
- Easily available in many fiber contents.
- Very slight ribbed texture.
- Tailors well.

Weaknesses
- Rayon or cotton fiber fabrics wrinkle badly.
- Easy to confuse with square weave.
- Ribbed surface subject to abrasion.

Usual fiber content
- Cotton fiber fabrics often use a mercerized finish to enhance the luster and strength of the fabric.
- Polyester/cotton fiber blends are used for better wrinkle resistance.
- Rayon or polyester/rayon fibers are used for inexpensive fabrics that are very soft and drapey.
- Silk fiber is used for heavyweight silk broadcloth.

Pima cotton broadcloth
Most commonly used in men's dress shirts, high-quality Pima cotton fiber will give a lustrous, smooth surface and a soft hand to the broadcloth.

Yarn-dyed cotton broadcloth
Dyeing yarn before weaving helps to keep color in the fabric longer. Yarn dyeing requires more time and is considered a higher quality than printing.

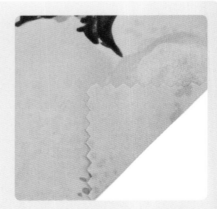

Silk broadcloth
Lustrous silk filament yarns are often used to create luxurious broadcloth for tailored shirts and dresses. The unbalanced, ribbed plain weave contributes to this fabric's crisp hand.

Poplin

One of the most versatile fabrics used today, poplin is an unbalanced plain weave, resulting in a cross-grain ribbed surface texture. The rib is more visible than in broadcloth, so the weft yarn is larger than in broadcloth.

One of the reasons why poplin has become such a versatile fabric is the way it is produced. The textile mill can use the same fine warp yarns and change the weft yarn according to the customer's order. Fabric weights range from top weights for shirts, blouses, and very lightweight bottoms, to medium weights for jackets, pants, and skirts.

Because of the ease with which the weft yarn is changed, poplins are most likely blended fabrics, with the warp yarns one fiber content, and the larger weft yarns another fiber content. Fiber content and yarn size will determine the end use of the poplin.

This solid-color poplin fabric is a common fiber mixture, combining 100 percent nylon warp yarns and 100 percent cotton weft yarns. This poplin is widely used in outerwear and casual pants, shorts, and skirts.

DESIGN RESPONSIBLY

Blending nonabsorbent fiber like nylon or other quick-drying fiber like hemp with cotton fiber will result in reduced energy required for drying fabric.

Facts and figures

Distinctive features
- Visible horizontal (cross-grain) ribbed texture.
- Stiff hand depending on the yarn size and fiber content in the weft direction.

Strengths
- Crisp hand (nylon blend adds more stiffness).
- Easily available in many fiber contents and prices.
- Visible ribbed texture.

Weaknesses
- Cotton fiber fabrics wrinkle badly.
- Ribbed surface subject to abrasion.

Usual fiber content
- 55 percent cotton (weft)/45 percent nylon (warp)—jackets/pants or shirts in lighter weight.
- 55 percent polyester (weft)/45 percent nylon (warp)—outerwear.
- 100 percent polyester—outerwear.
- 100 percent nylon—outerwear.
- 100 percent cotton.

Nylon/cotton poplin
Because of the nylon warp, this medium-weight poplin is very strong and is considered an important fabric for men's casual jackets and pants. This sample has a water-resistant coating on the back.

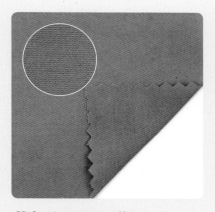

Nylon/cotton poplin
This poplin is frequently used in pants and shorts. The nylon fiber content allows the fabric to dry quickly. There is no coating.

100 percent cotton, printed stripe poplin
This is a low-quality poplin because the yarns are not tightly compacted together. The stripe has been printed onto the fabric.

Checks and plaids

Geometric images produced in multiple colors in fabric are generally called either a check or a plaid.

Check fabrics are usually two colors, and plaids are three or more colors with a more intricate use of color and spacing. Both types of images were originally created using dyed yarns and weaving them into fabrics to create the check or the plaid. However, the process of dyeing yarn first and then producing only woven fabric is slow and limiting. Today, checks and plaids can be produced as a printed image on any fabric, created using a cross-dyed method, or continuing the traditional yarn-dyed method.

Traditional yarn-dyed fabric, including Madras plaids, which were developed long ago in India, are still produced in low-cost labor countries. However, due to the continuing issue of water contamination from the dyeing processes, more and more low-cost fabrics will use pigment-printed checks and plaids, which do not require slow production, intensive labor, and wastewater concerns. Yarn-dyed fabrics continue to be used in men's dress shirts and high-quality women's blouses and shirts. For low-cost fashion items, most suppliers have switched to pigment printing to create the check or plaid.

This Madras plaid fabric is actually a patchwork of many squares of plaid fabric machine-sewn together to create a continuous patchwork roll. The plaids are compatible but different, so there is no attempt to match each design with the others.

Designer's tips:
- Checks and plaids must be "matched" at the seams to avoid visual confusion in the garment design, creating an unbalanced or disjointed appearance.
- Loss of color through washing (bleeding) or rubbing (crocking) is a common problem in color patterns on fabric. Dyeing yarn first before making it into fabric will improve colorfastness.

Gingham check
Gingham, always just two colors, is a square weave, so the check shape is always a square shape. Gingham is always used on lightweight or medium-weight fabrics.

Cross-dyed plaid
This fabric, produced from three different fiber yarns, is dyed all at once in one dye bath, resulting in each different yarn accepting a different dye, for a multicolor plaid effect.

Yarn-dyed windowpane check
This yarn-dyed twill-weave flannelette shows the square box that is characteristic of a windowpane check.

Facts and figures

Distinctive features
- Very noticeable and pleasing fabric image in a variety of colors.
- Can be either a square or rectangular geometric image.

Strengths
- Great variety of design images.
- Can use wide variety of fiber contents and yarns.
- Flexibility in image production—woven in or printed.

Weaknesses
- May lose color, depending on how the fabric was produced.
- Must match or balance check or plaid image.
- Unbalanced (rectangle) plaid cannot be used in bias garments.

Usual fiber content
- All types of fiber in unlimited blends and variations.

Matched and unmatched plaid

To maintain a harmonious design, plaids and checks must be handled differently from solid-color fabrics. It is important to be sure pattern pieces are lined up for continuous, matched and balanced images that draw attention to the garment design. Bias and straight grain use of the plaid pattern is used effectively in the coat on the far left, while the men's blazer is a patchwork of many different plaids.

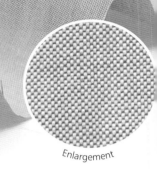

The yarns used in this red/white chambray Oxford are combed cotton. The fabric surface is smooth and somewhat lustrous due to the finishing technique.

Oxford

Oxford cloth fabrics are some of the most popular tailored shirting fabrics, particularly for menswear. The texture is achieved through an unbalanced basketweave, using one large filling yarn and pairs of smaller warp yarns.

Oxford cloth is always a top-weight fabric and is sometimes used in dresses. It cuts easily, holds seams very well, and can be easily topstitched. It is a traditional fabric in menswear, used for more casual, button-down collared shirts.

Although this fabric is often produced as a solid color (most frequently white or pastel colors), the warp yarns can be dyed a color, and the larger, less tightly spun weft yarn dyed white. The result creates a subtle two-color visual texture on the fabric surface known as the "chambray effect," which has a less formal appearance than a solid color.

Oxford cloth's quality is determined by the yarn size, so the smaller the yarns used, the higher the quality of the fabric. Pinpoint Oxford is considered a high-quality fabric because long staple cotton

fiber is required to produce the fine, lustrous spun yarns. The surface of the fabric is lustrous and the yarns are more tightly woven together. The same basketweave is used, but the beautiful luster and silky smooth hand of the fabric is achieved entirely from the high-quality cotton fiber that is used.

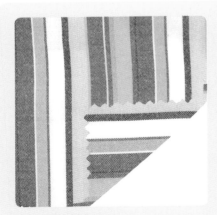

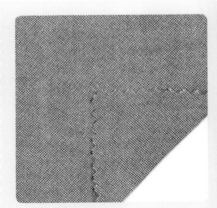

Striped Oxford
Oxford is sometimes produced in yarn-dyed stripes, as shown here. Oxford stripes place the colored yarns differently, so warp yarns are both colored and white. Weft yarn is always white to give the chambray effect. The face and back are the same.

Chambray pinpoint Oxford
High-quality cotton fiber must be used for this fabric, resulting in a luxurious smooth hand and lustrous visual appeal. The fine, high-twist cotton yarns used here distinguish this Oxford.

Chambray Oxford
This fabric uses blue yarns interlaced with white yarns, creating the chambray appearance. While most Oxfords are chambray weaves, solid-color Oxfords are also available.

Facts and figures
Distinctive features
- Pastel colors or two-color chambray color effect. Almost always frosty pastel colors on a subtle, textured surface.
- Pastel chambray blue Oxford is equal in popularity to solid white.
- Always an unbalanced basketweave, using paired warp yarns and usually one large weft yarn.
- Pinpoint Oxford follows the same yarn pattern as regular Oxford, but yarn size is finer and the fabric surface is lustrous and silky smooth.

Strengths
- Easily available fabric available at reasonable prices.
- Easily recognizable.
- Pinpoint Oxford is highly prized in menswear shirting.

Weaknesses
- Cotton/polyester blends pill noticeably.
- Low-quality Oxfords can cause seam slippage.

Usual fiber content
- 100 percent cotton or cotton/polyester blend.

Oxford cloth shirt
This fabric presses well and can be topstitched easily. The results are clean, crisp finished edges on the design, highly suitable for men's dress shirts.

Surface shine: ciré and chintz

Shine or luster is a very desirable fabric characteristic that communicates expense or higher quality. Imitating more expensive shiny or lustrous fabrics through the use of chintz and ciré finishes have been important ways for designers to find cheaper alternatives.

Using smooth-surface square-weave cotton fabrics, such as lawn or calico, the chintz finish is applied for a lustrous surface. Unfortunately, the chintz finish will only last one washing. The term "chintzy" comes from this finish name. Inexpensive calico cotton fabric was "improved" with this lustrous finish. After one washing, the luster was gone. More durable chintz finishes are now available, but are more expensive than the original. The ciré finish, used only on polyester square weaves, imparts a very glossy finish, looking almost "wet." The ciré finish is very durable.

This low-quality, red cotton fabric has a more luxurious appearance because of its very lustrous chintz finish. This shiny finish also adds stiffness to the fabric, improving its structure qualities.

Facts and figures

Distinctive features

- Lustrous, smooth surface for cotton fabrics.
- "Wet-look," very glossy, smooth surface for polyester fabrics.
- Both have a somewhat crisp hand, due to the finishing.

Strengths

- Lustrous or shiny surface.
- Crisp hand.
- Ciré is a very durable finish.

Weaknesses

- Chintz is a temporary finish, lasting only one washing or dry cleaning.
- Sewing tension is difficult to control on both fabrics, so seams often are puckered due to stitching.
- The fabric cannot be re-sewn, as original stitching holes may show in chintzed fabric.

Usual fiber content

- 100 percent cotton for chintz.
- 100 percent polyester for ciré.

Ciré back on this moiré fabric
A ciré finish can be applied to almost any smooth polyester surface. This sample has an embossed "wood-grain" appearance on the face and a ciré finish on the back.

Metallic finish for shine
This rayon/cotton fabric has a metallic heat transfer applied to the fabric surface. For the best application, a fabric blend that contains polyester or nylon is recommended.

Printed chintz
This square-weave, printed cotton fabric has been finished with a lustrous, though temporary, finish. The luster will be removed after a single washing.

Puckered surface: seersucker and plissé

Seersucker's special puckered appearance, usually produced in striped or plaid patterns, has traditionally been used for hot-weather apparel.

Although produced most often in 100 percent cotton, the puckered surface requires little or no ironing. No wrinkle-resistant finishing is applied. Fabrics are often striped, but checks or plaids are also available, with the puckers running in the straight grain direction. Polyester/cotton-blended fabric can be less expensive than 100 percent cotton seersucker. In medium weights, seersucker is used for summer suiting, including blazers and slacks.

Another puckered-surface fabric, plissé, imitates the more expensive seersucker weave. Plissé is always a lightweight fabric and is most often used in summer apparel. Using square-weave fabrics, such as lawn or sheeting, the fabric surface is heated or chemically treated to produce the puckered appearance. Plissé is often used in children's clothing and inexpensive women's tops.

This medium-weight, multicolored striped seersucker can be used in summer suiting or dresses. The puckered surface texture tailors well, adding a more pronounced structural characteristic to the fabric.

Facts and figures

Distinctive features
- Puckered surface appearance, always in the straight grain direction.
- Seersucker is usually produced in yarn-dyed stripes, checks, or multicolored plaids.
- Plissé is always a top-weight fabric, produced in both solid colors and prints.

Strengths
- Puckered surface doesn't require ironing.
- Crisp hand.
- Pleasing textured surface.
- If a woven seersucker, the puckered surface doesn't deteriorate over time.

Weaknesses
- Chemically finished cotton and cotton/polyester blend plissé puckered surface diminishes over time.
- Polyester plissé is heat-sensitive and can be uncomfortable in hot weather.

Usual fiber content
- For seersucker 100 percent cotton or cotton/polyester blends.
- For plissé 100 percent cotton, cotton/polyester blends, or 100 percent polyester.

Medium-weight seersucker for suiting
This yarn-dyed striped seersucker is typically used for suiting. It is a medium-weight seersucker fabric.

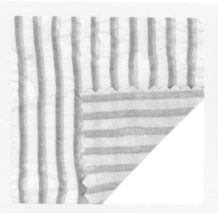

100 percent cotton plissé
A chemical finish is printed onto this lawn fabric. The printed portions of the fabric shrink, causing a puckered effect. Chemical puckered effect seems to flatten out over time.

Plaid seersucker
This yarn-dyed plaid uses four or more different yarn colors. The plaid must be balanced or matched in design and construction.

Dobby weaves

Novelty woven fabrics create surface texture based on how the fabric is woven. The leno weave always creates little holes in the fabric. You can see the holes woven into the fabric below, left.

The "white-on-white" pattern woven into this fabric is created by combining satin-weave stripes and groups of warp yarns in vertical arrangements with a balanced plain weave. There is a noticeable surface texture in the geometric stripe pattern.

These fabrics are most often used in summer apparel but tend to be more expensive compared to more basic weaves because they are more complex to produce. Dobby weaves combine several weaves, resulting in small, geometric patterns woven into the fabric. The dobby weave can have many different weave combinations, but the resulting fabric always has small geometric shapes woven into the fabric. For example, a fabric can have a balanced square weave, a satin weave, and a ribbed weave, all combined together to create a textured satin-stripe dobby, as the fabric example on the opposite page shows.

The dobby weave allows for great creativity in geometric surface textures for shirtings, and is used extensively in high-quality men's and women's shirts. The dobby weave can also be indistinguishable in weave construction, but it always creates surface texture. Dobby only occurs in weaving, not knitting.

White-on-white leno dobby
The surface texture in this leno dobby adds interest for a lightweight summer shirt.

Dobby stripe with metallic yarn stripes
In dressy shirt fabrics, dobby stripes are very common. This pattern uses a metallic yarn in the stripe.

Diamond dobby
This sample shows an interesting geometric pattern and stripes. This fabric will most likely be used in a men's or women's casual shirt.

Facts and figures

Distinctive features

- Small geometric patterns create beautiful surface texture.
- Large variety of fabric designs.
- Surface texture provides depth.

Strengths

- Great variety of woven patterns and textures.
- Variety of colors, both yarn and fabric dyed.

Weaknesses

- Cotton/polyester blends pill noticeably.
- Sometimes limited availability, especially in higher-quality cotton dobbies.

Usual fiber content

- 100 percent cotton, cotton/polyester blends—tailored blouses and shirts.
- 100 percent polyester or blended with rayon—same as above or soft dressy tops and dresses.
- Sometimes special yarns are added for a unique appearance.

"High-low" shadowed texture

Combining several weaves within a fabric produced this striped "high-low" shadowed texture. The tone-on-tone color appears to give a positive and negative color effect on the face and back of the top-weight fabric.

Enlargement

Taffeta

Taffeta is one of the more recognized fabric names. The fabric has a characteristic rustling noise, sometimes called "schroop," and a fine, cross-grain ribbed weave. The yarns are very tightly woven together, always using simple multifilament yarns. The hand is very crisp, making this fabric ideal for full skirts and dresses, and other formal occasion women's clothing.

This elegant, deeply toned taffeta combines two different color yarns, black and burgundy red, for a subdued eveningwear color. The distinctive crisp hand of taffeta is perfect for full silhouettes and sharply folded design details.

One of the visually appealing aspects of taffeta is the use of color in the yarns. Taffeta in iridescent colors, used in women's formal dresses and outerwear, is especially popular. Iridescence is achieved by using different yarn colors in the warp and weft, similar to chambray (see page 64). However, the bright multifilament yarns reflect light differently as the fabric's angle to the light changes—as the fabric moves, its color changes. The fabric shown above is an example of iridescent coloring.

Taffeta is very similar to a poplin weave (see page 61). In the textile industry, taffeta is always made from multifilament yarns; very "bright" (shiny) yarns are used for women's formal wear, and dull multifilament yarns are used for snowsports apparel and other outerwear uses.

Stripe taffeta design
Taffeta can be produced in plaids, stripes, or checks. They are always yarn-dyed.

Taffeta for ski or snowboard apparel
Because taffeta is such a tightly woven fabric, it functions well in water-resistant clothing such as ski or snowboard jackets. The hand is much softer, and noise is reduced because the yarns used are less stiff and duller than the nylon/polyester taffeta used in women's clothing. This is a recycled polyester Eco-Circle® taffeta.

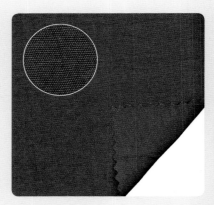

Crinkled taffeta
A crinkle finish has been applied by heat to this taffeta. This finish will be durable unless subjected to high heat, which will relax the crinkles.

Facts and figures

Distinctive features

- Lustrous surface with fine, cross-grain ribbed texture.
- Crisp hand, especially in nylon blends.
- Characteristic noise or "rustle" when fabric moves.
- Iridescent colors often used.

Strengths

- The crisp hand is ideal for full, exaggerated-silhouette designs.
- The ribbed texture and lustrous, sometimes iridescent, color is highly valued for women's formal apparel.
- Can be calendered for more surface luster or have patterns embossed into the ribbed surface.
- Excellent fabric for outerwear in polyester/nylon blends.

Weaknesses

- Noise or "rustle" of the fabric can be undesirable.
- Limited use—difficult to use in tailored designs.
- May wrinkle badly.

Usual fiber content

- Originally produced in silk fiber, polyester and nylon are now frequently used for more affordable, functional, easily maintained fabric.
- Polyester microfiber yarns are often used in athletic or outdoor apparel; the characteristic "rustle" is much reduced, however.
- Acetate can also be used.

Taffeta jacket
The deep tone in this taffeta jacket highlights the lustrous surface of the fabric. Taffeta is generally a stiff fabric, and the jacket design is unfitted, so the fabric stands away from the body.

Faille and bengaline

Faille (pronounced "file") is similar to taffeta (see page 70), although the cross-grain ribs are more pronounced. Bengaline is nearly the same as faille, although the ribs may be larger.

Multifilament warp yarns are always used in faille. Larger weft spun yarns, plied yarns, or several yarns grouped together are woven into a single weft rib. Faille is always considered a dressy or more formal fabric, no matter what fibers are used. Because of the pronounced rib, the hand of the fabric is quite crisp.

The lustrous appearance and crisp hand, like taffeta, make faille a good choice for tailored designs such as suits and sculptured silhouettes. However, faille is not as popular as taffeta because the more obvious ribbed surface may present design challenges, such as matching and balancing concerns. Faille fabric is not as tightly woven as taffeta, so slippage may also be a concern.

This ribbed weave is noticeable, not only because of the large weft yarns that create the ribs, but also because another colored yarn was combined with the filling yarn. This larger rib makes the fabric much stiffer than smaller ribbed weave fabric.

Facts and figures

Distinctive features

- Pronounced cross-grain ribbed surface, with less tightly woven surface and ribs more visible than in taffeta.
- Lustrous appearance.
- Crisp or stiff hand.
- Rustle or "noise" is less obvious, especially if using spun yarns in ribs.

Strengths

- The crisp hand is ideal for full, exaggerated silhouette designs.
- The ribbed texture and lustrous, sometimes iridescent, color is highly valued for women's and men's formal apparel.

Weaknesses

- Pronounced horizontal rib may be difficult to match or balance.
- Seam slippage likely, so fitted silhouettes are discouraged.
- May wrinkle badly.

Usual fiber content

- Silk in warp; cotton or wool in weft direction.
- Polyester/nylon/acetate/rayon blends, using spun yarns in the weft direction.
- Nearly always multifilament yarns in the warp direction.

Balanced effect
Balanced placement of pattern pieces will keep the horizontal lines moving in the same rhythm for the viewer.

Unbalanced effect
Horizontal faille lines must be placed carefully to keep the design from looking unbalanced.

Shantung

Shantung uses irregularly shaped yarns, creating thickened "slubs" on the fabric surface. Similar to taffeta (see page 70), its main difference is the use of this special yarn to create a different texture to taffeta.

Silk fiber was originally used to make shantung, although today the same texture can be imitated in polyester, acetate, and rayon fiber yarns. Slubbed yarns can add stiffness to the fabric, making it a good for sculptured, rounded silhouettes. Because of the slubbed surface, the cross-grain is quite visible. The issue of balancing is a concern in the design process; however, since the slub texture appears randomly throughout the fabric, matching is not a problem. Dupioni silk fiber, irregularly-shaped fiber produced from a pair of silk worms instead of a single worm, can be used in shantung for a heavier weight fabric.

Silk shantung uses slubbed (irregularly twisted) yarns that create a horizontally textured surface. The fabric shown here is stiff, and very lustrous, due to the 100 percent silk fiber content.

Facts and figures

Distinctive features
- Slubbed, cross-grain textured surface.
- Easily recognizable, especially when using silk fiber.
- Lustrous appearance.
- Crisp or stiff hand.

Strengths
- The crisp hand is ideal for full, rounded-silhouette designs.
- The slubbed texture and lustrous quality is highly valued for women's and men's formal apparel.

Weaknesses
- The distinctive slubbed surface must be balanced.
- Seam slippage is likely, so fitted silhouettes are discouraged.
- Slubs make sewing difficult and may degrade the surface durability.
- May wrinkle badly.

Usual fiber content
- Silk, using waste silk or other silk fibers that create irregular shaped yarn.
- Silk blends with polyester, rayon, or acetate.
- Polyester or rayon, imitating the slubbed appearance.

Balancing angled slubbed fabric at the seams

Balanced effect
Though impossible to match the irregular thickness of the slubbed yarns on the fabric surface, the linear ribbed texture must be balanced to avoid a lopsided effect.

Unbalanced effect
The two side panels show how a symmetrical design can look unbalanced, due to the different linear angles of the ribbed surface.

Multicolored silk shantung
This multicolored, yarn-dyed shantung gives depth to the fabric. The luster of the shantung is not so obvious due to the variety of colors introduced.

Sateen

Sateen fabrics always use spun yarns. The lustrous, smooth surface of cotton-fiber sateen is highly recognizable.

The more highly twisted spun yarns will create a more lustrous surface than loosely twisted yarns. Top-weight sateens, though available, often are costly due to the small yarn size. The majority of sateen fabrics are medium- to bottom-weight and are used for a softer, yet tailored silhouette. Sateen fabric, with its natural luster, is often used for tailored suiting or pants when cotton fiber is used, for a slightly more formal appearance.

Printed images on sateen are clear and well defined due to the smooth, lustrous surface. The contrasting colors look vibrant on this sateen fabric.

Designer's tip: A very sharp, silicone-coated or ballpoint sewing needle is required to avoid snagging long floating yarns. Also, seam slippage may result if sateen is not tightly woven.

Facts and figures

Distinctive features
- Lustrous, smooth surface, although short fibers are noticeable on the surface.
- The hand is soft, although stiffer in the cross-grain direction.
- Shows seam design detail well.

Strengths
- The luster is very durable.
- Holds its shape easily.
- A good fabric for fitted designs.

Weaknesses
- If polyester or a polyester blend is used, pilling shows easily on the smooth, lustrous surface.
- Wrinkles are very noticeable.
- Floating yarns are subject to snagging, which will reduce the durability of the fabric.

Usual fiber content
- Any spun fiber yarn can be used.
- All cotton. If mercerized cotton is used, the luster and hand are enhanced.
- Polyester and cotton blends are frequently used to lower cost and improve wrinkle resistance.

Sateen
This very lustrous sateen is actually polyester float yarns on the face but cotton yarns on the back side, which is why the back side looks so dull.

Pigment-printed sateen
This sateen has been pigment printed. Note that there is almost no image showing through to the back side. This is characteristic of a pigment (dry process) print.

Wet-printed sateen
This sateen has been wet printed (see the image on the back side, which occurs when the fabric is wet and the image is printed on the fabric).

Bridal satin

Satin fabric, using long floating yarns on the face, is easily snagged. Bridal satin, a densely woven satin, limits snagging by using shorter floats and more tightly woven yarns.

Texturized multifilament fiber yarns are always used in bridal satin. The lustrous surface is usually subdued, due to the shorter floating yarns and very dense weave. Bridal satin's heavier weight makes it an excellent fabric for bridal gowns or other formal dresses that require full silhouettes with minimum support. This fabric holds its shape very well and is used for sculptured designs. Seam details show very well. However, stitching may leave needle holes if sewing errors are made.

Designer's tip: Floating yarns are subject to snagging, especially in the sewing process. A very sharp, silicone-coated or ballpoint sewing needle is required. Also, a no-drag, silicone-coated sewing foot is essential.

Full-bodied bridal satin is used for sculpted silhouettes. The fabric is lustrous rather than shiny. This pink bridal satin is a good choice for jackets, full skirts, and design details that require minimum support.

Facts and figures
Distinctive features
- Lustrous, smooth surface, though short fibers are noticeable on the surface.
- The hand is soft, although stiffer in the cross-grain direction.
- Shows design seaming detail well.

Strengths
- The luster is very durable.
- Holds its shape easily.
- A good fabric for semi-fitted designs.
- Fabric hand is very smooth and luxurious.

Weaknesses
- The sewing process may snag the fabric.
- Sewing errors cannot be easily erased from the surface.
- Wrinkles are very noticeable.

Usual fiber content
- Polyester multifilament yarns, often texturized, and sometimes microfiber.
- Silk multifilament yarns.
- Acetate can also be used.

Ivory bridal satin
The densely woven, shorter float yarns produce a more substantial-feeling fabric that snags much less than more common satin fabrics.

Weighted satin
This lightweight, pale-blue satin fabric, using smaller yarns than bridal satin, has been finished with a resin to add a stiff hand, similar to the real bridal satin. It is less expensive than bridal satin.

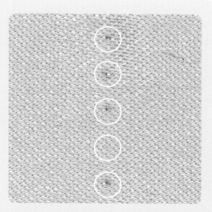

After-sewing error correction (enlarged image)
If the fabric is to be re-sewn, sometimes the satin face will show the former stitching holes and disturbed floating yarns.

Flannel

Flannel, a square, plain-weave fabric, is used for suiting and slacks, using wool-carded yarns to create soft, woven fabrics. Finished with a light brushed finish on both sides for a fuzzy surface, both the face and back look the same.

The weight of the fabric is dependent on the size of the spun yarn and how densely the yarns are compacted into the weave. Tropical, a summer-weight suiting fabric, also uses the same square weave, but without the brushed surface. Both flannel and tropical are available in many colors and patterns.

Flannel is an evenly textured, warm-hand fabric that is easy to use for beginners; it can be molded and beautifully tailored with fitted lines. It is a forgiving fabric, so sewing mistakes can be easily reworked without spoiling the visual appeal of the fabric.

Designer's tip: Top-weight "flannel" fabrics are usually a fine twill weave, not square plain-weave flannels. These lightweight fabrics have the same distinctive brushed finish but on the face side only.

This blue wool flannel fabric is typical of bottom-weight flannel. Its slightly brushed surface masks the square weave construction. The fabric weight makes it an excellent choice for jackets and winter-weight skirts and slacks.

Facts and figures

Distinctive features
- The square weave is very noticeable.
- An even-textured brushed surface in wool and wool blends.
- Tropical, which uses fine yarns, is less bulky than flannel and does not have a brushed finish.

Strengths
- The face and back look the same.
- Easy sewing and tailoring.
- Widely available in wool and other fiber blends.
- Soft hand.
- Durable fabric.

Weaknesses
- The name is sometimes confused with top-weight "flannel."
- Except for tropical, flannel is a cold-weather fabric only.

Usual fiber content
- Wool or wool-blended fabrics.
- Polyester/rayon blends, especially for tropical (no brushed finishing).

Plaid flannel
This plaid flannel, though a twill weave, is generally accepted as a flannel; the original plaids were all wool fiber. Today, flannel plaids are a variety of fiber contents.

Summer-weight tropical suiting
This balanced, plain weave fabric used in suiting was originally produced in high-quality, worsted wool yarns for summer weight. This pinstripe tropical fabric is a rayon/polyester blend, imitating the summer-weight wool tropical flannel.

All-season tropical suiting
A tighter weave than the pinstripe tropical, this tropical weave can span all seasons in a moderate climate. This polyester/rayon blend fabric is included in the "tropical" category, although it is actually a fine poplin weave.

Flannelette

Flannelette uses the same square weave construction that is used in flannel (opposite). However, flannelette uses cotton fiber and is brushed mostly on the face side only.

Flannelette imitates the more expensive wool flannel. The inexpensive yarns used to make it are produced using carded cotton fiber, producing a low-cost fabric. Soft flannelette is a popular choice for infants' clothing, sleepwear, warm sheets, and tops for women's and children's wear.

The brushed finish reduces the durability of the carded cotton yarns. More brushing gives a softer finish but increases the amount of shrinkage from laundering and weakens the fabric resistance to tearing and abrasion.

Caution: Flannelette is extremely flammable. If used in children's sleepwear, a flame-resistant finish is required in the United States.

The soft, brushed surface of flannelette is often printed. This printed flannelette would most likely be used for sleepwear or other inexpensive tops.

Facts and figures

Distinctive features
- Soft, brushed surface, generally face side only.
- Always cotton hand.
- Usually printed.
- Inexpensive.

Strengths
- Soft cotton hand.
- Very comfortable against the skin.
- Easy sewing and construction.
- Inexpensive, easily available fabric.

Weaknesses
- Shrinks easily.
- Brushing can weaken the fabric's durability.
- Pills easily.
- The brushed finish is extremely flammable in 100 percent cotton fiber content.

Usual fiber content
- Cotton.
- Cotton/polyester blends.

DESIGN RESPONSIBLY

While U.S. federal safety requirements demand a flame-retardant finish on children's sleepwear fabrics, the finishes themselves may expose children to harmful chemicals and heavy metals used in the finishing. More research is needed to confirm the long-term, low-exposure health effects of flame-retardant finishes on children. These same chemicals may also have a long-term negative impact on the environment.

Solid-color flannelette
This fabric-dyed flannelette shows the brushed face and unbrushed back.

Yarn-dyed plaid flannelette
This yarn-dyed plaid flannelette is a twill weave, similar to wool plaid flannel. Plaids are often more interesting designs if produced in a twill weave.

Linen

Butcher linen or linen-like

Linen fabrics, produced from flax fiber, are very popular for spring and summer apparel.

Because the flax fiber is a stem or bast fiber, the fibers are long, stiff, and irregular in shape. It is these irregular-shaped yarns, containing lumps or "slubs," that give this fabric its appearance. The yarn size and density of the weave will determine how the fabric is used. Suiting-weight fabric will use very thick yarns as compared to handkerchief linen. The thicker the yarn, the more pronounced are the slubs and irregularities.

Today, linen fabrics are used for suiting, pants, dresses, and jackets. While it has a crisp hand for tailored apparel, sometimes linen is soft-finished for a very drapable hand. However, linen fabrics have very poor resilience, so garment designs must consider severe wrinkling, unless a wrinkle-resistant finish is added. When using linen-like fabrics (imitation linen fabric using manufactured fiber), the wrinkling problem can be nearly eliminated.

This bottom-weight white linen fabric has a very crisp hand yet is not tightly woven. This means the translucency of the fabric should be carefully considered when designing a garment. The garment must be fully lined if this translucency is undesirable.

Designer's tip: The term "linen" can be applied only to fabric that is 100 percent flax or at least 50 percent in a blend. Sometimes "butcher linen" is used to describe a fabric using rayon fiber to imitate the look of linen fabric.

Linen fabric
This linen fabric is a lighter weight than the fabric shown above, and it is often used to make skirts and shorts. In addition, this lightweight linen has been finished with a softener for an extra-soft hand.

Linen-like fabric
Sometimes called "butcher linen," which isn't linen at all, this fabric uses 100 percent rayon, polyester, or polyester/rayon blend. The visual appearance is very similar to linen fabric.

Printed linen, using digital printing method
Linen can be printed, although the irregular surface makes fine image printing more complex. This fabric has been printed using inkjet printing technology.

Facts and figures

Distinctive features

- Slubbed yarns in warp and weft.
- The surface appearance is irregular due to different yarn shapes.
- Sometimes lustrous appearance, especially if beetled or otherwise calendered.
- A crisp hand when first produced.

Strengths

- Slubbed texture.
- Crisp hand.
- Very durable.
- Softens with more washings.

Weaknesses

- Poor wrinkle resistance.
- Folded edges do not resist abrasion and break apart.
- Can be expensive for a spring or summer fabric.

Usual fiber content

- Flax fiber or flax fiber blended with rayon or polyester.
- 100 percent rayon or polyester or blended polyester/rayon (butcher linen).

DESIGN RESPONSIBLY

Flax plants, as with all stem fiber plants, are very resistant to pests, so pesticides and herbicides are mostly unnecessary. Also, they don't require irrigation and they produce large amounts of usable fiber per acre/hectare.

Linen bias-cut suit

This linen suit, cut on the bias with unfinished raw edges, has a soft, washed finish. Traditionally expected to have a crisp, somewhat stiff hand, linen is a washable fabric that can be quite soft when washed multiple times. The softened finish can be commercially accelerated by adding enzymes or silicone to the wash.

Sheeting

Percale

Sheeting is one of the most common fabrics used today for casual apparel. Always a smooth surface, using evenly twisted spun yarns, sheeting quality is dependent on the fineness of the yarns.

Fine yarns create lighter-weight fabrics used especially for tops, although there is little distinction between calico (mostly printed) and solid-color sheeting. Percale is the term used to describe bedding fabrics, and it uses finer yarns compacted together. Thicker yarns create heavier fabrics used in skirts, dresses, and pants, and sheeting is a popular fabric for inexpensive casual clothing.

Medium-weight sheeting can be finished with a crinkled finish or wrinkle-resistant finish. It is used for embroidery or other embellishments to produce varied appearances in different apparel designs.

This inexpensive 100 percent cotton square weave is made from low-quality, carded cotton yarn. The fabric surface becomes softer after several washes and can be a wonderful fabric for ladies' casual blouses.

Facts and figures

Distinctive features
- Balanced weave—the face and back look the same.
- Smooth, even surface.
- All yarns look the same on the surface.
- Always cotton hand.

Strengths
- Tailors well.
- Soft hand.
- Durable.
- Good wrinkle resistance if blended with polyester.
- Adaptable fabric for a variety of finishes.

Weaknesses
- Fair durability when a low yarn count is used for inexpensive fabric.
- Sometimes shrinks badly after washing.

Usual fiber content
- 100 percent cotton or cotton blends.

Crinkled sheeting
A crinkled finish produces an appealing texture. This finish is used in both lighter- and heavier-weight sheeting.

Twill weaves used in sheets
This twill fabric is often used in producing bedsheets. Fine twill fabrics add variety to the fabric surface. This fabric is produced from bamboo rayon and has an antibacterial characteristic.

Cotton/polyester sheeting
This blended fabric is used for low-quality sheeting but is faster drying compared to 100 percent cotton sheets. Energy savings are significant if using a machine dryer.

Muslin

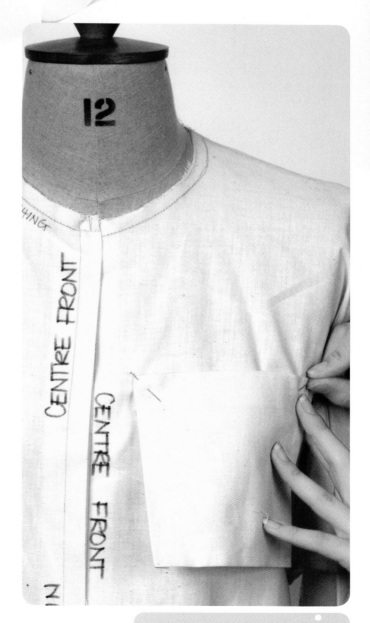

This medium-weight muslin has a crisp resin finish applied to the fabric. Design students should be careful in pressing and steaming their first designs using muslin to avoid fabric shrinkage.

Design students are introduced to muslin at the start of their training. The fabric, available in a variety of medium to light weights, is the artistic medium used to interpret apparel designs initially.

Primarily used undyed, the purpose of this fabric in design is to provide a neutral fabric for developing the garment vision. Muslin is an unfinished fabric, so it is subject to shrinkage during the pressing/steaming process. Care should be taken to avoid too much steam heat while developing design ideas. The hand is generally somewhat stiff, as some muslins have an added resin.

Preshrunk muslin is sometimes used as an interlining for tailored garments. However, because of the shrinkage problem, it is not recommended for this purpose.

Facts and figures

Distinctive features
- Even surface texture.
- Usually unbleached natural color, often with cotton "trash" still visible on the surface.
- Slightly crisp hand, usually due to resin finish.

Strengths
- Easy fabric to cut and sew.
- Can be draped during the design process due to the balanced weave.

Weaknesses
- Shrinks easily in the steaming process.
- Sometimes stretches because the fabric is unfinished.

Usual fiber content
- 100 percent cotton.

Muslin being draped on a dress form
Using muslin to envisage the designer's idea is often the first step toward design development.

Canvas

Duck, sailcloth

Canvas is a heavyweight fabric used for casual pants and jackets, bags, shoes, workwear, furniture coverings, drapes, and awnings.

Although canvas is the most common name for this basketweave fabric, there are two other fabrics that look quite similar: sailcloth and duck. They all have a similar surface; all are strong and reasonably abrasion-resistant.

In apparel, canvas is an alternative to denim (see page 86). Canvas in jeans or other casual bottoms and jackets is usually a lighter weight and lower cost than the denim fabrics used for the same designs. Therefore, if the designer wants a fabric with a similar use to denim, but a different color and texture, canvas can provide an interesting alternative.

Canvas has a naturally stiff hand, so it is a great fabric for seaming and topstitching detail. Canvas has a cross-grain ribbed texture, and the hand of the fabric is usually softened, either as fabric, or more commonly, in garment washing after being sewn. Pigment dyeing is especially popular for a soft, "worn" appearance after washing.

Enlargement

This canvas fabric is an unbalanced basketweave using a pair of fine yarns in the warp, and a single, thicker yarn in the weft. This large weft yarn contributes to the stiffness and heavy weight of the fabric.

Sailcloth fabric
Sailcloth is the lightest of the three fabrics and is commonly used in apparel.

Duck fabric
Duck is the coarsest and heaviest of the three basketweaves in this category. It is often used for bags or other products that require heavy weight and durability.

Recycled cotton canvas
Canvas uses finer yarns than duck, is more compactly woven, and is heavier. This sample was produced from recycled cotton fiber and spun with acrylic for strength. The cotton is already colored, so it does not need to be dyed. Recycled cotton yarn is not high-quality, but energy and water are conserved using this method of recycling.

Facts and figures

Distinctive features

- A crisp, stiff hand when first produced.
- Bulky fabric in heaviest weights.
- Slightly ribbed surface, but paired warp yarns add unique basketweave surface texture.
- Easily available and a well-recognized fabric.

Strengths

- A very strong and durable fabric.
- Softens with wear and washing.
- Tailors well.
- Even surface texture shows design seam details.

Weaknesses

- Cross-grain ribbed surface can weaken if the fabric is subjected to constant abrasion (rubbing against the fabric).
- Nylon canvas is very stiff.

Usual fiber content

- 100 percent cotton; becomes softer when washed.
- Hemp/cotton blends; flax/cotton blends are becoming more popular and have a similar hand to all-cotton.
- Polyester/cotton blends feel lighter in weight and sometimes pill. However, they are much more wrinkle-resistant than cotton or hemp/flax/cotton blends.
- 100 percent polyester or nylon; often used for industrial purposes, such as furniture and awnings for more strength and durability.

DESIGN RESPONSIBLY

The use of hemp fiber in canvas has historic significance. All ship sails were produced from hemp because the fiber was fast-drying and resisted mildew and other moisture damage. Our collective memory knows only cotton fiber for canvas in apparel. However, with the new innovations to "cottonize" hemp into softer fiber, its expanded use in canvas products seems a practical alternative to cotton fiber, which dries slowly and is not mildew-resistant.

Canvas shoes

Canvas clothing has an even surface texture, and the garment design can use many seaming details. Canvas is a signature fabric for casual shoes, bags, and beach apparel.

Homespun

A common fabric for handweaving, homespun uses large yarns for a coarsely textured square weave.

No matter what fiber is used, the result always looks less refined than fabrics that use finer yarns and tighter weaves. However, hand-woven homespun fabrics are often highly prized for blazers and coats.

A rugged fabric that is very durable, homespun is used for casual apparel or, if using wool fiber, career wear. Its coarse surface texture usually limits seam lines as design features. Too many seam lines on this coarse fabric will add bulk.

This 100 percent cotton homespun is typical of the coarsely spun yarns and loose balanced weave. Originally a hand-woven fabric, this sample retains the stiff hand that is important for structural fabrics.

Facts and figures

Distinctive features
- Coarse-textured, even surface, where yarns are distinct and visible.
- The face and back look the same.
- Often appears handwoven.
- Yarns can be loosely woven or a little more tightly woven, but not dense.

Strengths
- Balanced weave that tailors well.
- Look of hand-woven fabric.
- Good surface texture.
- Good durability.

Weaknesses
- Unrefined in appearance.
- In lighter weights may be less abrasion resistant.
- Not easily available for large production.

Usual fiber content
- 100 percent wool or wool blends—suiting, jackets, and coats.
- 100 percent cotton or cotton blends—spring/summer-weight casual sportswear and jackets.
- Polyester/rayon blends or linen blends—sometimes used for nonseasonal fabric.

Cotton homespun
Cotton homespun may be used in unstructured pants and jackets, though shrinkage is a concern. This sample includes embroidered dots on the surface.

Polyester/rayon homespun
This fiber blend is often substituted for wool homespun and is used in similar products, such as suiting, tailored jackets, and slacks.

Wool homespun
The coarse, handwoven look of this wool homespun uses low-spun woolen yarns that have flecks of color spun into the yarn. The result is a "rustic" fabric that is visually unrefined.

Hopsacking

Wool fiber hopsacking is a balanced basketweave, using small paired warp and weft yarn to create the fine texture.

Often used in men's suiting to create a different texture than the usual flannel or twill surface texture, hopsacking is especially popular in the spring and summer seasons. Although originally used to carry hops for producing beer, hopsack fabric is now used in fine suits, jackets, and pants. The basketweave texture is not so tightly woven like a usual plain weave or twill, so there is more breathability. Linen hopsacking is very comfortable in hot weather.

Basketweave texture is tightly woven in this fiber-dyed wool hopsack. It is used for casual men's sports jackets or topcoats.

Facts and figures

Distinctive features
- Basketweave fine texture.
- All-over even texture.
- More loosely woven than flannel for a more open texture.

Strengths
- Tailors extremely well.
- Good drape.
- Spring fabric.
- In linen, can be somewhat lustrous.

Weaknesses
- Limited availability in linen and wool blends.
- Appropriate for fall/winter seasons only.
- If linen, will wrinkle badly.

Usual fiber content
- 100 percent flax for linen hopsacking.
- 100 percent wool for fine wool, lightweight suiting.

Linen hopsacking
More traditional fabric in linen hopsacking shows flax fiber's lustrous character. Notice the basketweave texture.

Worsted wool hopsack
This tightly woven basketweave can have a "sheen," or luster, due to the highly twisted worsted yarns. However, due to the small yarns used, this hopsack fabric will have a more refined surface.

Woolen hopsack
This rustic-looking woolen yarn hopsack has a coarse hand, similar to the original hand-woven hopsack. The fabric is now woven as a balanced or unbalanced basketweave.

Denim

Denim has become the most important fabric used for apparel today. Its universal appeal transcends culture and tradition.

Although invented in Nîmes, France, denim is now viewed as an American fabric popularized in the 1960s. As denim retailer Gap ascended in the 1980s, denim jeans came to represent rugged individuality and self-reliance worldwide.

Designers now view denim as a canvas to communicate style, status, and character. The wide variety of denim finishes available provides a different level of expression beyond jean design.

Because of the importance of denim, four pages are devoted to this fabric—first, to discuss the various types of denim and fiber contents, and second, to provide information on finishing as well as the social and environmental impact of denim jeans production.

Denim's unique diagonal surface texture can be in a left-hand or a right-hand direction. Although there can be different angles of the diagonal texture and varying density in the weave that will change the fabric weight, all denims have a similar look. The size of the yarns used can influence the hand and drape of the fabric, but the diagonal weave direction doesn't change the softness of the fabric. Soft hand is governed almost completely by the finishing process used, which will be discussed on pages 88–89.

Denim is an extremely durable yet flexible fabric used in apparel. A heavy, temporary resin finish adds stiffness.

Facts and figures

Distinctive features

- Always dark blue indigo warp yarns on fabric face with white weft yarns behind blue yarns. Denim is never one color.
- Diagonal surface texture on face side only.
- The face is darker, the back a lighter color.
- A very stiff hand when first produced.

Strengths

- Rugged, very durable fabric, particularly against abrasion.
- Softens when washed many times.
- Diagonal texture aids the drapability of the fabric.
- More wrinkle-resistant than bottom-weight canvas.

Weaknesses

- Indigo dye is not dyefast and bleeds/crocks easily.
- Folded fabric edges wear out quickly.
- Stiff, heavy fabric requires special sewing equipment, such as a "walking foot" to sew more than two layers of fabric.

Usual fiber content

- 100 percent cotton.
- Cotton/spandex blend.
- Cotton with hemp or flax blend.
- 100 percent hemp or linen (may be used more in future denim fabrics).

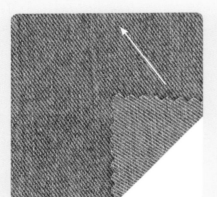

Left-hand twill

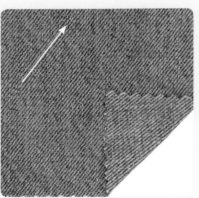

Right-hand twill

DESIGN RESPONSIBLY

Designers have come to assume that cotton fiber is the best fiber choice for denim fabric. Remember that cotton fiber production is high maintenance, susceptible to pests, and requires large quantities of water for dependable crop yields. "Cottonized" hemp fiber, a naturally pest-resistant, drought-tolerant fiber whose crop yields surpass cotton, is one of several alternative fibers to cotton. Conserving water use and reducing chemical use in production will help sustain the fiber supply chain.

Denim from recycled cotton fiber

This denim fabric is produced using cotton fiber reclaimed from cutting waste. By "opening" the scraps back into fiber and spinning the fiber into new cotton yarn, the blue color yarn is ready for weaving. The white yarn is also recycled cotton fiber. By eliminating yarn dyeing, this fabric eliminates the water used and the waste from dyeing.

Hemp drill or bull denim

Heavy twill fabric dyed one color is called drill or bull denim. This fabric is produced from cottonized hemp that has nearly the same hand as cotton fiber. Hemp is also produced in denim fabrics.

Red selvage denim

This red color at the selvage is an American tradition, now transferred to Japanese-produced denim. The selvage is sometimes used as a design element. The color used doesn't have to be red.

Denim dress

Fashion denim can either be washed to create the desired finish or, as with this designer dress, areas of the fabric can be "distressed," in this case the pockets, to achieve a certain look. The fabric edges on this garment have been left unfinished so that they ravel, a deliberate choice on the part of the designer.

Denim finishing

The designer is deeply involved in creating new denim jean finishes or adopting a new finishing technique. In general, the designer's goal is to create a "look" that will reflect current trends. It is also the designer's responsibility to consider social (labor intensiveness) and environmental (water and chemical pollution) consequences of the latest denim finishing procedures.

The appearance and soft hand of denim jeans is the result of washing the jeans in a unique blend of water, chemicals (especially bleach), mechanical abrasives, and heat. These chemical finishes are often proprietary, much like a secret recipe, and are closely guarded, as the resulting finish often defines a jeans brand and may be the reason a customer purchases and remains loyal to a company's jeans.

Here are a few suggestions that you might make when working with a jeans manufacturer to achieve the desired look and yet lessen the impact on workers and the environment:

- If bleach is used, choose a non-chlorine bleach. Do not use chlorine bleach, which is a toxin, especially for the workers at the factory.

- Use enzymes or other alternatives to bleach, which often take longer to produce the desired effect but have significantly less impact on workers and the local water supply.

- The less washing the better, which means the jeans will be a darker blue color. Avoid light color denim—it means more washing and more dye removed into the local wastewater system.

Finishing denim requires a rugged fabric, even for denim. Therefore, it is important to know the various bottom weights used and whether they can withstand the finishing process:

- 8 oz per square yard (227 g per square meter)—soft skirts and dresses.
- 10 oz and 12 oz per square yard (283 g and 340 g per square meter—lightweight pants.

  These fabrics cannot withstand such abrasive washing treatment and will wear out easily. In all cases, laundering with simple softeners is best. Additional abrasives should be tested.

- 14 oz per square yard (397 g per square meter)—jean construction. 14+oz per square yard (397+g per square meter) is available but seldom used.

  This weight is the fabric of choice for most extensively washed/treated finishes. Due to this processing, the final jeans will lose fabric weight and become lighter in weight after chemicals are applied and washing is completed.

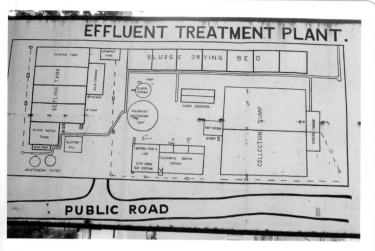

Wastewater treatment

This factory has installed simple wastewater treatment to clean the water as it leaves the denim washing facility. Designers should ask suppliers how they manage their wastewater and request production teams to personally inspect the factory site for responsible water and waste management.

Hand-painting bleach onto jeans

Many denim washes are labor-intensive and may require individuals to hand-apply chemicals before washing. The designer needs to understand the amount of labor that will be required to produce the proprietary "washed" appearance of their latest denim wash.

DESIGN RESPONSIBLY

The following are innovations in denim finishing:
- New silicone finishes that reduce water use.
- Use of a laser to "print" denim finishing marks without the use of water.
- Non-bleach finishing.

Types of denim washes

The recipes used in garment-washing jeans are considered intellectual property. Certain chemicals, hand applications, and machinery are used to achieve specific appearances and fabric hand, and the procedures are closely guarded secrets of the manufacturers. These are the basic washes:

Light-blue color wash

Heavily washed denim often uses extra chemicals to remove color and add softness. The most dye is removed during this process, which must then be cleaned from the wastewater.

Medium-blue color wash

Less dye is removed, and washing time is generally less than for the light-blue wash; however, a significant amount of dye and bleaching chemicals must still be removed from the wastewater.

Dark-blue or "raw" color wash

Only lightly washed in order to remove the fabric resin and slightly soften the fabric. The least amount of dye is removed in the garment-washing process.

Gabardine

A tightly woven fabric, the twill-weave texture appears as fine, diagonal lines that are close together. Gabardine is so tightly woven that it can sometimes resist water.

Produced using worsted yarns, wool gabardine is a good choice for outerwear coats. Regardless of the fiber content, all gabardine fabrics have good drapability, excellent wrinkle resistance, and wonderful tailoring quality for designs that require seaming detail. The flexibility of gabardine produces beautiful rolled shawl collars and lapels, slim skirts, and both flat and pleated-front slacks. It is one of the most versatile fabrics used in suits, blazers, skirts, dresses, and other tailored clothing.

Although gabardine is very densely woven, using smooth, high-quality spun yarns or more complex multifilament yarns, the result is a finely textured fabric that is easily manipulated in tailoring.

Designer's tip: Because of the even, flat surface, it is important to use a press cloth and avoid hard pressing, as the seam lines will show through to the surface.

This white, worsted wool gabardine has a smooth, somewhat lustrous surface, due to the highly twisted worsted yarns and the tightly woven diagonal textured surface. It drapes well and tailors into beautiful blazers and slacks.

Facts and figures
Distinctive features
- Fine, diagonal-textured surface; sometimes the diagonal is difficult to recognize.
- Densely woven for a good "body."
- Good drape for tailoring.
- Wrinkle-resistant, regardless of the fiber content.

Strengths
- Very durable fabric—especially abrasion-resistant.
- Resists wrinkles easily.
- Dense weave can resist light rain.
- Fine diagonal lines are an appealing texture in high-quality suits.

Weaknesses
- Usually a more expensive fabric than flannel or bottom-weight poplin.
- Polyester or polyester/rayon blends result in pilling.
- A difficult fabric to press without seam allowances showing through to the face, essential to use a pressing cloth.

Usual fiber content
- 100 percent high-quality wool, sometimes blended with mohair or cashmere.
- 100 percent multifilament textured polyester.
- 50 percent polyester/50 percent rayon spun-fiber blend to imitate wool.
- Cotton and cotton/polyester blends.

Cotton gabardine
The fine diagonal twill surface, produced using highly twisted, high-quality, worsted wool yarns, is a popular choice for tailored jackets and slacks—particularly in the herringbone pattern shown here.

Lyocell gabardine
Sustainable lyocell fiber is produced in a "closed loop" manufacturing process (see page 30). The fiber choice in this twill fabric creates a soft, wool-like surface that is resilient, and it can be a year-round fabric.

Worsted wool striped herringbone gabardine
This lightweight worsted wool fabric is usually used for men's tailored suits. The herringbone twill is a very popular pattern in suiting.

Chino

A popular twill weave, chino is always produced with cotton fiber. Not as densely woven as gabardine (see left), the diagonal twill texture is more noticeable and less fine than gabardine.

Chino is one of the most popular fabrics used in men's slacks, providing an alternative to dressier wool-blend gabardine, for more casual wear-to-work slacks. The twill weave makes the fabric more drapable than canvas or bottom-weight poplin.

Chino quality can vary according to how densely the fabric is woven. The more tightly woven the fabric, the finer the diagonal surface. The looser the weave, the coarser the appearance of the diagonal surface. Coarse-weave chinos are less expensive than more tightly woven chinos.

Slacks produced from chino fabric, after sewing is completed, are most often garment-finished with wrinkle-resistant and stain-resistant finishes for easy care and maintenance. Today, most cotton chino garments are also garment washed to achieve a soft hand. The cotton twill fabrics shown below are often considered very similar to chino.

This gray cotton chino is a popular fabric for men's casual slacks that can move from the golf course to a business meeting. Its smooth surface and drapable hand is ideal for tailoring casual jackets, pants, and skirts.

Facts and figures

Distinctive features
- Fine, diagonal-line surface texture.
- Good drape.
- Smooth surface.

Strengths
- Very durable fabric, especially abrasion-resistant.
- Easily available fabric.
- Good fabric for tailoring.
- Drapes well.

Weaknesses
- Looser weaves are not durable
- Must be preshrunk before sewing.
- Dark colors are not colorfast.

Usual fiber content
- 100 percent cotton.
- Cotton/polyester blends.

DESIGN RESPONSIBLY

The popularity of cotton chino pant fabrics for men's and women's slacks has been accelerated by offering garment finishing using nano-finishes. While the obvious benefits have made caring for 100 percent cotton slacks much easier, no effort has been made to understand whether nano-finishing is harmful to the environment or the wearer. Nano-molecules used in these convenience finishes have not been studied to determine whether they pose a health risk when they enter the water supply or are absorbed into the wearer's skin.

High-quality cotton twill
Note the steep angle of the diagonal texture of this cotton twill, which is typical of a more densely woven chino. This sample has a washed finish.

More pronounced cotton twill
This loosely woven fabric uses larger cotton yarns to widen the spaces between the diagonal lines of the twill, producing a lower-quality chino than the sample on the left.

Serge

Serge is used for high-quality wool suits. Its tightly woven surface requires very high-quality wool fiber, spun into worsted yarns.

The fine, diagonal lines on the fabric surface create a smooth, slightly lustrous surface. Serge is used for men's and women's high-quality suits, blazers, skirts, and slacks. The fabric hand tends to feel crisp or "hard." Some serge fabrics have a more defined twill surface but are not as fine as gabardine (see page 90).

Serge can also be produced using different colored yarns to create stripes, often called pinstripes. See the center photo below. Pinstriped serge is a typical fabric for more conservative business attire.

This serge fabric is ideal for high-quality men's suits. Tightly woven for a steeply diagonal twill surface, serge is an extremely durable suiting fabric that tailors well.

Facts and figures

Distinctive features
- Fine, diagonal-lined fabric face.
- Smooth, crisp hand.
- Drapes very well.
- Sometimes lustrous surface.

Strengths
- Excellent fabric for molding and tailoring.
- Excellent resilience.
- Tailors very well.

Weaknesses
- Fabric face can develop an undesirable "shine."
- Expensive.

Usual fiber content
- Fine, 100 percent wool.
- High-quality wool blend, sometimes with cashmere.

Fiber-dyed serge
Fiber is dyed before the yarn is spun. Sometimes several different colors of fiber are spun together in one yarn. The result is a "heather" effect of several colors of fibers in one fabric.

Pinstriped serge
Introducing lighter-colored warp yarns to the serge twill will produce a striped effect, known as a pinstripe. The crisp hand of serge in a pinstripe pattern is a very good choice for tailored clothing.

Tricotine
Tricotine is a type of twill weave that produces a flat-looking twill texture. This sample is a spun woolen yarn; sometimes textured multifilament crêpe yarns are used.

Cavalry twill

This fabric was used in cavalry uniforms, from where the name originates.

The raised, very pronounced diagonal twill surface is easily recognized. The high–low effect of the raised diagonal line followed by the contrasting low surface accentuates the texture. The fabric has a surprisingly soft drape, which makes it very comfortable to wear.

Cavalry twill is used for riding pants or other uniquely tailored jackets and pants. The raised textured surface supports rounded shaping. This fabric will support more exaggerated silhouettes. It is sometimes used for tailored men's and women's suits. Its surface texture is very noticeable, from fine lines to very pronounced diagonal lines.

The high–low diagonal texture of a cavalry twill calls for a simple garment design. Its soft drape allows for easy movement and beautiful tailoring details.

Facts and figures

Distinctive features
- Pronounced, raised diagonal surface.
- High–low surface.

Strengths
- Good drape for such a textured fabric.
- Strong fabric.
- Very interesting texture.

Weaknesses
- The pronounced diagonal surface sometimes creates a matching problem for designs using many seams.
- May snag easily on the raised diagonal lines.
- Not easily available.

Usual fiber content
- 100 percent wool or wool blend.
- 100 percent cotton or cotton/blend.

Wool cavalry twill
Wool cavalry twill has a soft hand. This sample has a subtle diagonal high–low texture.

Cotton cavalry twill
Cotton cavalry twill is often used in distinctive casual twill slacks and jackets. It has a tactile hand and, if a garment is washed, the surface texture will develop quite a soft hand.

Two-tone cavalry twill
This two-tone cotton cavalry twill is not as soft as wool twill but makes an interesting texture for sportswear. The pronounced high–low diagonal surface texture is emphasized by the two colors of yarn used.

Ripstop

Ripstop fabric was designed to prevent fabric from ripping or tearing. It has been used extensively in the military for extremely durable field uniforms, parachutes, tents, and other equipment that requires excellent durability.

This versatile fabric is used for camping gear and apparel, as well as for bags and other products that require strength and durability. The balanced square weave has an extra set of warp and weft yarns that are larger than the rest of the warp and weft yarns. The resulting "squared" texture on the fabric surface creates extra reinforcement for tearing resistance. Because of its traditional use by the military, ripstop has become a favorite for "extreme" wear clothing. Designers find the squared texture an interesting change from the usual twill of denim (see page 86) or the ribbed appearance of canvas (see page 82).

This yellow ripstop has a crisp hand due to the heavier yarns woven into its compact weave. Nylon ripstop is often used for lightweight casual jackets or accessories.

Facts and figures

Distinctive features
- Square, raised, woven-in pattern.
- Slightly stiff hand where the heavier yarns are interlaced.

Strengths
- Very durable, especially strong fabric.
- Very interesting square texture.
- If cotton fiber is used, the cross-hatched "squared" fabric surface is more exaggerated and the fabric is bulkier than nylon or polyester ripstop fabrics.
- Nylon and polyester ripstop is a lightweight yet strong fabric for pants and jackets.

Weaknesses
- Polyester and nylon fiber fabrics are somewhat limited in product use.
- Cotton ripstop is not easily available for commercial use.

Usual fiber content
- 100 percent cotton, cotton/polyester, or cotton/nylon blends.
- 100 percent polyester.
- 100 percent nylon.

Cotton ripstop fabric
Cotton ripstop fabric is often used in men's casual pants and vests. A very durable fabric, the square texture of the ripstop fabric provides a contrast to the usual twill or canvas surfaces for casual pant fabrics.

Ripstop with embossed face
This polyester ripstop is often used for outerwear. The circular pattern embossed on the fabric face adds an additional texture combined with the square ripstop weaving pattern. There is a lightweight water-resistant coating on the back of this fabric.

Recycled polyester ripstop
This fine-denier yarn fabric is completely recyclable. The polyester microporous membrane, which is water-resistant and breathable, and the polyester ECO CIRCLE™ fabric are produced from recycled polyester garments.

 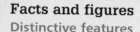

Ottoman

Ottoman fabric has a pronounced cross-grain rib. It is formed by very fine warp yarns, almost always multifilament yarns, interlacing with large weft yarns that are quite "plump."

As the fine warp yarns slide over and under the large weft yarns, the resulting texture is heavily ribbed, but with a smooth, sometimes lustrous surface. The rib and luster of ottoman can vary in size, but it always has a firm (stiff) hand.

Ottoman is most commonly used for furniture upholstery, but occasionally it is used to make women's suits or separate fashion jackets. The stiff hand of the fabric governs the type of garment silhouette. Closely fitted silhouettes are generally not advised. It can be used to create sculptural silhouettes that stand away from the body. The fabric may be prone to slippage, depending on the width of the ribs.

Ottoman fabric has a stiff hand due to the large horizontal ribbed texture. It's popular for upholstery fabric and sometimes for jackets and coats.

Facts and figures

Distinctive features
- Very pronounced cross-grain rib.
- Firm or stiff hand.
- Can have a somewhat lustrous surface.

Strengths
- Excellent cross-grain texture.
- Good choice for sculptural shapes.

Weaknesses
- Not wrinkle-resistant.
- Bulky, sometimes stiff.
- Unstable fabric when sewing as weft yarns can pull out.
- If extremely large rib, may require matching/balancing design.

Usual fiber content
- 100 percent cotton.
- Fine silk warp with large wool weft yarns or large cotton weft yarns.

How to "balance" a pronounced ottoman rib

Such exaggerated ribbed surface texture will require matching and balancing. The top photo shows how the side panels have not been cut with the ribbed surface at the same angle. When sewn into a garment, these ribbed fabric lines will distract from the design and sometimes influence the fit. Cut carefully and plan how the ribbed surface is to be balanced in the design.

Balanced

Unbalanced

Printed ottoman rib

This is a wet-printing process, so the fabric is moistened before the dye is applied to the fabric surface, then it is chemically "fixed" to be more dyefast and rinsed to remove excess dye. Notice how the image colors soak through to the back side.

Dobby weaves
for suiting

Fabrics used for suits have evolved into a wide variety of unique weaving patterns. The fabric surface texture is created by combining different weaves and using different types and colors of yarn in the woven-in geometric patterns.

This satin-stripe dobby suiting has a lustrous and matte texture to the fabric surface due to the combination of satin and plain weaves used in its construction. The satin stripes stand higher on the surface than the matte plain-weave areas.

Similar to the weaving style in top-weight dobby weaves (see page 68), bottom-weight dobby weaves provide interesting texture and pattern on the fabric surface. The designer who is attracted to these weaves is usually envisaging stylish suiting and elegant attire in general.

Dobby weaves in bottom weights are used almost exclusively for women's and men's suiting, dressy jackets, dresses, and pants. These fabrics often have contrasting matte and lustrous surfaces woven into the designs. The result often creates surface texture or color patterns by combining satin, plain, and twill weaves, using different types and colors of yarn, in the woven-in dobby designs.

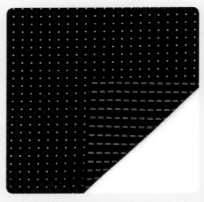

Mitered-stripe sewn design in a jacket
A stripe design can be sewn together at matched angles to create a chevron or "V" shape. Designers will sometimes use a striped dobby fabric in order to incorporate the mitered-stripe effect into their garment design.

Patterned dobby
Bouclé yarns provide surface texture along with varied interlacings of different sizes of yarns. This fabric is similar to the fabrics popularized by Chanel suits.

Pin dot dobby weave suiting fabric
Notice the use of colored yarn that emphasizes the woven-in texture in a horizontal texture and contrasting pin dot detail.

Facts and figures

Distinctive features
- Interesting geometric patterns and texture woven into the fabric surface.
- Full-bodied fabric that holds the silhouette shape.
- Drapes very well.

Strengths
- Excellent fabric for tailoring.
- Generally good resilience.
- Great variety of textures in different weave combinations.
- Textures are specific to the geometric woven-in designs.

Weaknesses
- Fabrics are not always easily available.
- The texture can be easily snagged.
- Can be expensive.

Usual fiber content
- Fine, 100 percent wool.
- Wool/silk blends.
- High-quality wool blend, sometimes with polyester or rayon.
- 100 percent polyester or polyester/acetate blends.
- Rayon and acetate/rayon blends.

Women's suit using a dobby-patterned suiting fabric
This elegant, lustrous, and matte geometric pattern is achieved by combining satin and plain weaves in alternating stripes adjacent to duller, plain-weave areas.

Tweeds

Tweed fabric is not a weave. The tweed look is achieved by combining various colored fibers into multicolored, irregularly spun yarns, and then weaving these yarns into fabric.

The description "tweed" can also be applied to tweed (multicolored, irregularly spun) yarn knitted into sweaters. It is also possible to create tweed fabrics using solid-color yarn and weaving specific patterns, such as herringbone (see photo above). It is a broken (or reverse) twill weave but is traditionally called a herringbone tweed if produced in a wool blend or wool-like blend. Plain weave fabric, using the tweed yarns mentioned above, can also be called tweed.

Although the original tweed look seems to originate from the British Isles, the look of tweed fabrics is produced in many countries. Tweed-like fabrics are produced in multiple fiber contents, with the end result a subtle, multicolored surface effect.

Some tweeds are actually patterns of yarns (usually wool or wool blend) woven together to create checks and plaids. Every designer should be able to recognize houndstooth check and glen plaid, which are well-known patterns. Although technically not a tweed, plaid fabrics often use tweed yarns and are woven together to create square or rectangular patterns of color.

This fabric is produced from 75 percent recycled cotton fiber, spun with acrylic fiber for strength. The fiber is already colored, so the fabric is already dyed when weaving is completed. Using recycled cotton fabric conserves energy and water as no additional dyeing is required.

Facts and figures

Distinctive features
- Subtle, multicolored yarns woven into twill or plain weave fabrics.
- Specific checks and plaids identified with "tweed."
- Usually coarse wool texture, not refined.

Strengths
- Beautiful, multicolored fiber yarns producing a variety of solid colors, checks, or plaids.
- Wool hand is preferred.
- Wool fabrics are quite durable and even moisture-resistant if tightly woven.

Weaknesses
- Manufactured fiber blends have the look of the wool tweeds but are much less durable.
- Plaid or check pattern will require matching seams.

Usual fiber content
- 100 percent wool.
- Wool/rayon and wool/acrylic blends.
- Acrylic, polyester, and nylon blends.

Twill weaves using multicolored tweed yarns for a patterned tweed

Houndstooth check
Houndstooth check is a highly recognizable fabric, created by weaving together solid colored and tweed yarns.

Multicolored plaid
An example of a plaid pattern, created by interlacing dyed solid colored and tweed yarns together.

Tweed jackets
Traditionally a bottom-weight fabric, tweeds that use multicolored yarns are best in tailored blazers and coats. These fabrics tailor beautifully, and the multicolored patterns provide their own style.

Weaves using multicolored tweed yarns for an "allover" tweed effect

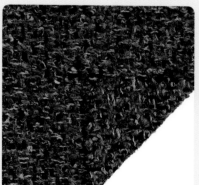

Glen plaid
Another highly recognizable fabric pattern is Glen plaid.

Donegal tweed
The Donegal tweed pattern requires multicolored, irregularly spun yarn that is woven into a plain-weave fabric.

Generic "tweed" fabric
Although not an identifiable tweed fabric, this fabric shows the two characteristics of a tweed fabric: multicolored fiber yarn and multiple colors of yarn, all woven together to create a subtle pattern.

Jacquard weaves

Jacquard weaves are the most complex woven fabrics used today. The fabrics are characterized by curved, intricate images woven into the fabric, often using different colored yarns.

This brocade fabric, using a jacquard weave, shows the lustrous and varied patterns and textures that are so characteristic of the jacquard weaving technique.

The apparel industry uses these fabrics with great care and uses them sparingly because they are slow to produce and expensive to purchase. There are three major groups of jacquard weaves:

Tapestry: Machine-produced tapestry tries to imitate hand-woven tapestry. The result is a flat, tightly woven unbalanced plain weave, using different colored yarns in the weft, to create the surface image.

Brocade: Detailed design that results in high–low woven-in images, designed especially to resemble embroidery on the fabric surface. Heavy, sometimes metallic, yarns are introduced into the fabric.

Damask: Generally using one color or limited colors, the images are woven in combinations of satin weaves and plain ribbed weaves. Fine yarns are nearly always used because the goal is to weave lustrous images into the fabric. Woven-in images are usually floral, but stripes are sometimes introduced into the generally luxurious designs.

Designer's tip: The fabric image may be positioned for use in one direction, called a "one-way" design. It is important to review carefully so the fabric image will be positioned in a way to balance and match the image on the garment design.

Tapestry
Example of machine-produced tapestry.

Brocade
The detailed design of brocade resembles embroidery on the fabric surface. Brocade tends to be heavier than damask and lighter than tapestry, but there are exceptions.

Damask
Example of the luxurious designs that are woven to produce damask.

Facts and figures

Distinctive features

- Always curved in shape, intricate images woven into the fabric, imitating embroidered or hand-woven fabrics.
- Luxurious in appearance.
- Highly recognizable, used for high social-status products.

Strengths

- The beautiful woven-in images make simple styling a must, which means less complicated sewing construction.
- The fabric design sells itself, so garment design is often secondary.
- Bottom-weight jacquards are firm fabrics, holding seaming detail very well.

Weaknesses

- Cutting the fabric incorrectly can cause it to become less stable, sometimes encouraging seam slippage.
- Unless tightly woven tapestry, the fabric can have poor abrasion resistance, particularly around the satin weave portions of the woven-in design.
- Expensive.
- Difficult to match and balance along the seams.

Usual fiber content

- 100 percent wool or wool blends.
- Silk blends, with wool, rayon, or cotton.
- Cotton blends, with rayon, silk, or polyester.

DESIGN RESPONSIBLY

Jacquard weave fabrics impart elegance and a feeling of investment in the clothing. Rarely, if ever, used in inexpensive "fast fashion," jacquard fabrics are more costly than the usual fabrics selected for inexpensive clothing. Therefore, using jacquard fabrics is likely to send the message to the consumer that the fabric is valuable and should be kept and passed on. The consumer may be motivated to keep the garment for other uses instead of discarding it.

Tapestry and brocade garments

The tapestry fabric design used in the pants above has such a large woven-in design that one part of the fabric can be used for each pant leg. The silver brocade fabric used for the outfit to the right shows the curved design in metallic yarns in both the jacket and contrasting slacks.

Enlargement
Velveteen has a matte look, but the cut pile emphasizes how the light is absorbed or reflected. This depth of color contrast creates a luxurious appearance and soft hand.

Velveteen

This luxurious fabric has a deep, napped surface created by bringing cut yarn ends to the surface—called a cut-pile surface. The resulting fibers on the surface create a velvet-like surface, but a shorter napped surface than velvet (see page 186).

Cutting the yarns or shearing the surface is a complex finishing process, so velveteen is considered a luxurious, expensive fabric. It is used for jackets, skirts, dresses, and pants. The nap is sometimes flattened, changing the light reflection on the cut-pile surface.

Nap and color

An important concept to understand when selecting velveteen for a design is how the direction of the nap will influence the color of the fabric surface. The position of the nap direction during cutting will determine the color that the garment will appear when sewing is completed. In the warp direction of the nap, light can appear to reflect away from the surface (lighter color) or be absorbed into the surface (darker color).

Positioning the pattern pieces so that all are using the same nap direction will ensure that the sewn garment will appear to be the same color all over.

Flocked fabrics

Flocked fabrics are produced to imitate velveteen as follows: tiny fibers, usually rayon fibers, are glued or otherwise attached to a square, plain-weave, cotton ground fabric. The result is a smooth, soft surface that has a similar hand to velveteen but is stiffer and less bulky. It is inexpensive, and the flocked surface can be removed by abrasion. Usually produced in dark or deep-toned colors, crocking is often a problem. Washing is not advised. Flocked fabrics don't have a nap direction, so they can be very economical in production. These fabrics can be used in all the same products as velveteen.

Nap "up" direction
The garment will appear darker in color to the wearer, as light appears to be absorbed by the surface. The fabric will seem rougher because the nap direction is pointing away from the ground.

Nap "down" direction
The garment will appear lighter to the wearer, as light appears to bounce off the fabric to the wearer's eye. The fabric will seem smoother because the nap direction is pointed toward the ground.

Two-tone velveteen
Two-tone velveteen sample to show a different surface appearance. This sample has a more casual appearance than the solid-color velveteen.

Facts and figures

Distinctive features

- Luxurious, deep, even-cut pile (napped) surface.
- Always produced as a solid color, often deep tones.
- Bulky hand because of the napped surface.

Strengths

- Deep, luxurious, cut-pile surface.
- Strong fabric.
- Easily available.

Weaknesses

- Pile surface is not abrasion-resistant.
- Expensive and slow to produce.
- Nap direction is important in production. Can cause excessive fabric waste in cutting due to adjusting the pattern placement for nap direction.
- Washing may damage the pile.
- Nap is subject to being flattened during wear.

Usual fiber content

- 100 percent cotton (usually high-quality cotton fiber).
- Cotton blend, using cotton nap and polyester/cotton back.

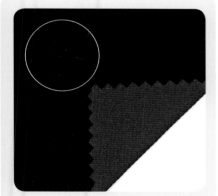

Flocked velveteen

Imitation velveteen made using the "flocking" process, where fibers are glued to a backing fabric. A less expensive, yet similar, appearance to velveteen.

DESIGN RESPONSIBLY

Sometimes recycled fibers are used in flocking. Therefore, the idea of flocking could be explored as a new fabric production method that uses existing fiber. This is a new area of study and is worthy of further exploration.

Velveteen jacket

This long, fly-front closure jacket illustrates the luxurious luster characteristic of velveteen. The fabric has been cut in the nap "up" direction to enhance the deep brown color. A less expensive, yet similar, appearance can be produced using flocked velveteen.

This 22-wale corduroy pile is produced from bamboo rayon, giving a lustrous, soft surface.

Corduroy

One of the most versatile cut-pile fabrics, corduroy is used in casual slacks and jeans, jackets, and skirts.

Corduroy is produced by introducing extra yarns in regular row intervals that are cut and brushed, creating the brushed rows, or "wales." The rows are always produced in the warp direction, so the nap direction must also be considered in garment design and production (see Velveteen, page 102).

The number of wales in a corduroy fabric helps determine its appearance and use. The fewer wales per inch, the bulkier the fabric. The more wales per inch, the finer the wale and the lighter the weight of the fabric. There is a great variety of corduroy wale design, the most common are:

- 8–10-wale: outerwear, jackets, and casual pants.
- 16-wale: most common corduroy; pants, jackets, skirts, vests.
- 21–22-wale, sometimes called "pinwale": used in shirts and dresses or soft-silhouette skirts; it often has a lustrous wale.

Although most frequently used in casual clothing that has a soft, comfortable hand, corduroy garments are washed for further softening before retail distribution. The washing process can be simply laundering for a little softness or a more proprietary "recipe" washing for a specific appearance.

8-wale corduroy
8-wale corduroy is the most commonly used corduroy. This fabric is used in particular for men's pants and jackets. The two-tone color adds a more casual appearance to the fabric.

5-wale corduroy
5-wale fabric is used for men's pants. Its softness is due to the wide wale that adds a velvety hand.

Thick and thin corduroy
There are many variations of corduroy construction. Thick and thin, shown here, is one example of corduroy wale variety.

Facts and figures

Distinctive features
- Warp-direction wales.
- Soft hand, luxurious cut pile.
- Almost exclusively cotton-fiber cut pile.

Strengths
- Wales provide surface design interest.
- Soft hand and pleasing surface texture.
- Easily available in common wale counts.

Weaknesses
- Not a durable fabric—the napped surface wears out easily.
- Nap direction must be considered; may add to fabric cut waste during garment production.

Usual fiber content
- 100 percent cotton or cotton/ polyester blends.
- Rayon and rayon/cotton blends.

Men's corduroy coat
The fine-wale corduroy used for this coat is almost velveteen in appearance but keeps its casual, rustic hand. The wales add texture and volume to the surface—a great combination with denim jeans.

Brushed fabrics

Unlike cut-pile fabrics, brushed fabrics roughen the smooth fabric surface for the purpose of creating a hairy or fuzzy third dimension, called a "napped" surface. Napping will feel warm to the touch, so a warm hand can be a functional result of this finish.

Brushed or napped fabric nearly always has a soft hand. This cotton fabric has been brushed to imitate suede leather. Sometimes the fabric is "sanded" to achieve the suede surface.

Brushing, or napping, can result in several types of finishes; some have only recently been developed:

Brushed finish: the fabric is brushed, and a somewhat irregular hairy surface is the result. This finish is popular for the brushed back of fleece (see page 182) or bull denim (see page 86), flannel (see page 76), or flannelette (see page 77).

Peached finish: the fabric is brushed and then shaved to produce an even, short, hairy surface. The point of this finish is that it should feel like the skin of a peach. It was invented in the late 1980s in Japan.

Sheared and brushed: After a pile weave is sheared (or cut), the cut yarns are brushed to create an even finish of separate fibers for a soft pile. Corduroy (see page 104) and velveteen (page 102) are both sheared and then brushed for the expected pile finish.

Sanded finish: produced by fine emery rollers, beginning with a fine texture and using successively grainier emery rollers. Fibers are often split into finer segments to create a very soft surface. Often applied to top-weight and medium-weight fabrics. Sanding on twill fabrics is especially appealing because of the short floating yarns.

Sueded finish: produced in a similar manner as above but usually applied to bottom-weight fabrics. The result of this finish is to look and feel like sueded leather.

Fleece
Brushed fleece will pill badly. 100 percent cotton brushed fleece is considered a fire hazard. When producing a cotton-hand fleece, polyester is almost always blended with cotton fiber to reduce the flammability of brushed cotton fiber.

Peached finish
Peaching, a brushed finish that is shaved to imitate the skin of a peach, is now applied to cotton blended fabrics, rayons, and microfiber polyester fabrics.

Brushed back canvas
This canvas has a polyester face and cotton yarns on the back side that have been brushed for a soft hand on the inside of the fabric.

Facts and figures

Distinctive features

- Soft, hairy surface, with a warm hand.
- Sueded fabric will feel like skin.
- Brushed finish adds bulk to the fabric for a feeling of quality.

Strengths

- Luxurious, warm hand.
- Firm, bulky hand.
- Can imitate suede leather very well in certain fabrics.
- Variety of napped finishes are available.

Weaknesses

- Brushed finish in cotton fabrics will cause significant shrinkage in the laundry.
- Brushing will reduce the durability of the fabric, both the strength and abrasion resistance.
- Brushed finishes should be applied to high-quality top weights or medium-quality bottom weights.

Usual fiber content

- 100 percent wool.
- 100 percent cotton and cotton/polyester blends.
- 100 percent microfiber polyester.

Brushed cotton jodhpurs

Cotton suede cloth was selected for these jodhpur-style men's pants. The brushed surface adds bulk to the fabric and will help maintain the wide silhouette.

Wrapped pile fabric suit

This wrapped jacket suit uses contrasting pile fabric surfaces to provide design interest and soft texture. The fabric resembles suede leather but is a much lighter-weight fabric that drapes well for this soft-silhouette suit.

Felt fabric, such as this pink cloth, can be steam-molded into a shape or easily sewn into three-dimensional forms. The fabric edges do not ravel.

Fabrics from fiber

Felt and other non-wovens

Fabrics produced directly from fiber are known as nonwoven fabrics. This category also includes nonwoven (massed fiber) fabrics other than felt.

Felted fabrics are produced in a similar manner to paper: fiber is massed together; moisture, heat, and pressure are applied; and the fibers shrink together to create a tangled fiber mass. No yarn is required. Fabric can be produced directly from fiber. The fabric is usually stiff and bulky in medium to bottom weights.

Wool fiber is most often used to create felt. It will continue to shrink and can be molded for hats and other three-dimensional shapes using steam and pressure.

Rayon fiber is sometimes blended for added softness, although 100 percent wool fiber is best for molding into shapes.

Thermoplastic fibers, especially polyester, are used to produce nonwoven fabrics for interlinings, packaging, and other industrial uses. These fabrics can be formed by applying heat and pressure only, slightly melting the fibers together to form the surface. There are some new developments in textile design, using the felting or fiber-massing techniques, applying heat and pressure and other materials to increase fabric strength.

Faux suede
The mass-fiber construction of the faux suede aids in the skinlike hand of the fabric. This sample was produced using the principles of the massed fiber process, using polyester microfiber, heat and pressure, and suede sanding to create the fabric.

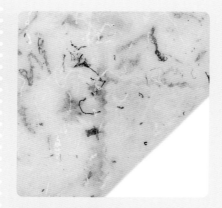

Massed polyester
This experimental fabric uses recycled and shredded plastic bags in the fabric surface to add color and texture. The heat used to shred the bags seems to have melted the plastic; however, the needle-punched fabric remains soft to the touch.

Spunlace
Some massed fiber fabrics can create open, "lacy" patterns by massing fiber together in interesting patterns. These fabrics are not so durable but offer new methods of creating lacy fabrics.

Facts and figures

Distinctive features
- Stiff and bulky fabric.
- Can be molded into three-dimensional shapes using steam and heat.
- Both face and back of the fabric can be used.

Strengths
- Wide variety of textures, all showing a nondirectional surface.
- Some manufactured massed fiber fabrics are very strong and abrasion-resistant.
- Can be molded (if wool blend).

Weaknesses
- Drapes poorly.
- Most felted fabrics have poor strength and low abrasion resistance.
- Sewing stitching holes will further weaken the fabric.

Usual fiber content
- 100 percent wool or wool/rayon blends.
- 100 percent polyester.
- Polyester/rayon/olefin blend.

DESIGN RESPONSIBLY

There is some experimentation in textile designs using recycled fiber, especially wool blended with polyester, to create new types of felted nonwoven fabric produced from postconsumer garments. At this moment, the idea of using postconsumer fiber is only conceptual, but the idea of nonwoven fabric produced from garneted postconsumer clothing is intriguing.

Felted hat
Felt fabric can be molded into three-dimensional shapes, like this runway fashion hat. This hat can be re-formed into another silhouette by re-blocking, using pressurized steam on a hat block.

Melton

Melton is most commonly used to make heavy winter coats and overcoats. Its dense structure is ideally suited to keeping out cold air and moisture.

Melton wool is one of the most versatile coat fabrics. It can be steam-shaped and tailored easily. Melton is nearly always a thick, warm fabric for fall and winter.

Melton is often slightly brushed and then sheared for an even, non-lustrous surface. One of the important features of melton fabric is its denseness. A tightly woven fabric, either plain weave or twill weave, the fabric is heavily fulled (preshrunk). This process will compact the fabric to the point where it may look and feel like felt. This tightly compacted fabric is ideal for outerwear, and it has been the fabric of choice for coats and overcoats in the fashion industry.

Meltons today are often wool blends, using rayon, cashmere, vicuna, and sometimes polyester and nylon, but the density of the fabric is always its distinguishing feature. Most often dyed solid colors, some meltons are dyed to show a "heather" effect.

Medium-weight melton
Both the face and back sides of this medium-weight melton can be used. It is durable and warm. The fabric color—the fiber was dyed before being spun into yarn—shows the heather effect well.

Double-weave melton
This melton was specially produced to have a different color on each side to create a reversible coat.

Finely felted melton
This fabric probably used virgin wool fiber, not recycled wool, which is so often used in melton fabrics. This sample uses a tightly woven construction, and the surface has been carefully brushed.

Shaped melton coat

Melton is an ideal fabric for a shaped winter coat; the fabric tailors very well and its dense weave provides good protection from wind and moisture. The peacoat, which originated in the Navy, was produced from the same fabric dyed dark blue.

Facts and figures

Distinctive features

- Smooth, densely woven fabric.
- Usually solid color.
- Wool or wool blends.

Strengths

- Dense, tightly woven fabric is extremely durable.
- Excellent tailoring fabric.
- Smooth, brushed, and sheared surface.
- Medium-weight fabric is highly desired for fashion coats.
- Shows design seaming detail well.

Weaknesses

- Often shows "water spots" on the fabric surface.
- Snags easily on the fabric surface.
- Sewing requires very sharp needle or ballpoint needle to avoid snagging.
- Must use nonstick sewing foot to avoid snagging fabric surface.
- Lustrous, smooth surface, though short fibers are noticeable on the surface.
- The hand is soft, although stiffer in the cross-grain direction.

Usual fiber content

- 100 percent wool or wool/rayon blends.
- Wool blends combined with cashmere or vicuna.
- Wool/polyester/nylon blends.

DESIGN RESPONSIBLY

The fiber used in melton fabrics can be recycled wool fiber; after garneting, the fiber is spun into new yarn. After weaving, the fabric is dyed a solid color and is heavily fulled (steamed to shrink). The resulting fabric is tightly woven and very warm. Until the 1940s, recycling wool garments back into fiber and weaving it into new fabric was a usual practice in the textile industry. Melton fabric can be produced from postconsumer wool garments.

Double knits
Bottom weight Ponte di Roma, piqué

Double knits produced as bottom-weight fabrics are created by knitting two fabrics together at the same time. Always a weft knit, it is produced as yardage, not garment pieces that will later be stitched together.

This vintage plaid double knit reflects the colors and feeling of the late 1970s. It's a very durable knit, without much stretch, that can be used for a tailored jacket or casual pants.

Although the popularity of heavy double knits has waned, it was very popular in the 1960s and 1970s, when clothing design was dominated by bottom-weight double knits, often made in manufactured fiber.

Knitted bottom-weight fabric is popular for tailored suits, pants, and jackets. Double knits are very resilient and stable fabrics and are almost rigid, like a woven fabric. These knits can create interesting textured surfaces, such as piqué or other textures. Wool fiber was quickly replaced by textured multifilament polyester yarns and spun acrylic yarns to imitate the natural wool fiber. Today, double knit fabrics are still used and are mostly polyester fiber fabrics. All images knitted into double knit fabric are produced using jacquard knitting techniques. Using dyed yarn, geometric and curved designs can be produced. It is important to know this distinction as compared to woven-in images, as mentioned earlier in this section (see page 100).

Double knits do not drape well but are very easy to cut and sew. The fabric is very stable and doesn't roll up at the fabric edge when cut, which is a problem for single knit jersey (see page 150). Ballpoint needles are best to avoid snagging yarns. Otherwise, seam detail and pressing can be managed well. The manufactured fiber fabrics mentioned above can be laundered easily, depending on the garment construction tailoring details.

Double knit piqué
Piqué double knit has an ideal texture for casual apparel. Piqué knits are usually medium-weight. This sample shows how two yarns, one colored, the other white, are used to create this double knit: the white yarns are used only on the back side, and the colored yarns are used only on the face.

Double knit Ponte di Roma
This Ponte di Roma double knit in a solid color has an even surface, which is great for tailoring. It looks the same on the face and back sides.

Double knit jacquard pattern
This knitted-in design can be either a curved design or a geometric design. All knitted-in designs are considered jacquard knits.

Facts and figures

Distinctive features

- Firm hand yet soft knit touch.
- Varied surface texture, from smooth, even surface to significant texturing.
- Wrinkle resistant—sometimes "springy."

Strengths

- Tightly knitted fabric that seems like a heavyweight woven fabric.
- Very resilient.
- Easy to cut and sew.
- Variety of surface textures available.
- Can be reversible, depending on the fabric design.

Weaknesses

- Can be snagged easily, like any knit surface.
- Mostly manufactured fibers used, especially textured polyester fiber.
- Availability is limited.

Usual fiber content

- 100 percent wool or wool/ polyester blends.
- 100 percent polyester.
- Acrylic or acrylic/polyester blends.

1970s double knit suit
Double knit fabric is especially comfortable for garments where there is need for subtle expansion. It is a great fabric for tailoring.

Coated fabrics

Fabrics can be coated with other materials to change the basic character of the original fabric. For example, a cotton poplin fabric (see page 61), which does not resist moisture, can be transformed into a water-resistant fabric by adding a specific coating, such as a waxed coating.

This printed fabric has a clear coating on the face side and is intended to be used for children's raincoats. The coating on the fabric adds stiffness to a lightweight cotton broadcloth.

A coating is applied for different reasons, so durability is often related to the coating's purpose. The coating is applied as a liquid and spread across the fabric surface; it is then heated or cured to adhere the coating to the fabric surface. The coating remains somewhat flexible so the fabric can be sewn and worn comfortably. Oilskin, wax, and liquid rubber are all natural coatings applied to fabrics (mostly plain weave fabrics). These coatings make a fabric water resistant but vary widely in their durability and ability to maintain water resistance. A polyurethane foam coating (synthetic petroleum-based coating) added to the back of the fabric provides padding and insulation.

A coating can change the texture, hand, and weight of a fabric. Usually, a coated fabric is less flexible (it has a stiff hand), heavier, and often has a more lustrous surface. Coated fabrics are used almost exclusively for outerwear garments: raincoats, ski wear, snowboard apparel, and other outdoor clothing.

Contrast color coating
This foam coating to taffeta is an opaque coating. It can be colored to add contrast for design detail. Some foam-coated fabrics use the coated side as the face side. This coating is nonporous and is a good water-resistant fabric.

Matched color coating
This fabric color is the same as the foam coating. Color-matched coating is a design concept that gives a more subtle garment appearance while still retaining the water-resistant function.

Wax-coated poplin
Wax-coated fabrics show creases easily if the fabric is crushed. Notice the crease marks on this cotton poplin fabric surface. Some designers consider these crease marks desirable for their design.

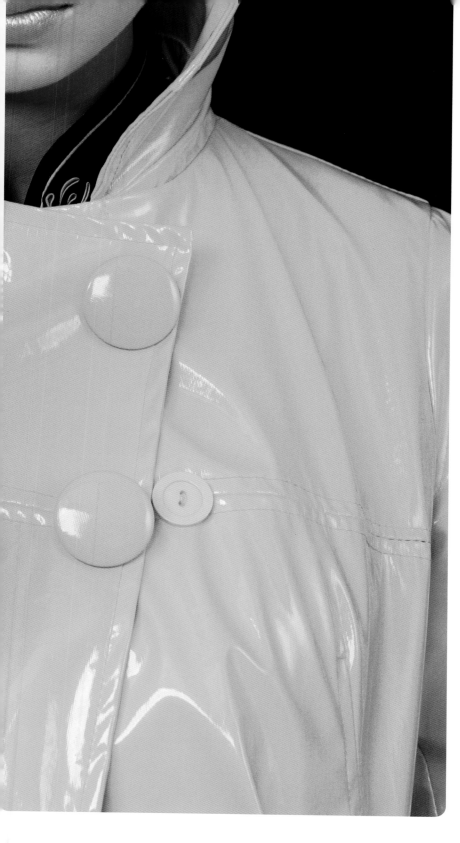

Facts and figures

Distinctive features

- Crisp, stiff hand.
- Lustrous or shiny surface.
- Water-resistant in most cases.

Strengths

- Wide variety of coating options.
- Adds weight to an inexpensive fabric.
- Excellent weather protection fabric.

Weaknesses

- Stiff hand makes design details difficult to sew.
- Stitching holes cannot be removed. Perforations weaken the fabric.
- Coatings are often not porous, so they can be uncomfortable next to the skin.
- Heat-sensitive—they dry out and crack the surface.
- Wrinkle easily.

Usual fiber content

- Ground fabric is usually polyester or polyester/coat blend.
- Coating can be liquid material that is spread on the fabric and cured to stay on the surface: liquid rubber, oil, wax, PVC (petroleum-based polyvinyl chloride) liquid, or foam.

DESIGN RESPONSIBLY

Polyurethane foam fabric coatings provide a good water-resistance function on cotton ground fabrics. Wax, oilcloth, and liquid rubber are water-resistant yet do not produce excessive emissions like petroleum-based polyurethane foam. Coating selection is often based on durability, and only polyurethane coatings are very durable. Consider the environmental consequence of your coating selection.

Raincoat

The soft and supple surface appearance of this raincoat is the result of the coating application. The coating is applied as a liquid, spread as an opaque coating across the lightweight knitted ground fabric. The result is a soft, somewhat flexible fabric with a wonderful shiny surface.

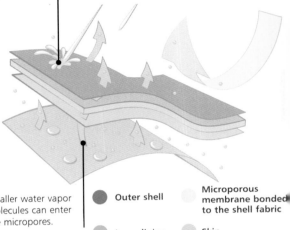

Microporous laminated fabrics

Lightweight, tightly woven fabrics using nonabsorbent fiber are used for these high-performance fabrics. The microporous membrane applied to the back side of this jacket fabric adds weight and moisture-management function.

The dream of outdoor enthusiasts was to have a fabric that resisted moisture yet allowed the body to expel perspiration through the fabric. Such a fabric was invented over 30 years ago, and was called a microporous membrane fabric.

A nonabsorbent outside (shell) fabric was fused to a polyurethane membrane that contained billions of micropores (pores too small for water molecules to pass through but large enough for water vapor molecules to enter). The result was a fabric that was water-resistant and breathable (it allowed air to pass through). This innovation transformed outdoor clothing, ski and snowboard wear, rain gear, and coats. Microporous membranes bonded to a shell fabric provide water resistance and breathability to create a fabric that is lighter in weight and that can be used to create comfortable, functional clothing.

Larger water molecules cannot pass through the micropores.

Smaller water vapor molecules can enter the micropores.

● **Outer shell**

● **Inner lining**

○ **Microporous membrane bonded to the shell fabric**

○ **Skin**

Taffeta/microporous membrane
Taffeta is a fabric commonly bonded to a membrane. This sample bonds three layers: taffeta shell, microporous membrane, and a tricot lining. This ECO STORM™ fabric, made using only polyester materials, is recyclable into ECO CIRCLE™ polyester fiber.

Polyester poplin microporous membrane on polyester fabric
New microporous membrane ECO STORM™ fabrics are produced entirely from polyester materials and are now recyclable into high-quality ECO CIRCLE™ fiber after the garment is discarded.

Heat-sealed seams
This jacket, intended for outdoor activities, has functional fabric seams, heat-sealed to resist moisture at stitching holes. Special equipment is required to seal the sewn seams.

Microporous membrane fabrics are designed to function at various levels of water resistance, suitable for both the casual hiker and the extreme athlete. Shell fabrics bonded to membranes are usually lightweight, tightly woven taffeta, poplin, or twill, and sometimes satin weave. A smooth, flat surface is a must for reliable bonding of the laminate.

The microporous laminate is heat-bonded to the shell fabric. Laminated fabrics are very heat-sensitive and should never be placed in a heated dryer or hot water. Heat will degrade the fabric bond and cause the fabrics to separate.

Designer's tip: The term "waterproof/breathable" is often used when describing this functional fabric. Remember that microporous membranes are not waterproof but resist moisture very well.

Facts and figures

Distinctive features
- Crisp, stiff hand.
- Lightweight fabric.
- Smooth surface, sometimes lustrous.

Strengths
- Wide variety of microporous membrane functional options.
- Adds weight to inexpensive fabric.
- Excellent weather-protection fabric.

Weaknesses
- Stiff hand makes design details difficult to sew.
- Stitching holes cannot be removed. Perforations weaken fabric.
- Heat-sensitive—function will be reduced.
- Expensive when compared to less functional fabrics.

Usual fiber content
- GrouShell fabric is nearly always polyester or nylon, or a blend of both.
- Cotton blended with nylon or polyester is occasionally used.
- Laminate is usually polyurethane, although new innovations now include polyester microporous membranes.

DESIGN RESPONSIBLY

Polyester garments are now recyclable into new, high-quality fiber and fabrics. Therefore, whenever possible, design your garments to be recyclable into new fiber and fabric. Using polyurethane membrane or mixing fiber contents in your apparel will make recycling your design impossible.

Snowboarding/ski wear
Water-resistant yet breathable microporous membrane fabric is lightweight and doesn't weigh you down. It is ideal for when you're participating in winter sports.

Film fabric

Plastic sheets

Film, usually produced from a plastic material, is not made from fiber at all. Although still a two-dimensional surface like other fabrics, film is neither porous nor breathable.

This plastic film can be sewn or otherwise attached to another fabric to create accessories or rainwear.

This fabric can be very uncomfortable to wear, because body perspiration does not evaporate, so garments produced from film become wet on the inside. Care must be taken to add absorbent fabrics to the inside of these nonporous fabrics.

Film fabrics are used in shower curtains, accessories, footwear, and rain gear. Most common materials are polyurethane or polyvinylchloride (PVC). Latex, a natural rubber, is also used.

Bonded fabrics often combine film and another fabric for functional use. For example, film can be laminated to the face of a cotton calico fabric (see page 57) for a water-resistant fabric in children's rain gear. Thin foam layers can be laminated to a polyester tricot for added weight and thermal insulation.

Another use of film is to emboss the surface to imitate leather grain or other fabric surfaces. These embossed surfaces are then bonded to a fabric backing and are used for the fabric face. See Faux leather and suede on pages 124–125 for more information. Embossed film fabric is a common bonded fabric used in accessories, handbags, shoes/boots, and jackets.

Finally, film fabrics can be bonded to many different fabrics, such as mesh, plain weaves, and tricot knits. Highly textured surfaces do not bond well at all.

Film embossed to look like denim
The twill-like surface embossed onto this film is bonded to a lightweight fabric to add strength. The embossing can also encourage flexibility in a usually stiff plastic surface. Due to the nonporous film, an absorbent fiber lining is recommended.

Embossed face on bonded film
Note the embossed texture that imitates a woven fabric surface. The film has been bonded to a knitted interlock backing.

Clear film on cashmere
This matte-finish film is bonded to a soft cashmere fabric to create a water-resistant surface and soft inside for a novelty outerwear coat.

Facts and figures

Distinctive features

- Very stiff, "plastic" hand.
- Can be embossed, matte, or shiny surface.
- Water-resistant or nonporous.

Strengths

- Wide variety of film face options.
- Bonding can strengthen film face.
- Excellent weather-protection fabric.
- Can provide thermal insulation if foam is used.

Weaknesses

- Stiff hand makes design details difficult to sew.
- Stitching holes cannot be removed. Perforations weaken fabric.
- Can be uncomfortable—not breathable next to skin.
- Heat-sensitive—dries out and cracks surface.

Usual fiber content

- Ground fabric is usually polyester, although cotton or nylon are sometimes used.
- Film is polyurethane or PVC. Polyester film is encouraged, as it can be recycled.

DESIGN RESPONSIBLY

Most film fabrics are not recyclable. Those produced from plastic materials are often bonded to fabrics that also cannot be recycled. Limit the selection of these fabrics, and develop designs that can be reused easily.

Film fabric used in a garment

This film fabric, with its crinkled, shiny surface texture, is very lightweight, creating a complex jacket silhouette with interesting trim details that would not be possible in a crisp, handwoven fabric.

Leather

Leather has an uneven surface and thickness. This cowhide has been split so it is much thinner and easier to sew than the original hide.

Leather is the skin of an animal that is used in clothing and is divided into two categories—hides and skins.

Hides are from large animals such as cows and are thicker than skins. Skins are from small animals, such as sheep or goats, and are thinner than hides. Top-grain refers to the outside skin. If a thick hide is split, the leather is called split hide and is usually napped to produce a soft surface. Top-grain leather is the best quality and most durable.

Leather is tanned and chemically treated to maintain and soften it while preserving the material. Leather is irregular in thickness, depending on the area of the skin that is used. It is also important to remember that leather is not yardage, so the available surface area is dependent on the size of the skin or hide.

Leather can be tanned and finished to be:
- Patent—shiny, glossy surface.
- Glacé—hard, polished surface.
- Natural grain surface—natural skin surface.
- Embossed—image pressed into the surface.

Leather finishing is extremely varied, and different finishing techniques are applied that reflect the current fashion trends. Once the leather has been tanned, dyes and surface treatments are added.

Patent leather
Patent leather has a stiff hand and high-gloss surface. The leather can often crack when folded repeatedly.

Cowhide vs. calfskin
Calfskin (right) is a leather selected for its soft, pliable hand. It is a thin skin, not thick like cowhide (left). Note the fine grain on this top-grain surface, compared to the older, adult cowhide.

Embossed leather
Embossing on leather is usually a decorative touch. This sample has been embossed to resemble ostrich leather.

Facts and figures

Distinctive features

- Recognizable surface grain and noticeable "skin" touch.
- Pliable surface (depending on the finishing process).
- Permeable surface that is comfortable to wear.

Strengths

- Permeable surface.
- Desirable grain or other textured surface.
- Somewhat water-resistant.
- Usually durable surface.

Weaknesses

- Difficult to match all the pattern pieces, especially if more than one skin is required for a single garment.
- Requires a "walking foot" sewing machine to sew the garment.
- Finishing used on surface may increase cutting and sewing difficulty.
- Labor-intensive cutting and sewing.
- Color may crock off the surface or backside.

DESIGN RESPONSIBLY

Leather and suede require tanning to preserve the skin, which is one of the most polluting textile processes. Ask for enzyme tanning or other newly developed tanning procedures that are less polluting.

Leather fashion garments

This leather dress and skirt, finished with interesting cutouts (far left) or a pearlized surface (left), are designed with numerous sewn seams, reflecting the size of the skins used. Each pattern piece is often cut individually, taking care to match skin texture, thickness, and color. There is usually more waste in leather cutting due to these matching issues.

Suede leather

Suede is a leather that has been brushed or otherwise napped for a soft, velvet-like texture. It is considered a luxurious material because of its soft hand and its pliable drape.

Suede leather can be various thicknesses, depending on the origin of the leather. This soft suede is pigskin and is stiffer than sueded calfskin or lambskin.

The soft hand of suede makes it an ideal choice for accessories and fashion apparel. Gloves, small accessories, and fitted garments are often produced with suede. Compared to thick cowhide, suede is thinner and somewhat easier to sew. Fine suede garments usually contain many seams because the skins of small animals, such as lambs and calves, are used. The garment design must consider the skin size to accommodate the pattern pieces. Suede is usually lined to prevent direct contact with the wearer's skin and avoid crocking and discomfort.

Two main types of suede are produced:
Split cowhide: Usually a coarser, brushed, textured finish that is not generally used in fine apparel, but rather for more casual apparel and accessories.

Sueded calfskin, lambskin, and pigskin: Thinner leather napped to produce a finely brushed surface that is very desirable.

Because of the napped surface, dyes on suede leather tend to crock easily. It is important to consider the color of suede because darker colors are more likely to show the color rubbed off. Pastel colors are frequently used in suede because they show the napped surface better, but also because color crocking is less noticeable.

Split cowhide
Note the more textured napped surface, which shows the brushed leather fibers on the surface.

Sueded/printed and embossed
Sueded pigskin that has been embossed and printed with a deep red color to resemble a reptile-skin surface.

Sueded pigskin
Sueded pigskin still shows the pores on the skin surface through the sueded texture.

Facts and figures

Distinctive features
- Beautiful soft, brushed surface.
- Pliable, "skin" texture.
- Luxurious, substantial feeling.

Strengths
- Excellent fabric for molding and tailoring.
- Generally good resilience.
- Great variety of textures in different weave combinations.
- Textures are specific to the geometric woven-in designs.

Weaknesses
- Fabrics are not always easily available.
- Texture can be easily snagged.
- Can be expensive.

Suede jacket and skirt

There is no fabric like suede leather for a luxurious, soft surface, yet full-bodied weight. The soft textured material can be a little bulky, like this men's suede jacket (for a more casual appearance) or finer, like this soft, supple suede skirt (for a refined look).

Faux leather and suede

The purpose of these fabrics is to imitate animal leather or suede, and they are designed to closely resemble the natural material.

The reasons for designing faux fabrics are: the lower cost of the material; the ease of cutting and sewing; the fact that they are more available than leather or suede; and animal treatment and environmental concerns. They are also designed to go beyond the limitations of leather and suede by creating "unnatural" colors and textures.

Faux leather and suede can be used on all the same products as real leather and suede, such as shoes, handbags, accessories, jackets, pants, and skirts. The hand and weight of these fabrics are quite similar to the natural material. In fact, it is sometimes difficult to distinguish faux from real leather. The two main differences between the natural material and faux material are:

This imitation alligator leather is actually three layers of fabric bonded together to give the same thick, leathery texture of the real alligator skin.

- Faux leather is nonporous, so the fabric doesn't allow air to pass through. Therefore, it can be uncomfortably hot compared to leather that is porous. It sometimes has a "plastic" odor.

- Fabric backing is required to support the embossed plastic face. This backing is usually a top-weight interlock knit (see page 152) that keeps the bonded fabric as flexible as possible to imitate real leather.

Patchwork faux leather
This faux leather can be distinguished by a fabric backing on the back side. This fabric backing is an interlock knit that provides flexibility and strength, similar to real leather.

Embossed faux suede (sueded finish woven cotton)
This brushed-surface woven fabric has been embossed with a printed black film that resembles a reptile-skin pattern. The brushed surface, combined with the printed film, has a skin-like texture.

Printed faux leather
This faux leather has a distinctive lambskin appearance except for the houndstooth printed pattern on the surface. However, looking at the back side will always distinguish the real from the faux.

Facts and figures

Distinctive features

- Usually a very good imitation of real leather or suede.
- Can show "unnatural" adaptations of color and texture.
- No irregularities on the fabric surface, common in natural materials.

Strengths

- Wide range of surface textures and colors.
- Good imitation of leather, but available in yardage.
- No irregularities in fabric thickness or surface.
- Less expensive than leather.
- Ease of production cutting and sewing.
- Color and texture matching is not a problem.

Weaknesses

- Nonporous—not breathable.
- Dry-cleaning chemicals may damage or destroy plastic film.
- Cannot be re-sewn. Needle holes cannot be repaired.
- Plastic surface may cause "noise" or adhere together easily.
- Extremely heat-sensitive.

Usual fiber content

Face:
- Usually polyurethane (PU) or polyvinylchloride (PVC) film; polyester film, which is recyclable, may be available.

Backing:
- 100 percent polyester interlock knit or polyester/cotton blend square plain weave.

Women's faux leather jacket and skirt

The smooth plastic surface of this jacket and skirt has been crinkled in a way not possible with real leather; the thin film is heat-sensitive. When this fabric is backed with a thermoplastic 100 percent polyester interlock, a malleable material that can be sewn with tailored details and hardware is produced. The resulting design has great visual appeal and is lighter in weight, more flexible, and less expensive than leather.

Bonded and fused fabrics

Bonding two fabrics together will create a fabric that can be reversible or two-sided. The technique of adhering two fabrics together can provide the designer with new fabrics that could not otherwise be produced in one fabric.

This fabric was created by bonding a napped sueded cotton fabric to a heavy canvas fabric. The new bottom-weight fabric is great for structured handbags.

The designer can select two different fabrics for their garment and bond the two fabrics together to create a single textile. The bonding process can be either an adhesive glue application between the two fabrics or placing a double-sided fusible web between two fabrics. In both applications, heat and pressure are necessary to finish the bonding process.

Bonded fabrics provide new options for designers. It is possible to develop new fabrics by combining different types together.

Bonding will always add weight and stiffness to the final fabric. Therefore, bonded fabrics are usually for outerwear garments or suit jackets. However, lining fabric are sometimes bonded to face fabrics to eliminate sewing labor for linings or to add bulk. Shoes and handbags often use bonded fabrics because of the additional stiffness required to their shape.

Jacquard tapestry with tricot lining
This tapestry fabric can be lined before sewing. The tricot knit lining will stay flexible and help stabilize the tapestry for outerwear or accessories.

Soft pile with vinyl
This bulky faux mouton has been fused to a vinyl fabric for a reversible fabric. It imitates a sheared sheepskin.

Taffeta with polar fleece
Taffeta fabric bonded to a polar fleece fabric can produce a wonderful fabric for fashion coats.

Facts and figures

Distinctive features

- Face and back of fabric can be utilized.
- Often-bulky fabric with a stiff hand.

Strengths

- A wide variety of fabrics can be bonded together.
- Excellent weight and hand for structured garments.
- New fabrics can be simply created from existing fabrics.

Weaknesses

- Fabrics can be separated if exposed to high heat or chemicals.
- Bulky, sometimes difficult to sew. May need a walking foot.

Usual fiber content

Face fabrics:
- Can be any fiber content, although polyester fiber blends are preferred.

Fusible inside layer:
- 100 percent polyester spunbonded or spunlaced fabrics with heat-sensitive adhesive applied to both sides.

Long faux sheepskin coat
This long, cream-colored jacket uses a faux shearling knitted pile fabric and a faux suede fabric to mimic a real sheep's skin. Using a bonded fabric to imitate animal skin is one example of its possible applications. The bonded fabric is often intended to be reversible.

Supporting structure

Designers find interlinings mysterious—fabrics that are never seen yet are intrinsically a part of the designer's final product.

In a finely tailored suit, interlinings are chosen carefully and can mean the difference between a well-rolled lapel and a flat lapel. The following pages will introduce the designer to the types of interlinings available and why they are selected for various purposes. The correct interlining choice should not be overlooked when selecting fabric for the design.

The function of interlining is to provide support for those parts of the design that need reinforcement. These parts include collars, cuffs, button plackets, jacket lapels, and hemlines, to name a few. The designer will determine where interlinings are needed to achieve the desired shape or silhouette. Selection of the interlining requires experience, often via the method of trial and error. This section is intended to provide information to help with selection, but ultimately, the designer must consider several interlining choices and test them with the fabric selected for the design. The fabric used for the garment and the amount of support required will determine the type of interlining needed, as well as whether the interlining will be applied using heat-sensitive adhesive or by sewing it in.

Interlining fabric choices

There are three main categories of interlining. All categories can be applied as fusible (with a heat-sensitive adhesive) or non-fusible (without this adhesive):
- Woven interlinings.
- Knitted tricot interlinings.
- Spunlaced or spunbonded webs of fiber, usually nylon or polyester fiber.

Casual ensemble: interlining

There are several areas on these garments that will require support: the jacket lapel, front closure and hem; the striped top collar and button placket; the pant waistband and pocket edge.

The purpose of interlining

Interlining has three main functions:
- Adding weight or backing to a lightweight shell fabric.
- Sustaining a silhouette for a design element of a garment, such as a collar.
- Supporting a design element that needs to be shaped or "encouraged" to perform a certain way, such as the soft fold on a suit jacket lapel.

Selecting an interlining

The key to selecting the right interlining for the design is in understanding how an interlining will change the character of the fabric. In most cases, the fabric should not be substantially changed (weight, hand, texture) when an interlining is applied. The designer should always test a variety of interlinings on fabric samples to better understand what type of interlining should be selected for the design. Here are a few guidelines to assist in the selection process.

When to use a fusible interlining:

- To achieve a firm shape or silhouette, such as a shirt collar.
- As a fast way to add firmness to the body of a jacket (often added to the front of a jacket only for less expensive production).
- For firm waistbands, belts, and handbags.
- For hemline support.

When to use a non-fusible interlining:

- When producing high-quality suiting—hand-stitching in lapels and the jacket body replaces the adhesive, and the final effect will be soft shaping, not stiffness.
- For adding support or weight without disclosing the interlining.

Smart ensemble: interlining

This crisp shirt collar and cuff have interlining to support their sculpted appearance. The button front closure also needs interlining to support this soft, silky shirt fabric. The tie requires a soft, lofty, resilient interlining that doesn't wrinkle after being tied and untied. The waistband and pocket edges also require interlining for added support.

Interlinings for structure

Interlinings vary widely in price and availability. Price often determines which interlining is used.

The lowest cost interlinings are the fiberwebs, either spunlace or spunbonded. Tricot knits are also inexpensive. Woven interlinings, cotton plain weaves, wool canvas, or hair canvas, which come in a variety of weights, are the most expensive. High-quality production uses canvas, and low-quality production uses fiberwebs or tricot. The type of fabric used for the design and the type of design will always guide the designer on what interlining to use.

The traditional method of applying the interlining is to hand-sew using stitches that cannot be seen from the face of the fabric. However, with the introduction of heat-sensitive adhesives, the application process is faster and less labor-intensive. Heat and pressure will adhere the interlining to the fabric back without sewing. Experimentation with interlinings is important, and the final choice is the designer's. It is important to remember that interlinings, if 100 percent polyester, can be recycled, but must be placed in the same fiber-content garment.

Hair canvas uses horsehair, wool, and other fiber blends to provide a stiffness that will not soften over time. This interlining is used in high-quality tailored suiting.

Facts and figures

Strengths

- Canvas is an excellent interlining for wool suiting.
- Wool canvas is excellent for men's ties or other unpressed designs.
- Tricot is excellent for soft, structured designs.
- Fiberwebs come in a wide variety of weights and can be used with fiber-content fabrics.
- Neither tricot nor fiberwebs shrink easily.

Weaknesses

- Cotton- or wool-blend canvas can shrink inside the garment if subjected to laundry or steam heat.
- Fiber webs are not abrasion-resistant and pill/degrade inside the garment.

Usual fiber content

- 100 percent wool or wool blend.
- 100 percent cotton.
- 100 percent polyester.
- 100 percent nylon or polyester/nylon blends.

How interlinings are applied

Before application: Interlinings function without being seen, so it is important to choose an interlining that will not be noticed.

This tricot knit interlining has a heat-sensitive adhesive that is activated when heat and pressure are applied.

After application: The softness of this interlining will not add stiffness to the wool melton fabric—only reinforcement.

Spunbonded fiber-web
This fiberweb shows the dots of adhesive on one side; it is unmarked on the other side.

Tricot without adhesive
Tricot interlining is very stable (it doesn't stretch) yet can keep the shell fabric more flexible than most other interlinings. This sample shows the adhesive dots on one side.

Wool canvas
Wool canvas is never fused. Its main purpose is as interlining in men's ties or for additional lift in a tailored suit.

Wool canvas interlining in a men's tie
The bias-cut wool canvas adds loft and flexibility inside the tie for added resilience after knotting the tie.

Fluidity

The designer's goal is to select a fluid fabric that follows the curve of the human form. There is a sensuousness to letting the body create the design form, and the fabric chosen for this purpose should communicate this sensuality.

Almost like water flowing over the body, fluid fabrics have a liveliness that helps the designer to breathe life into the sewn garment. Soft, drapable fabrics that cannot support themselves are ideal. Fabrics that fall in a heap and fabrics that easily slip away are examples of fluid fabrics that will allow the human form to emerge in the context of the designer's vision.

Wide variety of fluid fabrics

Designers will have their own particular understanding of fluidity both in how the fabric moves and drapes.

The Paris-based Premiere Vision® textile show has created the Seduction® section to display the majority of these sensuous, fluid fabrics. How a fluid fabric performs is directly related to the type of yarn that is used to construct the fabric. Pay close attention to the types of yarns used in fluid fabrics—these give the drape, weight, and a liveliness to the fabric that is not possible in a structured fabric. Highly twisted yarns, both spun and multifilament yarns, are key to the performance of these fluid fabrics. Fiber content is less important, although filament fibers tend to be more

Satin on the bias
The designer cut this soft satin fabric on the bias to emphasize the drape effect of this dress design. The soft folds stay close to the body, like flowing water.

How fluid fabrics work

Most fluid fabrics perform like a liquid. The human form provides the shape, and the fabric flows over it. The special "flowing" feature of these fabrics requires certain fabric characteristics for them to perform at their best:

Drape: The fabric falls over the body like a stream flowing over a stone in the center of the stream. The fabric must follow the form of the body. Seaming details can be complex to sew, as the fabric is often difficult to keep in place during the cutting and sewing process.

Weight: Fluid fabrics are often not heavy, as their function is to drape and flow. In general, top-weight or medium-weight fabrics are considered fluid fabrics.

Movement: Fabric movement is unique to fluid fabrics. They possess a liveliness or "springiness" that is characteristic of many fluid fabrics. The designer can choose a variety of fabrics that both flow and move and have a personality.

A fluid fabric can have many forms

The key to selecting the right fabric for a sensuous or elegant design that shows off the human form is to understand how yarn and fabric construction techniques influence fabric performance. Watch for examples of how the same fabric construction can morph into a completely different fabric by changing the yarn.

Innovation in fiber and finishing for structure

There have been many innovations in fluid fabrics because these fabrics are often used in athletics. Their drapability and movement are designed for active body movement, so there are yarn and finishing details that will appear on certain pages in this chapter. Stay alert for these important details.

Back detailing
The center-back clasp on this dress provides focus, to draw up the soft fabric drapes that then cascade over the body.

Fluidity
This chiffon fabric is airborne, conforming to airflow rather than the body. Notice the attempt to create structure by folding and stitching the chiffon in geometric blocks down the bodice and skirt. Much sewing labor was needed to achieve structure, for which chiffon is ill-suited.

Chiffon

This beautiful, sheer fabric is one of the most recognized of all fabrics. Chiffon is very lightweight, and often used as an outside layer for a multilayered evening or bridal gown.

A square weave, always using multifilament yarns, chiffon is loosely woven to achieve its sheer, see-through appearance. It is most often used in formal evening dresses and blouses. However, chiffon is also used in lingerie, nightgown and robe sets, and undergarments. Chiffon is often designed into full silhouettes but is also selected for simple bias-cut dresses, with a lining underslip.

This chiffon uses metallic yarns in the warp but retains its soft, liquid drape characteristic of all chiffon fabrics.

Designer's tip: Never design a form-fitting, structured garment with chiffon. The loosely woven, square weave construction will easily "slip" (yarns pull away from seams) when being worn. Therefore, always support chiffon with a lining fabric to strengthen this weak fabric. Always keep silhouettes loose-fitting—that's the way this fabric was designed to be used.

Facts and figures

Distinctive features
- Lightweight, sheer fabric.
- Soft hand.
- Lustrous—as always, a multifilament yarn is used.

Strengths
- Sheer and very lightweight.
- Drapable and soft.
- If using polyester fiber, fabric will be more wrinkle-resistant than silk fiber.

Weaknesses
- Weak fabric. Seams easily "slip" (fabric pulls away at the seams, leaving one set of yarns, which are easily broken or torn).
- Not suitable for tight-fitting garments.

Usual fiber content
- 100 percent silk.
- 100 percent polyester.
- 100 percent rayon.

Printed chiffon
This printed sheer fabric is extremely lightweight. The soft rayon fabric has a beautiful soft hand. Printed chiffon is common in dresses, using a solid color lining.

Burn-out chiffon
Chiffon is used as the base cloth for this fabric that was produced with a satin face. It was printed with acid to achieve the "burn-out" design.

Chiffon with embroidery
Solid-color chiffon is used as the base cloth for embroidery.

Georgette
Single georgette

Georgette, often called single georgette, is sometimes confused with chiffon (see left). The difference is the hand—georgette has a somewhat rough surface texture and is very drapey. Chiffon has a much smoother surface and is not as drapey as georgette.

The key to the difference in texture and drape is the type of high twist yarn. The more complex twisted yarns in georgette make this fabric more expensive than chiffon. Georgette can be produced in a variety of sheerness and textures due to the yarn type and how densely the yarns are woven together. However, georgette can be used instead of chiffon, creating a more drapable fabric that has a liveliness to it. Georgette will follow the body's curves more successfully than chiffon because of its drapable qualities. The designs for georgette usually include formal occasion dresses and blouses that are not form-fitting but drape on the body.

This georgette has a "bounce" when worn, typical of all georgettes, due to the crêpe-twist yarns used in the fabric production.

Facts and figures

Distinctive features
- Lightweight, sheer fabric.
- Somewhat rough surface.
- Excellent drape.

Strengths
- Sheer and very lightweight.
- Drapes on the body very well.
- Gathers and pleats well; not suitable for tight-fitting garments.
- The textured surface may snag.

Weaknesses
- Weak fabric. Seams easily "slip" (fabric pulls away at the seams, leaving one set of yarns, which are easily broken or torn).

Usual fiber content
- 100 percent polyester or polyester/rayon blends.
- 100 percent rayon.
- 100 percent silk.

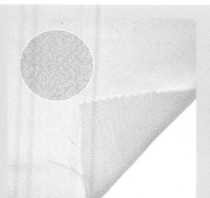

Double georgette
As a plain weave fabric, georgette will look the same on both sides, so this fabric is reversible and heavier.

Iridescent georgette
Using one color in the warp and another in the weft can create an iridescent effect.

Georgette jacquard
The sheerness of georgette jacquard can show a beautiful pattern in the fabric. This sample is iridescent, using two colors—blue in the warp and red in the weft—so the fabric changes color as it moves.

Voile

For apparel, voile is most commonly produced in spun yarns, specifically higher-quality cotton or worsted yarns that have been highly twisted.

Voile is somewhat sheer, although not as sheer as chiffon or georgette (see pages 136 and 137) because the spun yarns are thicker than the multifilament yarns used in those two fabrics. Again, voile has a beautiful drape when compared to lawn (see page 56), where the yarns are less highly twisted.

Highly twisted yarns are a feature of many fluid fabrics. This is an important point when the designer chooses between lawn or voile, because the voile may cost more due to the yarns used.

Cotton voile is used for summer blouses and dresses. Its drape works very well for soft pleating and gathers. Wool voile is not as commonly used. It is not as sheer and is a little heavier, but it can be used for dresses, blouses, and skirts.

The soft hand of this fabric is achieved by high-twist cotton yarns that are loosely woven. The fabric is a popular choice for hot weather.

Wool voile
Wool voile is not in common use. Notice how the high-twist worsted yarns are widely spaced.

Printed cotton voile
Voile's sheer surface limits printing or other finishing capabilities. This soft-finish floral print doesn't show bright colors because the porous fabric surface reduces color intensity.

Cotton voile with dots
The sheerness of voile makes lining this fabric important. Used primarily as a spring/summer fabric, most designers will add a lining behind sheer voile for modesty.

Gauze

Gauze is a sheer cotton fabric that is very low-quality. Using simple, low-spun yarns, loosely woven gauze provides a soft, absorbent surface that is especially used in accessories or women's fashion tops.

Gauze is sometimes confused with voile (see opposite). Gauze is always a low-quality cotton fabric that will need special attention in finishing to be sure the fabric performs as expected in a garment. This fabric is recommended for loose-fitting tops, dresses, or skirts only.

Designer's tip: Gauze is very weak. Always design a product that will support gauze with another more stable fabric, or create a design that is wrapped, rather than sewn.

This loosely woven fabric is actually a dobby weave. Irregularly floating yarns provide a more stable fabric than a more traditional, balanced, plain-weave gauze.

Facts and figures

Distinctive features
- Coarsely woven, sheer fabric.
- Lightweight.
- Very soft hand.

Strengths
- Soft hand.
- Drapes on the body very well.
- Gathers well.

Weaknesses
- Weak fabric. Seams easily "slip" (fabric pulls away at the seams, leaving one set of yarns, which are easily broken or torn).
- Not suitable for tight-fitting garments.
- Shrinks easily.

Usual fiber content
- 100 percent cotton or cotton/polyester blends.

Solid-color gauze
Gauze is often dyed deeply toned colors. This balanced plain weave is more tightly woven than some other gauzes.

Printed gauze
With additional sizing resin, gauze can be printed. This sample has been wet-printed, not dry-pigment printed. (Notice the color of the dye showing through on the reverse side of the fabric.)

Striped gauze
This plain weave fabric has a textured surface, due to the different sizes and irregular spacing of the interlaced yarns. The loose and irregular weave of this fabric is enhanced by the different color warp yarns.

Lining

Linings cover the inside of a garment, to conceal raw seam edges, and to reduce friction when putting on a garment. With these two functions in mind, lining fabrics are always lightweight with a smooth surface.

The best-performing lining fabrics are produced from multifilament yarns that give a silk or silk-like appearance to the inside of the garment. Lining fabrics often add a decorative element to the garment. Designers sometimes select a printed lining or a contrast-color lining to supplement their design vision. Fabrics normally used for garments can also be used for lining. For example, wool plaids (see page 62), fleece (see page 182), or velvet (see page 186) can all be introduced for contrasting textured lining.

Designer's tip: Lining fabrics should never shrink when the garment is cleaned, so preshrinking or testing for shrinkage will ensure that the final garment will retain its shape after being cleaned. Colorfastness should also be tested.

This cotton twill, windowpane check lining fabric was a design choice to enhance the men's jacket design. Lining provides designers with an opportunity to add contrast or energy to their garments.

Facts and figures

Strengths
- Polyester linings are colorfast in most conditions.
- Polyester linings are not affected by dry-cleaning chemicals or body perspiration.
- A wide variety of weaves, colors, and special effects for linings.

Weaknesses
- Rayon, acetate, and silk fiber linings are subject to color fading or bleeding from dry-cleaning chemicals or perspiration.
- Rayon, acetate, and silk fiber linings weaken and tear easily after absorbing perspiration.
- Seam slippage is common in all lining fabrics except tricot.
- Cotton lining must be preshrunk.

Usual fiber content
- 100 percent polyester.
- 100 percent rayon or acetate.
- 100 percent silk.
- 100 percent cotton.

Printed square weave lining
This 100 percent polyester square weave is printed using a digital inkjet printing technique. The result is extremely dyefast. If using silk fiber, this lightweight fabric is called "China silk."

Tricot lining
Tricot knit lining is well suited to an activewear garment, allowing flexibility in garment stretch and recovery.

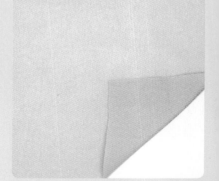

Satin
Satin lining, regardless of the fiber content, always provides a smooth, shiny surface. A silk satin will have more drape than an acetate satin.

Selecting linings

The fabric used for the body of a garment can determine the type of lining fabric selected. Here is guide to selecting a lining.

Cotton-plaid jacket lining

Using almost any smooth woven surface texture, plaid linings can provide a distinctive appearance to a tailored suit or jacket.

Athletics jacket lining

Activewear knit jackets and pants often use lightweight tricot knits or mesh knits to provide wicking moisture control for perspiration from exercise.

Twill-weave jacket lining

Twill weaves, tightly woven using lustrous multifilament yarns, produce luxurious linings. They are most often used in men's tailored jackets and coats.

Lined coat

The "secret" of this coat is the flash of a red velvet lining when the garment is open. Great drama can be added to a design by using a contrasting lining that reflects the designer's attitude.

Satin

The smooth, shiny surface of satin fabric is one of the most recognized fabrics in fashion. Designers often confuse satin weave with silk fiber. Satin is a weave, not a fiber.

Satin fabrics are produced in many different fiber contents but always with the same result—a smooth and lustrous surface. Satin fabrics use multifilament yarns only. They are usually very flexible or drapey compared to stiffer structure fabrics, such as bridal satin or sateen. The degree of drapability is related to the type of yarns used. Satin fabrics with highly twisted multifilament yarns will have more drape than satin fabrics using simple multifilament yarns.

Because of its smooth, lustrous surface, satin fabric is nearly always selected for dressy blouses and dresses. However, its sensual drape also makes it a popular choice for lingerie and undergarments.

The fiber content of satin fabrics vary widely. Rayon, acetate, polyester, and silk multifilament yarns will all produce a lustrous surface. The hand of the satin fabric will vary depending on the fiber content and degree of yarn twist. The quality of satin is related to the density of the satin weave. Resilience is also related to the fiber content.

This deep burgundy polyester satin fabric can be used for dresses, blouses, and linings. It is a washable fabric.

Facts and figures

Distinctive features

- Luxurious, lustrous surface.
- Smooth surface.
- Drapey.
- The hand is soft, although stiffer in the cross-grain direction.

Strengths

- Wonderful surface texture.
- Good spring/summer fabric.
- Good choice for dresses and blouses in silk and polyester fiber fabrics.
- It shows seaming detail well.

Weaknesses

- Often shows "water spots" on the fabric surface.
- Snags easily on the fabric surface.
- Sewing requires very sharp needle or ballpoint needle to avoid snagging.
- Must use nonstick sewing foot to avoid snagging fabric surface.

Usual fiber content

- 100 percent polyester, acetate, or rayon.
- 100 percent silk.

Printed satin
Satin fabrics are ideal for taking finely detailed prints. The smooth surface reflects color beautifully.

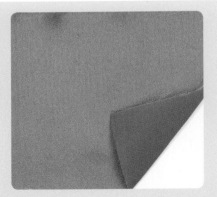

Charmeuse
Smooth, lustrous warp yarns are used on the fabric face and highly twisted crepe weft yarns on the back. The resulting fabric has a smooth satin surface and a back that resembles crêpe de Chine (see page 144).

Burnout satin
This satin face fabric, burned out in a pattern to show the georgette ground fabric, is unique in its construction, using both a satin face and a sheer georgette ground.

Satin gowns
The sensuous satin fabric used in these gowns demonstrates how flexible the fabric is, draping to show the form of the body.

Crêpe de Chine

(also known as faille crêpe)

Crêpe de Chine is a beautiful, lustrous, voluptuous fabric that hints at the body's shape as it slides over the form.

This ribbed weave includes very fine, textured horizontal ribs that are barely visible, and more pronounced, textured ribs similar to faille (see page 72). The textured rib is achieved by complex, highly twisted crêpe yarns, similar to georgette (see page 137), woven in the weft direction only and interlaced.

Crêpe de Chine fabrics are "lively," meaning they are springy when compressed and released. The high-twist yarns create this effect. These fabrics are a favorite in dressy blouses, dresses, and lingerie. It is possible to use very lightweight crêpe de Chine as a lining, but it is more expensive than lining fabrics. An important point about crêpe de Chine is its ability to hold a seam. Therefore, design elements can feature seaming structure as well as drape. Seam slippage is less likely to occur in a crêpe de Chine than in the more loosely woven fabrics or fabrics that use only low-twist yarns.

This white crêpe de Chine has a supple and lightweight hand, and can hold seams well; however, the white color can be somewhat sheer. Dark colors are less sheer.

Facts and figures

Distinctive features

- Horizontal (weft direction) fine texture or "pebbly" ribbed crêpe appearance.
- Lustrous surface; luster dependent on the fineness of the rib.
- Luxurious drape.

Strengths

- Lustrous, fine ribbed surface.
- Holds seams well.
- Drapes very well.
- Unlikely to slip.

Weaknesses

- In heavier weights can be difficult to cut accurately because the fabric slips.

Usual fiber content

- 100 percent polyester and polyester/rayon blends.
- 100 percent silk and silk blends.

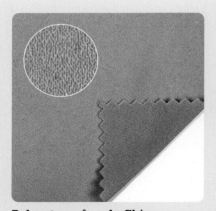

Polyester crêpe de Chine
All crêpe de Chine fabrics are reversible. This 100 percent polyester fabric is a good example.

Embroidered silk crêpe de Chine
The smooth, finely ribbed surface is well suited to fine machine embroidery. Lustrous rayon embroidery yarns are added after the fabric is dyed, finished, and cut into garment pattern pieces.

Printed crêpe de Chine
Crêpe de Chine printed fabrics are a favorite fabric for women's blouses. The fabric is lightweight and yet opaque for modesty. This fabric is printed using a wet print. The image is nearly the same on the back side as it is on the face.

Muted highlights

Crêpe de Chine has a characteristic "highlight"—focused areas of reflected light at the top of fabric folds. Unlike satin fabric surfaces, which are entirely shiny, crêpe de Chine fabric surfaces reflect light in a muted fashion.

Crinkled fabric

Crêpeon

Fabric with a warp-direction crinkled surface is generally referred to as a crêpeon fabric. Crêpeon fabrics can be any fiber content, but the result is always a lengthwise (warp-direction) crinkled surface texture.

This crinkled fabric is similar to gauze, but the wrinkled effect is due to the type of yarns used, resulting in deep crinkles in the texture of the fabric. This fabric is very loosely woven, but the crinkled surface is pronounced.

Although the term "crêpeon" is not used frequently in today's textile industry, suppliers will often refer to a fabric with a woven-in crinkled appearance as crêpeon weave.

Crinkled fabrics are varying top- and medium-weights primarily used for blouses, tops, dresses, and soft, lightweight pants and jackets. The main feature, this crinkled surface texture, which is created during the weaving process, will allow the fabric to retain its texture for the life of the garment.

The crinkled texture will limit the type of design. It is best to design with fewer seams and allow the soft, unstructured garment to drape on the body. Sewing seam details on a crêpeon fabric surface makes for a "busy" design that is difficult to sew and press.

Fabric hand will depend on the fiber content and type of yarns used. In general, spun cotton yarns and fabrics produce a very casual, somewhat rough texture, and polyester multifilament yarns produce a more dressy, smoother, softer texture.

Tightly woven polyester crêpeon
The fine, high-twist multifilament yarns are woven tightly together, creating the subtle crinkled surface of this lightweight crêpe fabric.

Loosely woven cotton crêpeon
The coarse, high-twist cotton yarns produce a pronounced warp-direction crinkled effect. This bottom-weight fabric is versatile, used for casual jackets, pants, and skirts, and has been a signature fabric for certain designers.

Dobby stripe crêpeon
This medium-weight dobby fabric combines twill weave, warp-direction stripes with plain weave stripes. The polyester/rayon blend crêpe yarns produce the crinkled effect across the fabric surface.

Facts and figures

Distinctive features

- Vertical (warp direction) all-over crinkled surface.
- Often loosely woven surface, so the fabric is somewhat see-through.

Strengths

- Wonderful surface texture.
- Good spring/summer fabric.
- Good choice for dresses and blouses in silk and polyester fiber fabrics.

Weaknesses

- Textured surface is difficult to cut accurately.
- Slippage can occur in more open-weave crêpeon fabrics.
- Pressing seams can be difficult.

Usual fiber content

Spun yarns:
- 100 percent cotton and cotton/ polyester blends.

Multifilament yarns:
- 100 percent polyester and polyester/ rayon blends.
- 100 percent silk and silk blends.

Crinkled wrap dress

This soft wrap dress needs few seams because the crinkle fabric texture adds drape and softness. The contrasting smooth shine in the medallion belt focuses the design at the wrap closure.

Challis

Challis (pronounced "shallee") is a square-weave woven fabric with a soft, slightly fuzzy surface. The yarns used are always spun, not multifilament. Today, most challis fabrics are rayon, which increases the soft hand.

Challis fabrics are most frequently used in prints, for children's and women's tops, dresses/skirts, blouses, and shirts. Rayon-blend challis prints are also often used in men's and women's Hawaiian-print shirts instead of cotton fiber. The rayon absorbs the dyes better than cotton, and the soft rayon hand makes a wonderful, cool fabric for a warm climate.

Challis's soft hand makes it an ideal fabric for soft pleats, soft gathers, or bias cutting for a loose-fitting design. Although the fabric will sew and press well, its softness makes it unsuitable for a fitted design.

Challis can be inexpensive because the spun yarns are not highly twisted. When polyester is blended with rayon, the result can be unsightly pilling. Remember to take care when selecting a fiber blend to understand whether pilling will be a concern for your design.

Always soft and lightweight, challis fabric can be either a balanced plain weave or a fine twill weave. This red fabric is a rayon challis in a twill weave. It has a lightly brushed surface to imitate the original wool challis.

Facts and figures

Distinctive features
- Finely woven, slightly hairy surface.
- Most frequently printed.

Strengths
- Very soft hand.
- Drapes on the body very well.
- Gathers well.
- Sews and presses well.
- Inexpensive fabric in rayon/polyester blends.

Weaknesses
- Not suitable for tight-fitting garments.
- Pills easily if using a polyester blend.
- Rayon fabrics wrinkle easily.

Usual fiber content
- 100 percent rayon or rayon/polyester blends.
- 100 percent cotton or cotton/polyester blends.

DESIGN RESPONSIBLY

100 percent rayon or polyester/rayon blended challis fabrics are a popular choice for inexpensive clothing. Produced mostly in developing countries, the viscose rayon uses production methods mostly banned in industrialized nations. These inexpensive viscose rayon or rayon/polyester fiber fabrics produce toxic emissions and chemical waste that is not regulated in the global textile industry. Although the low price of this fabric is hard to resist, remember that its production is no longer allowed in countries that have environmental regulations that limit toxic emissions and chemical waste.

Light-ground challis print
Challis fabrics are usually dark-colored prints. However, this cowboy printed challis is used for women's blouses, skirts, or sleepwear and has a lightly brushed surface for added softness.

Dark-print challis
Rayon challis is often used for printed shirts and blouses. Cool and soft to the touch, the rayon fiber accepts dyes very well, so dark-toned colors are often selected for wet-printed designs.

Surah

Surah is an elegant fabric, always using multifilament yarns, to create lustrous, finely woven twill fabric.

Surah's light weight and drape make it ideally suited to accessories, such as elegant scarves and men's neckties. It is occasionally used in lingerie or lining because of its light weight.

Surah is most often used as a printed fabric. The tightly woven diagonal twill surface provides an ideal surface on which to print detailed images, second only to satin as a printing medium. The soft drape, cut on the bias, produces elegant men's ties, usually printed with appropriate menswear designs. Solid colors show the distinctive twill texture. Women's designer scarves also use these finely woven surah fabrics. The soft drape of the fabric can only be achieved by this twill weave. A plain weave fabric will simply not have the same drape as surah.

Lightweight, lustrous, and tightly woven, surah is an elegant fabric for linings, men's ties, and scarves.

Facts and figures

Distinctive features
- Lustrous, finely woven diagonal surface effect.
- Lightweight and opaque.
- Very soft hand.

Strengths
- Lustrous surface.
- Soft hand, drapes very well.
- Gathers well.

Weaknesses
- May slip if sewn seams are used.
- Not suitable for tight-fitting garments.

Usual fiber content
- 100 percent multifilament silk or silk blends.
- 100 percent microdenier polyester or polyester blends.

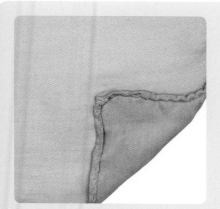

Solid-color surah
This fabric is not reversible. The fine diagonal texture on the fabric face is very appealing. This pocket square for a men's suit has been hand-rolled and hand-stitched to finish the cut edges.

White surah
Solid white surah is used for expensive lining or ties. It is an expensive fabric to produce, so it is rarely used in full garments.

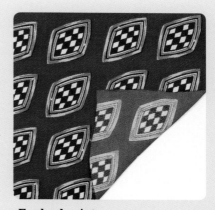

Foulard print
This foulard print (small geometric design) on surah is a typical print design for men's ties.

Jersey

Knitted jersey fabric is one of the most popular but least recognized fabrics in apparel. One of the most diverse fabrics used in the fashion industry, the size of the yarn can distract the designer from the fact that it is a jersey knit.

Fine yarns are used for very lightweight garments, hosiery, and underwear, and bulky yarns are used for sweaters, socks, and accessories, such as gloves, hats, and scarves.

A jersey fabric stretches out of shape easily, so this fabric should not be used for a fitted garment without the addition of an elastic yarn knitted into the fabric. Jersey fabrics are most commonly used in underwear, pajamas, lingerie, T-shirts, knit tops, and lightweight sweaters and dresses. Garment designs do not require exact fitting because jersey's stretchability allows for easy fitting on a variety of body types. The wide variety of jersey fabrics are distinguished by the different fiber blends used for texture and hand.

This jersey cotton fabric is one of the most popular fabrics used today. A lightweight fabric that doesn't hold its shape very well, it is up to the designer to create a garment that does not fit tightly on the body.

Designer's tip: Jersey also has an unusual characteristic: the fabric edge, when cut, will not stay flat but will roll. This characteristic is especially noticeable in lightweight cotton jersey. An anti-roll fabric finish should be applied to the fabric so it can be cut and sewn together more easily.

Tonal-color jersey
This three-color jersey fabric was created by combining three different colored yarns into the knitted fabric.

Wool jersey
The natural elasticity of wool helps this jersey fabric retain its shape. The lightweight single knit keeps the fabric lightweight compared to a woven wool fabric.

Wool-like polyester jersey
This loosely knitted jersey is produced from textured polyester multifilament yarns intended to imitate wool. However, this fabric doesn't possess the elasticity of tightly knitted wool jersey.

Facts and figures

Distinctive features

- Knit stitches on the face giving a flat surface.
- Purl stitches on the back giving a textured surface.
- Cut edges roll.

Strengths

- Wide variety of textures and hands.
- Easily available.
- Stretchable fabric, easy to fit.
- Good drape.
- Resilient, though fiber content will help resilience further.

Weaknesses

- Fabric is difficult to sew after cutting due to the rolled edges.
- Fabric stretches out of shape easily.
- Must use ballpoint needle.
- Fabric snags easily and, if yarn is broken, will cause a "run" (stitches are dropped and fabric de-knits).

Usual fiber content

- 100 percent cotton and cotton/polyester blends.
- Linen and ramie, blended with polyester.
- 100 percent wool or wool blends.
- 100 percent polyester and polyester/rayon blends.
- 100 percent silk and silk blends.
- 100 percent rayon and rayon blends.

Contrasting jersey garments

Jersey is usually known for its soft hand and its ability to drape. This jersey jumpsuit has a very soft appearance and drapes beautifully, showing the body's curves. In contrast, some jersey fabrics use simple spun yarns that do not enhance the fabric's drapability, as seen in this gray jersey top.

Interlock

Interlock is a knitted fabric that has the appearance of a jersey knit face (see page 150) on both sides of the fabric. A lightweight fabric that behaves somewhat like a woven fabric, it is quite rigid compared to a single-knit jersey.

The yarn will determine the drape of the fabric. Fine, multifilament yarns will add more drapability and softness. Spun yarns, such as cotton fiber or rayon, are usually bigger yarns than the multifilament yarns, so spun yarns will generally create a bulkier, less drapey fabric.

Men's polo knit shirts often use interlock because this fabric can hold the seams very well (like a woven fabric) and is less likely to stretch out of shape during the cutting and sewing process. However, interlocks do not have the same stretchability as jersey. Interlock knits are also used for dresses and blouses, especially when printed.

This cotton interlock fabric is more loosely knitted than most interlock fabrics. It still retains the stability of interlock knits but has a softer, more drapey hand.

Facts and figures

Distinctive features
- Flat surface showing only knit stitches.
- Lightweight and opaque.
- Drapey but more rigid in weft knit.

Strengths
- Smooth knit surface.
- Soft hand, drapes very well.
- Gathers well.
- Reversible.
- Cut edges do not roll.
- Easy knit fabric to cut and sew.

Weaknesses
- Surface can be snagged.
- Somewhat bulky fabric for its weight, though this is not always true.
- Broken yarn can cause a run on the fabric surface.

Usual fiber content
- 100 percent multifilament polyester, rayon, or silk, or blends.
- 100 percent microdenier polyester, especially for athletic apparel.
- 100 percent cotton, staple rayon; sometimes blended with polyester.

Cotton interlock
This tightly knitted fabric feels compact and rigid compared to cotton jersey. Cotton interlock is used for men's and women's casual shirts.

Bamboo rayon interlock
This interlock, using rayon produced from bamboo raw material, is extremely soft and drapey compared to a cotton interlock.

Polyester interlock
Because of the rigidness of interlock compared to jersey, interlock is often used as a base cloth for laminating film or faux leather and suede. The knit construction adds flexibility to stiff film laminates.

Matte jersey

Matte jersey is a lightweight, knitted fabric known for its drape and stability (little stretch).

Using high-twist crêpe yarns, matte jersey has a recognizable "crêpe" surface and hand. However, its knitted construction is generally much less expensive than woven crêpes are to produce. The surface texture will vary, depending on the type of crêpe yarns used.

Designers most often select matte jersey for dresses and blouses. Loungewear designers sometimes select matte jersey for drapey, sensuous robes. This fabric has the same "liveliness" as most woven fabrics but the stretchiness of a knit. Only multifilament yarns are used, which are necessary to create the high-twist crêpe yarns. It is most commonly used as a 100-percent polyester fabric and is frequently printed, using a variety of printing techniques.

The lively, soft drape of this fabric is ideal for dresses and blouses. It is stable, retaining its shape while being worn.

Facts and figures

Distinctive features
- Pebbly, crêpe-like surface.
- Has knitted surface flexibility.
- Drapey and lively.

Strengths
- Sews easily.
- Drapes very well.
- Gathers well.
- Cut edges do not roll.
- Can be elastic without being elastic yarn.

Weaknesses
- Surface snags easily.
- Cutting pattern pieces accurately can be difficult.
- Broken yarns may cause a run on the fabric surface.

Usual fiber content
- 100 percent polyester or rayon.
- 100 percent multifilament silk or silk blends.

Rayon matte jersey
The cool, soft drape of rayon fiber translates into an elegant fabric used for sensuous women's dresses, tops, and skirts.

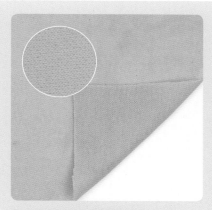

Polyester matte jersey
This matte jersey is one of the most common fabrics used in dresses, both as a solid color and as a print.

Printed polyester matte jersey
Because matte jersey is a more stable fabric than a single-knit, it is used extensively for printing. Stripes are particularly difficult to print, subject to curving (called "bowing").

Fine-gauge sweater knits

Sweater knits are always weft knits. Gauge refers to the number of stitches per inch used to produce the fabric. A fabric that is produced using many small stitches knitted together is referred to as a "fine-gauge" sweater knit.

Machine knitting is a highly technical but very creative field. For the designer not familiar with the full vocabulary of the knitting industry, recognizing a fine-gauge knit fabric is a key point. Remember, if the knit fabric face and back stitches are difficult to see, the fabric is fine-gauge.

Sweater knits that are full-fashioned will always be fine gauge. Similar to hand knitting, shaped, knitted garment pattern pieces are produced on a computerized flatbed knitting machine. The pattern pieces are then knitted together, not sewn together. The result is a full-fashioned garment, most commonly seen in fine-gauge sweaters. One of the advantages of full-fashioning sweaters is that there is no cut waste. Garments are designed, and the fabric is knitted to specification.

Fine-gauge knits show little surface texture. This sweater knit is an even-textured, smooth surface, probably 20 stitches per inch, that uses fine yarn.

Outside

Outside

Inside

Inside

Full-fashioned sleeve seam
Assembling a full-fashioned knit garment is expensive because the pieces are produced as their final shape first and then knitted together (rather than being cut into shape from rolls of knit fabric yardage). The benefit of a full-fashioned seam is that the knitted edges do not have bulky seam allowances.

Faux full-fashioned sweater
Because there is such value attached to a full-fashioned sweater, some designers will "fake" it and produce the distinctive full-fashioned surface stitches while sewing the entire garment.

Facts and figures

Distinctive features

- Very small knit stitches on the fabric surface that are not easily seen.
- The fabric surface is generally tightly knitted together.
- If the fabric is cut, the cut edge will roll.

Strengths

- Stretchable fabric, easy to fit.
- Good drape.
- Resilient, although the fiber content will help resilience further.

Weaknesses

- The fabric may stretch out of shape.
- If sewing is necessary, a ballpoint needle should be used.
- The fabric snags easily, and if the yarn is broken, a "run" will occur (stitches will be dropped and the fabric will ravel).

Usual fiber content

Spun yarns:
- 100 percent cotton and cotton/ polyester blends.
- Linen and ramie, blended with polyester.
- 100 percent wool or wool blends.

Simple multifilament yarns:
- 100 percent polyester and polyester/ rayon blends.
- 100 percent silk and silk blends.
- 100 percent rayon and rayon blends.

Fine-gauge sweater-knit garments
Fine-gauge sweater knits are always lightweight. Fine yarns are used for knitting and the resulting fabrics can be quite smooth, allowing for further ornamentation, as in the sequin-trimmed dress, right, or using contrasting satin-weave textures to enhance the final ensemble as in the fine-gauge knit vest, above.

Pointelle knits

Weft-knitted fabrics can be produced in a wide variety of textures and patterns. Pointelle knits have very noticeable characteristics, and designers have identified these fabrics for their designs.

Pointelle knits are designed using regular patterns of spaces, or holes, in the fabric. The spaces in the fabric are arranged in distinctive patterns, combined with other knit surface textures to produce beautiful, lightweight knits.

Pointelles are commonly used for camisoles, lingerie, underwear, infants' wear, and fashion knit shirts. Their variety of surface textures inspire designers, especially during the spring/summer season. Requiring a tightly knit fabric to control the open spaces in the fabric design, fine-gauge knits are required for pointelle knits. With a fine, small yarn size required, fine-quality cotton or wool yarns must be used. However, a great variety of fiber contents are used in producing pointelle knits.

The softness of this pointelle knit is enhanced by the subtle stripe and floral effect knitted into the fabric. Pointelle is created by knitting a pattern of open spaces (no yarn) into the fabric

Floral pointelle
The floral design knitted into this jersey fabric is created by knitting a series of "holes" into the fabric.

Shiny dot pointelle
Though not a real pointelle knit, the shiny rayon yarns woven into this jersey imitate the "spaces" produced in a true pointelle knit.

Ribbed pointelle
This ribbed pointelle is a fabric often used in infant apparel. The ribbed knit adds some elasticity, and the open spaces in the fabric keep the baby cool in hot weather.

Facts and figures
Distinctive features
- Knit stitches on the face and back.
- Specific pattern of spaces designed into the fabric for an openwork design, which is usually geometric.
- Fine-gauge knit.

Strengths
- Wide variety of patterns.
- Light and airy fabric designs.
- Stretchable fabric, which is easy to fit.
- Good drape.
- Resilient, although the fiber content will help resilience further.

Weaknesses
- The fabric is difficult to sew because of the spaces in the fabric texture.
- A ballpoint needle must be used.
- The fabric easily snags, and if the yarn is broken, a "run" will occur.

Usual fiber content
Spun yarns:
- 100 percent cotton and cotton/ polyester blends.
- Linen and ramie, blended with polyester.
- 100 percent wool or wool blends.

Simple multifilament yarns:
- 100 percent polyester and polyester/ rayon blends.
- 100 percent silk and silk blends.
- 100 percent rayon and rayon blends.

Women's dress
This knitted dress illustrates the great variety of light, open-stitched surfaces that a pointelle knit fabric can have. While pointelle knits are commonly used for lingerie, the light, airy feeling of this fabric makes it a popular choice for spring and summer casual clothing.

Mesh

A fabric that is mostly holes or spaces framed by tightly interlooped yarns, yet has a soft, stretchable hand, is a mesh fabric. The size and shape of the fabric holes and their spacing on the fabric surface can have great variety.

This lustrous warp-knit mesh is often called athletic mesh. Used for permeable fabrics that allow cooling air to pass through the fabric during athletic activity, it is a relatively durable fabric, though it is mostly enclosed holes.

Mesh fabrics have become an important fabric for athletic garments, women's lingerie, and underwear. They are inexpensive and can create very interesting texture. Because of the holes or open spaces that define a mesh fabric, this fabric is often used as a jacket or pant lining for comfort, avoiding skin contact with a less comfortable shell fabric. Mesh lining on functional snowboard apparel or cycling jackets may also act as a wicking layer, moving body moisture away from the body for fast evaporation.

Mesh fabrics always use simple multifilament yarns, from a variety of nonfunctional mesh to highly functional wicking and quick-drying fabric. As previously noted, mesh fabrics are most often selected for athletic sports apparel that requires quick cooling and drying functions. Depending on the style of the mesh, the designer can select a fabric for fashion or function.

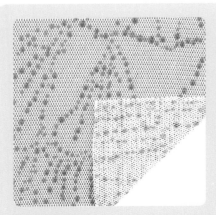

Small holes
Small holes, knitted closely together, produce less durable fabrics but are more sheer than large-hole fabrics. This small-hole mesh is often used for women's fashion tops, and it is often printed.

Medium holes
Medium-holed mesh is often used for linings in jackets and pants.

Large holes
Large holes are usually knitted far apart and create durable fabrics for athletic activity. These large-holed mesh fabrics are not sheer like the small-hole mesh knits.

White mesh top on tennis dress

Mesh fabric provides maximum air-flow for athletic designs. This warp-knit mesh has a slightly crisp hand to maintain the silhouette of the top of this tennis dress. This warp tricot knit mesh has almost no stretch in the straight grain (or vertical) direction.

Facts and figures

Distinctive features

- The surface is holes, framed by interlooping yarns.
- The straight-grain direction does not stretch or elongate very much.
- It nearly always has soft hand and drape.

Strengths

- Wide variety of hole size and luster.
- Easily available.
- Rigid in straight-grain direction.
- Good drape.
- Resilient.

Weaknesses

- The fabric is difficult to sew after cutting due to fabric holes.
- A ballpoint needle must be used.
- The fabric snags easily.
- The more holes in the fabric, the more difficult it is to cut accurately.

Usual fiber content

- 100 percent polyester.
- 100 percent microfiber polyester for wicking capability and quick drying.

Black mesh on shoulders

This black mesh, produced from widely spaced weft single-knit, is very soft, conforms easily to the body, and is likely to stretch out of shape easily. Adding spandex yarn will help sustain the shape of the shoulder.

Tricot

Tricot knits are among the most popular fabrics used in apparel. Most designers will not recognize a tricot fabric, but they are important in interlinings, linings, lingerie, underwear, swimwear, and athletic apparel.

Designers looking for an inexpensive, smooth-textured fabric that provides strength without weight will select tricot. Always using inexpensive multifilament yarn for fabric production, tricot fabrics provide strength in the straight-grain direction and expansion in the cross-grain direction, and are very lightweight. Polyester fiber content is most commonly used. Tricot fabrics, like nearly all knits, are soft and somewhat resilient. The drape is generally good, although yarn size will affect the quality of the drape. The bigger the yarn, the less drape there will be.

Tricot fabrics are often selected for pajamas, robes, nightgowns, inexpensive fashion tops, and dresses. Tricot is easily printed, especially when using heat-transfer printing. Tricot is especially important to the fast-fashion women's designer because the fabric is inexpensive, readily available, and easily transformed by dyeing, printing, and pleating.

Designer's tip: Tricot fabric may be subject to rolling, although it is much easier to control than jersey (see page 150). It may be useful to add an anti-roll finish to the fabric.

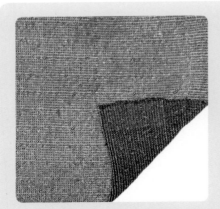

Tricot with metallic yarn fabric
Tricot is a lightweight fabric. Adding metallic yarn will create a sheer and less stretchy textile.

Tricot printed fabric
This printed tricot uses a thicker yarn that is a heavier weight than the yarn used for lingerie tricot fabric. This heavier type of tricot can be used as loose-fitting athletic apparel as well as for fashion.

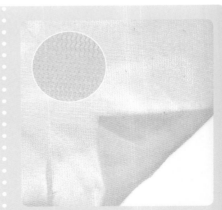

Tricot lining
Tricots can be inexpensive, base-cloth fabrics for laminating to film or for bonding to another fabric for increased weight. This type of tricot is usually sheer and very inexpensive.

Facts and figures

Distinctive features
- Smooth surface with slightly sheer appearance.
- Very rigid in the straight-grain direction.
- Expands in cross-grain direction.

Strengths
- Durable fabric.
- Easily available.
- Stretchable fabric, easy to fit.
- Good drape.
- Resilient, although the fiber content will help resilience further.

Weaknesses
- Fabric is difficult to sew after cutting due to slightly rolled edges.
- A ballpoint needle must be used.
- The fabric surface snags easily.

Usual fiber content
- 100 percent polyester.
- 100 percent nylon.

Slip with tricot and lace
The smooth surface of tricot fabric is ideal for undergarments like this lace-trimmed slip. This fabric is stable in the straight-grain direction and will keep the garment from stretching out of shape.

Traditional lace

Historically significant as one of the badges of class rank, handmade lace required great skill and much time to produce. Lace was available only to the very wealthy until the invention of machinery that could imitate the openwork thread designs in lace fabric.

This black lace is produced to imitate v expensive Alençon lace. The scalloped e has been machine-embroidered with a c wrapped rayon thread for a hand-embroide appearance. It is easily available by the yard, is unlikely to stretch out of shape ea

Most laces available for apparel are now machine-made and are available in many designs imitating the original handmade fabrics. The designer's choice of lace fabric is completely their own, as there are hundreds of lace designs and methods of production. It's important to look out for one-way designs that will require the pattern pieces to be lined up in the same grain direction. It will also be important to balance the lace design on the body, so that the garment does not appear lopsided. Busy lace patterns usually encourage the designer to minimize seaming details in their garments.

Most laces are drapey, folding elegantly against the body. Because most laces are also see-through and not very durable, lace fabrics are used sparingly and for one-off events. They are often lined with a lightweight lining fabric, and the under-fabric color will show through to the surface.

Machine-made lace fabrics intended to closely imitate the original handmade lace fabrics and are divided into three main groups:

- Embroidered lace (lace ground with embroidered thread stitched over the surface).
- Schiffli lace (all-over embroidered lace).
- Bobbin-type (thread twisted together to create a pattern).

Bobbin lace
Often called Cluny lace, the yarns that make up the fabric are twisted together in intricate, lacy patterns.

Schiffli lace
This fabric has a heavily embroidered and very textured lace surface.

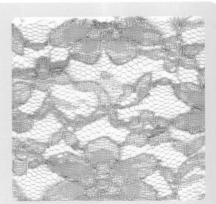

Gold lace
This gold-colored lace, similar to the black lace shown at the top, has an embroidered texture similar to Alençon lace. These expensive laces are generally only available in white and black, but occasionally can be found in fashion colors.

Facts and figures

Distinctive features
- Imitates handmade lace.
- Usually narrow width (36in/91cm).
- Highly textured, complex images.

Strengths
- Wide variety of textures, designs, and hand.
- Usually resilient.
- Lightweight and see-through qualities make lace a good fabric for layering with other lightweight fabrics.
- Usually soft drape.

Weaknesses
- Can snag easily.
- The irregular surface makes sewing lace uneven, and seams may come apart easily.
- Matching the design may cause extra fabric cutting waste.

Usual fiber content
- 100 percent polyester or polyester/ rayon blends.
- 100 percent silk.
- 100 percent cotton or cotton/ polyester blends.

Lace wedding gown
This Schiffli lace fabric is produced with a netting background, with large lace images repeated across the fabric. It was made with a scalloped edge, and the designer intended to place this scalloped edge at the neckline. Careful balancing and lace image-matching is an important part of this gown design.

Mass-market lace

The laces described here are produced on high-speed equipment for low-cost imitation laces. These lace fabrics are what most designers use in their designs, as they are readily available and inexpensive compared to the laces described on the previous two pages.

Flat-textured lacy designs using simple multifilament yarns produce fabrics ranging from lustrous to matte. Fabric width is wide for best fabric consumption in designs. There is great variety in lace pattern, colors, and flattened surface texture. These raschel laces are usually very lightweight yet quite strong in the straight-grain direction, unlike the more expensive laces on the previous pages. Therefore, these inexpensive knitted laces tend to be used more frequently and for a wide variety of uses.

Primarily used for inexpensive formal dresses, blouses, and sometimes window coverings and tablecloths, these lace fabrics are available in a variety of colors. Because of the flatness of the lace images, raschel laces are selected for lingerie and underwear.

In fashion colors, raschel laces are used in women's blouses, tops, and dresses.

Yarns used for lace production are always simple multifilament; spun yarns are not used. Fabrics nearly always have a good drape.

Printed stretch lace
This raschel lace has been screen-printed with a floral image on the lace design. The polyester/spandex blend is perfect for fitted women's fashion tops and camisoles.

Lightweight lace
This inexpensive lace pattern is used in lingerie and evening dresses.

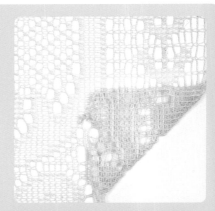

Raschel lace for interiors
Lace designs that imitate traditional, handmade tatting and embroidery are often used for table linens and window coverings today, and they have been adopted by some designers for apparel.

Facts and figures
Distinctive features
- Knit stitches on the face.
- Purl stitches on the back.
- Cut edges roll.

Strengths
- Readily available in a wide variety of designs.
- Easy to cut and sew.
- Rigid fabric in straight-grain direction.
- Usually very drapey fabric.
- If yarns break, fabric will not run.

Weaknesses
- May be difficult to sew if the lace design is very open.
- Snags easily.

Usual fiber content
- 100 percent polyester or polyester/ rayon blends.

Stretch lace
This stretch lace fabric has been blended with spandex yarns, an important feature in tops and dresses that are designed to fit closely to the body.

The metallic surface on this polyester/spandex-blend jersey has been applied by a heat transfer. The metallic film is elastic, like the knit fabric base, and it will expand and contract with the fabric.

Enlarge

Lamé

Lamé has a metallic surface, created by any type of construction. Although lamé originally used metal thread, now metallic surfaces are often applied by a resin coating or laminate.

All lamé fabrics are soft and appear to be "liquid" metal when worn. Used in very dressy knits or woven fabrics, these metallic fabrics radiate sparkle and shine.

Lightweight lamé, woven with monofilament metallic yarns, is somewhat drapey. This woven lamé is often used for costumes or trim but is not suitable for most apparel because it is weak.

A different method of producing a lamé surface is by the heat transfer of tiny metallic dots onto the surface of a knitted fabric. The dots are placed so close together that the surface appears to be a solid color.

Woven lamé
Flat monofilament metallic yarns are used in the weft direction, and thin, strong warp yarns are interlaced together. Only the shiny metallic yarns are visible on the surface.

Georgette lamé
Smoke-colored metallic yarns are inserted into this plain weave georgette fabric to create a pewter-colored metallic surface.

Pink lamé
Although lamé originally used gold, silver, and copper yarns, today, metallic surface fabrics can be many colors. This pink metallic film has been applied to a rose-colored knit.

Facts and figures

Distinctive features
- Metallic surface, any metal color.
- Very shiny metallic appearance.

Strengths
- Smooth metallic hand.
- Drapes well.
- Resilient.

Weaknesses
- May not be resewn. Stitching holes will show.
- Woven lamé is prone to seam slippage.
- Laminate lamé is heat-sensitive.

Usual fiber content
- 100 percent polyester.
- Nylon, polyester, metallic blends.
- Polyurethane laminate.

Lamé suit
The subtly shimmering surface of this lamé suit was produced by adding metallic yarns to the woven worsted wool fabric. It does not have the brilliant shine of a metallic coating.

Textured knits

Using different-colored yarns in a fabric can create the illusion of texture, and patterns of stitches in a knit can add depth to a mostly smooth fabric surface. These are both methods of providing variety in knit textiles. The end result will depend on the type and size of yarns used, as well as the stitching patterns.

Since knitting does not depend on tension, strong yarns are not required for producing knits. Therefore, the variety of yarns used can include textured yarns for surface interest. Only four textured knits are shown here, but there are hundreds more. Knit designers, using weft knits, can create beautiful textures by combining different colors and yarn types.

All knits have good drape, and top-weight textured knits create wonderful, soft-hand garments. Textured knits, in top and medium weights, are used for tops and women's dresses.

Almost any fiber content can be used for surface texture knits. Since producing the texture is the priority, fiber content can be used to enhance the surface.

Enlarged

The striped surface texture of this knit fabric is achieved by reversing the knit stitch; the purl stitch creates the broad bands of texture. The reverse side is a mirror image of the face side. Both sides of this fabric can be used.

Designer's tip: Textured surface knits are highly prone to snagging. Because the stitches are part of a network of yarns that are looped together, the yarns protruding on the surface are susceptible to being caught and pulled (snagged), creating unsightly puckering on the surface and a yarn being pulled from the fabric. If the yarn is broken, the stitch will be dropped and a "run" will form as more stitches are dropped.

Thermal double knit
Thermal double knits are used to retain body heat during cold weather if worn as the underlayer with several more layers to keep body heat from escaping. Thermal knits have this characteristic square-textured appearance.

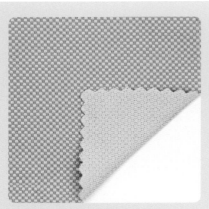

Two-color pique knit
This jacquard double knit produces a pixelated-effect check in two colors, but only one color shows on the back side. This effect can be useful in creating a reversible design.

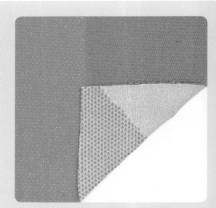

Reversible knitted texture
Unlike woven jacquards, knitted jacquards can have either geometric or curved designs. This sample uses three colors of yarn; the face shows the surface image and texture in two colors and the back side, the reverse image and texture in two colors.

Facts and figures

Distinctive features
- Great variety of surface textures available.
- Knit stitches on the face.
- Purl stitches on the back.
- Cut edges may roll.

Strengths
- Wide variety of textures.
- Easily available.
- Stretchable fabric, easy to fit.
- Good drape.
- The fabric retains its shape due to the alternating use of knit and purl stitches on the face and back.
- Resilient, although the fiber content will help resilience further.

Weaknesses
- The fabric requires a special sewing technique—flat-locking or chain-stitching—to allow the seams to expand with the wearer.
- A ballpoint needle must be used.
- The fabric snags easily, and if the yarn is broken, it will cause a "run" (stitches are dropped and the fabric de-knits).

Usual fiber content:
Spun yarns:
- 100 percent cotton and cotton/ polyester blends.
- Linen and ramie, blended with polyester.
- 100 percent wool or wool blends.
Simple multifilament yarns and texturized multifilament yarns:
- 100 percent polyester and polyester/ rayon blend.

Tweed sweater
Textured surfaces in knitting are achieved by combining different colored yarns into a variety of knit stitches that will produce an interesting texture. This tweed effect was produced by selecting slubbed, variegated-color yarns to be tightly knitted in textured wales. The result imitates a woven tweed fabric.

Designed knit surfaces

As mentioned on other pages, knitwear has infinite variety in weight, texture, and fit, based on the size and texture of the yarn used and how tightly the yarn is knitted together.

Designers are able to create very interesting sweaters using complex CAD (computer-aided design) software and flatbed computerized knitting machines; the importance of CAD to the knitwear industry cannot be overemphasized.

Designed knit surfaces can duplicate very traditional cable stitch designs or may be new surfaces only available from computerized knitting machines. There are only a handful of knit surface designs shown here, but unlimited design ideas can be produced.

The most common designed knit surface is cable knitting. The cables' soft, linear shapes that seem to twist on the surface can be produced in many styles and textures, depending on the size of the yarn and tightness of the weft knitting. Other designed knit surfaces are produced using raschel warp knitting. These fabrics are produced

This warp knit fabric's specific surface design combines mesh and chevron stitched construction not possible in woven fabrics.

as flat yardage and are cut and sewn into knit garments. Both geometric and lacy designed surfaces can be produced. Warp knits will be more rigid and less stretchy than weft knits.

Raschel herringbone
This herringbone surface is engineered to create a fitted sweater. It is a raschel warp-knit fabric that is cut into garment pieces and sewn together. It is an open-knit design, but the warp-knit construction is more stable than weft knits of a similar design.

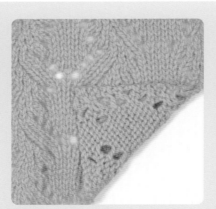

Subtle cable sweater surface
Cable stitches in sweaters are distinctive and are considered a traditional surface design. This flat, stylized cable design is an open design that is less stable than more tightly knitted cable would be. As a weft knit, shaped pieces can be knitted and then sewn together or produced as flat yardage.

"Bubble" knit surface
This "bubble"-shaped knitted surface, a weft knit, creates a pebbly surface. The loosely twisted spun yarns add "hairy" texture in addition to the bubble texture.

Facts and figures

Distinctive features

- Great variety of surface textures available.
- Knit stitches on the face.
- Purl stitches on the back.
- Cut edges may roll.

Strengths

- Wide variety of textures.
- Easily available.
- Stretchable fabric, easy to fit.
- Good drape.
- The fabric retains its shape due to the alternating use of knit and purl stitches on the face and back.
- Resilient, although the fiber content will help resilience further.

Weaknesses

- The fabric requires a special sewing technique—flat-locking or chain-stitching—to allow the seams to expand with the wearer.
- A ballpoint needle must be used.
- The fabric snags easily, and if the yarn is broken, it will cause a "run" (stitches are dropped and the fabric de-knits).

Usual fiber content

Spun yarns:
- 100 percent cotton and cotton/polyester blends.
- 100 percent wool and wool blends.
- Acrylic, rayon blends.

Multifilament yarns and texturized multifilament yarns:
- 100 percent polyester and polyester/rayon blends.
- 100 percent silk and silk blends.

Knitted dress

Men's sweaters use the designed knit surface especially well to create unusual textures and colors; however, this elegant, long, knitted dress also takes advantage of the chevron knitted pattern to create a varied surface through imaginative diagonal seaming.

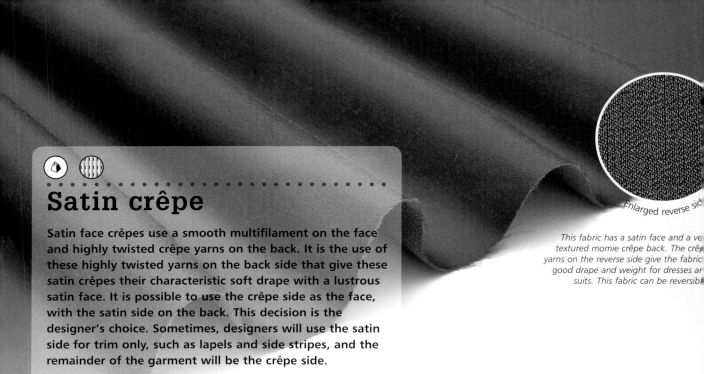

Satin crêpe

Satin face crêpes use a smooth multifilament on the face and highly twisted crêpe yarns on the back. It is the use of these highly twisted yarns on the back side that give these satin crêpes their characteristic soft drape with a lustrous satin face. It is possible to use the crêpe side as the face, with the satin side on the back. This decision is the designer's choice. Sometimes, designers will use the satin side for trim only, such as lapels and side stripes, and the remainder of the garment will be the crêpe side.

Enlarged reverse side

This fabric has a satin face and a ve
textured momie crêpe back. The crêp
yarns on the reverse side give the fabric
good drape and weight for dresses ar
suits. This fabric can be reversibl

Since satin crêpes can usually be used on either side, they can be called a satin-back crêpe (where the crêpe is the face side) or crêpe-back satin (where the satin is the face side).

Fabric content and the type of yarns used will determine what the surface looks like and the hand of the fabric. All satin crêpes have a soft drape. Most satin crêpes are used for dressy or more elegant apparel. Therefore, only multifilament yarns are used.

Faille-backed satin
This faille-backed satin shows the fine multifilament crêpe yarns on the back and the smooth multifilament yarns on the satin face.

Brushed-back satin
The brushed back is created by using a spun yarn behind the multifilament floating face yarn. This fabric is used for a warm lining fabric in a winter coat.

Pebble satin
The pebble satin face has an interesting surface texture, while the crêpe back side keeps the fabric soft and drapey.

Facts and figures

Distinctive features

- Always has satin face with crêpe (matte) back (can be reversed).
- Very soft drape.

Strengths

- Good drape.
- Beautiful, lustrous satin surface with matte surface on the back.
- Color matched if using both satin and crêpe sides on same garment.

Weaknesses

- Expensive fabric due to special yarns and construction.
- Must use very sharp sewing needle to prevent snagging when sewing.
- Fabric subject to stretching during sewing, due to highly twisted crêpe yarns used.

Usual fiber content

Simple multifilament yarns combined with high-twist crêpe yarns:

- 100 percent polyester and polyester/rayon blends.
- 100 percent silk and silk blends.
- 100 percent rayon and rayon blends.

Satin crêpe wrap dress
The weight of a satin fabric with a crêpe back keeps the fabric from moving too easily. The deep folds in this garment reflect the weight of the satin crêpe.

Textured crêpe suiting

Suiting crêpes are some of the most beautiful fabrics produced in women's apparel. Using complex multi-twisted multifilament yarns combined in a variety of weaves, the resulting textured surfaces provide fabrics that have liveliness and resilience for women's suiting apparel. Manufactured filament fibers are used almost exclusively.

Highly-textured suiting fabrics are almost always a crêpe fabric, but they have enough weight and volume to be used in tailored suiting apparel. This type of suiting fabric has became very popular for women entering senior management positions who want clothing different from traditional worsted wool menswear fabrics.

Textured-surface suiting crêpes add enough texture to look different from menswear fabrics and also can be used in more elegant apparel.

This medium-weight crêpe fabric is known as a moss crêpe double weave. With a textured face and smooth back side, it can be used on either side for contrasting surfaces

Designer's tip: These highly textured fabrics should be cut and sewn with caution, as the textured yarns can stretch when cut and sewn, causing fit problems.

Matelassé effect double-knit
This matelassé-effect (puckered surface) double-knit is heavy and rigid enough to be used as a suiting fabric. The textured surface, knitted to a flat knitted base, creates an interesting surface for suiting.

Moss crêpe
The highly twisted, textured crêpe yarns used in this fabric are woven in an irregular pattern to create a textured surface.

Striped dobby
This dobby weave shows a textured stripe. This crêpe has been fused with a tricot for extra body, a technique often applied for suit jackets.

Facts and figures

Distinctive features

- Interesting textured surface.
- Drapey fabric.
- Textured yarns create volume without weight.

Strengths

- Excellent drape, especially in a medium-weight fabric.
- Tailors/holds seams well.
- Resilient, though fiber content will help resilience further.

Weaknesses

- Fabric subject to stretching during the cutting/sewing process.
- Expensive fabric due to special yarns and production methods.
- Must use ballpoint needle, recommended to prevent snagging during production.

Usual fiber content

Simple multifilament yarns and high-twist crêpe yarns:

- 100 percent polyester and polyester/ rayon blends.
- 100 percent rayon and rayon blends.

Crêpe suit

The contrasting satin jacket and pant side stripe provide a "metallic" edge to the soft texture of the crêpe pants.

Smooth-surface crêpe

All crêpe fabrics use highly twisted crêpe yarns. Because the smooth surfaces shown on this page all have an even surface texture, the yarns used can be either highly spun yarns or multifilament yarns. The fabrics will retain their soft drape, and they perform very well in jackets and suiting apparel that require tailoring.

Wool crêpe is a popular, somewhat textured fabric, using highly twisted wool yarns. Most wool crêpes are produced as momie crêpes, which have a slightly bumpy, allover surface texture. A momie crêpe can be used on both sides.

Faille crêpes are often used as elegant matte surface fabrics for suiting or tailored long dresses. Silk faille has a beautiful drape and hand, and it is often used as a dinner suit fabric. There are polyester fiber alternatives, as silk faille can be very expensive.

There are other less-identifiable crêpes, but the surface of the fabric is always even and has a limited texture, using highly twisted spun or multifilament yarns. Silk filament yarns are almost never used in momie crêpe fabrics. Polyester multifilament yarns are often used in these crêpes, and are sometimes blended with wool or other fibers.

This rayon/polyester faille crêpe fabric uses a textured weft yarn to emphasize the ribbed weave. The crêpe weft yarns add softness and drape

Wool momie crêpe
This 100 percent wool momie crêpe shows fine, highly twisted wool yarns that are woven into this subtle momie weave. The fine wool yarns make this an expensive fabric.

Dobby weave crêpe
This fabric is a crêpe due to the highly twisted wool yarns used. The dobby weave used creates a geometric pattern on the surface, very typical of crêpe weaves.

Large yarn wool momie crêpe
The large wool yarns used in this crêpe provide a regular matte surface. The momie crêpe surface is more pronounced than the more finely woven momie crêpe shown in the red sample on the left.

Facts and figures

Distinctive features

- Even surface, either slightly pebbly or with a tiny rib.
- Excellent drape and good weight for jackets and bottoms.

Strengths

- The even texture shows seam details very well.
- Fabric will hold silhouette of design well, though it is drapey.
- Good drape.
- Resilient, though fiber content will help resilience further.

Weaknesses

- Expensive fabric.
- Fabric may stretch during cutting and sewing process.
- Fabric surface may snag.

Usual fiber content

Spun yarns:
- 100 percent wool or wool blends.
- Simple multifilament yarns and high-twist.

Multifilament crêpe yarns:
- 100 percent polyester and polyester/ rayon blends.
- 100 percent rayon and rayon blends.

Smooth-surface crêpe jacket
This gray-green jacket uses a smooth-surface crêpe fabric that has a little added stretch for a well-fitted garment. In addition, the fabric tailors extremely well, showing fit lines and pressing.

Tricot for athletics

Tricot warp knits always use multifilament yarns in the production of this smooth-surface fabric. Its lightweight and tightly knit smooth surface, plus its ability to dry very quickly, make tricot an ideal fabric for active sports.

Traditional wool or cotton fiber fabrics are almost unknown today in athletic apparel. Fibers that absorb moisture, like wool or cotton, do not release moisture (by evaporation) quickly. The fabric surface temperature becomes cool and sometimes results in muscle injury or uncomfortable conditions on the playing field.

Tricot fabrics come in a variety of surface textures for different athletic applications, and may also include Spandex for a compression fabric, which will be further discussed in the Compression chapter (see pages 260–287). Top-weight tricot fabrics are used for non-contact sports, such as tennis or golf. Contact sports, such as football or basketball, require a heavier weight tricot and often include tricot mesh fabrics as well.

Polyester microfibers have created high-performance fabrics by allowing moisture to wick to the surface and quickly evaporate. Fabrics that remain damp or wet longer can chafe against the skin and also add weight. Quick-drying fabrics are now a requirement for most athletic teams and now all polyester fabrics are recyclable.

This warp piqué knit was produced using high performance wicking yarn. The 100 percent polyester fabric will manage moisture by wicking it away from the body during athletic activity, keeping the athlete comfortable

Tricot with wicking quality
This 100 percent polyester fabric, using wicking fiber with a brushed back, will wick moisture away from the body and keep the athlete comfortable during active exertion.

Elastic tricot with brushed back
This tricot uses microfiber polyester blended with spandex; this fiber blend will produce a slim fit, hugging the body. The wicking characteristic will move perspiration away from the body, and the brushed back will be comfortable next to the skin during exercise.

Tricot with texture
It is unusual to produce a 100 percent cotton tricot fabric, but in golf apparel the cooling effect of cotton's slow evaporation process could be very comfortable on a hot, humid day on the golf course. This cotton tricot is yarn-dyed black and red.

Facts and figures

Distinctive features

- Can be either a lustrous or a matte surface, depending on the yarn used.
- Tricot mesh is a tightly knit fabric, too, like the solid tricot fabric.

Strengths

- Lustrous, smooth surface.
- Stable fabric that does not stretch out of shape easily.
- Expands with the body, but does not elongate in the straight-grain direction.
- Very durable fabric.

Weaknesses

- Surface can be snagged easily but doesn't impact durability of fabric.
- Must use a ballpoint sewing needle to avoid sewing snags.

Usual fiber content

Multifilament yarns:
- 100 percent microfiber polyester or regular-fiber polyester.
- 100 percent microfiber nylon or regular-fiber nylon.

Soccer kit

Tricot knits for athletes sustain garment shape during athletic activity, yet provide flexibility and stretch. Wicking polyester fiber is used to keep the athlete cool and dry while minimizing skin abrasion from cold, wet fabrics.

French terry

Fleece fabric and French terry are nearly the same fabric except for one important difference: fleece fabric always has a brushed back surface and French terry always maintains the looped pile surface on the fabric back.

Both fleece and terry fabrics always have a smooth knit stitch surface and a special looped pile that is added to the back side. They are among the most popular fabrics for producing "hoodie" sweatshirts or pullovers for casual wear. The brushed back of a fleece fabric adds a warm hand to the fabric and is frequently used to produce lightweight garments for the fall, winter, and spring. Used primarily in athletic apparel, for warm-up pants and tops, this fabric is now commonly used for casual, loose-fitting apparel in pants, skirts, jackets, and tops for men, women, and children.

Fiber content is always cotton or cotton/polyester blends. The 100 percent cotton content is acceptable for French terry, but an all-cotton fleece is considered a fire hazard and should never be used as a fleece fabric. Cotton/polyester fleece reduces the fire risk. Occasionally, 100 percent polyester is used for microfiber polyester, in producing high-tech, lightweight French terry fabrics for athletic use.

The distinctive looped-pile back and flat knit face of this fabric make it a favorite for casual, comfortable clothing. This organic cotton French terry performs in the same way as conventional cotton.

Facts and figures

Distinctive features
- Smooth knit face.
- Looped pile back for French terry.
- Brushed back for fleece.
- Soft hand.

Strengths
- Brushed back side is warm to the touch.
- Fabric is easily available and inexpensive.
- Soft hand.

Weaknesses
- Fleece side will pill easily.
- Must use ballpoint sewing needle, as snagging may occur.

Usual fiber content
- 100 percent cotton or cotton/polyester blends.
- 100 percent polyester.

Polyester fleece
This fleece fabric has a wool-like appearance on the face, but the brushed side is very soft. It will provide a warm hand on the inside of the garment.

Two-tone fleece
This sample was produced from 60 percent recycled cotton fiber, 20 percent acrylic, and 20 percent polyester. The cotton fiber was already dyed, so less chemical dye waste was produced during manufacturing.

Microfiber French terry
This pink French terry uses high-performance polyester microfiber for wicking moisture away from the body. The fine-gauge fabric is tightly knit and uses spandex fiber for added fit.

Gray ensemble

This designer has created a garment with simple lines and a snap closure because this fabric stretches out of shape easily during the sewing process. However, the soft drape is well understood for this design.

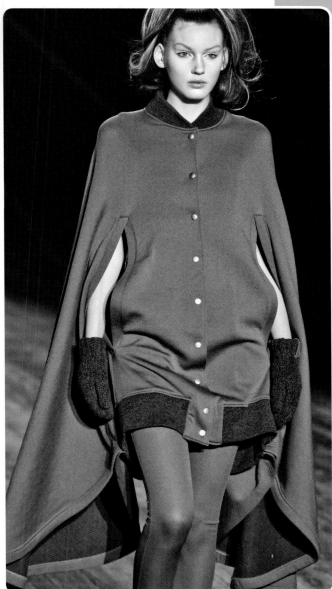

French terry "hoodie"

The roomy, slouchy appearance of this fabric is due to the unstable single knit. The fabric stretches out of shape easily but will return to its original shape after washing and drying. A looped pile is inserted on the back side and adds bulk to the fabric.

Polar fleece

Polar fleece fabric has revolutionized the outdoor apparel industry. Polar fleece almost always uses lightweight polyester fiber, either microfiber or regular polyester fiber.

This fabric has replaced heavy wool knitwear, which is a disadvantage on the hiking trail and is also susceptible to pests; a problem for long-term seasonal storage. Polar fleece is produced by creating a cut-pile face and brushed back. The result is a fabric that is lightweight and retains body heat, dries quickly, and resists pests.

Polar fleece has been the fabric of choice for pullovers and soft jackets in recent years. Durable and lighter in weight than wool, polar fleece has been adopted almost completely by outdoor apparel manufacturers. Polar fleece can be easily worn year-round and, by layering with a windbreaker jacket, can provide warmth in windy weather conditions.

Sometimes polar fleece can be used as a jacket lining instead of lightweight lining fabrics. The napped surface on both sides creates thermal insulation under the tightly woven jacket fabric.

PET polyester, produced from plastic bottles, is a low-quality polyester fiber that can be used to produce polar fleece fabric. However, PET polyester is a weak fiber and must be reinforced with acrylic, nylon, or virgin polyester fiber. PET polyester polar fleece is nearly always a fiber blend for this reason.

Polar fleece has a napped surface on b[...] sides; it must use the sheared surface on [...] garment face and the brushed surface on the ins[...] of the garment. This pink polar fleece could be use[...] warm linings or warm pullover to[...]

Lightweight polar fleece
Lightweight polar fleece, especially this microfiber polyester polar fleece, is a great fabric to produce seamed garment details. It is not as bulky as more traditional polyester fiber polar fleece.

PET polar fleece
PET polar fleece feels nearly the same as virgin polyester fiber polar fleece. PET fiber is from made recycled plastic bottles that have not been decolorized. PET fiber is a low-quality fiber, and nearly always requires another virgin fiber for added yarn strength.

Embossed polar fleece
After being sheared and brushed, polyester polar fleece can be embossed to show a different texture. An embossed, grid-like pattern has been applied here. Since the face is a cut pile, it is less likely to pill. The brushed back surface will be more likely to pill, which is always unsightly.

Polar fleece camping pullover
A double-face, napped fabric provides warmth yet is lightweight.

Facts and figures

Distinctive features
- Soft cut-pile of face and brushed fleece back.
- Bulky fabric that always feels soft.

Strengths
- Cut-pile face does not pill much.
- Back side is warm to the touch and is usually a brushed surface.
- Fabric is easily available.
- Microfiber polyester hand is extremely soft compared to regular polyester fiber.
- Flexible knit construction.

Weaknesses
- Must consider direction of nap when creating design and cutting fabric.
- Brushed fleece side will pill easily.
- Recommend ballpoint sewing needle, as snagging may occur, but is not required.

Usual fiber content
- 100 percent polyester microfiber or regular fiber.
- PET polyester fiber from plastic bottles.

DESIGN RESPONSIBLY

PET polyester fiber, a low-quality polyester fiber used in many fleece garments, can be recycled into new PET fiber. It can be continuously recycled. However, PET fiber is currently not recycled after it has been made into a garment. Therefore, recycled plastic bottles, which are the raw material for making PET polyester, are simply diverted from the landfill for a little while rather than integrated into the fiber supply chain. PET polyester fleece garments will end up in the landfill until the garment industry organizes the collection and recycling of such useful fabrics into new PET polyester fiber.

Velour

Velour is produced two ways: it can be knitted or woven. It is recognized by its longer (deeper) nap compared to velveteen (see page 102), which has a shorter (shallower) nap.

This polyester/spandex-blend velour produces deep, rich pile that is elastic. The fabric can be easily fitted to the body because of this elasticity.

Knitted velour is less expensive and more widely available than woven velour. The knit construction makes the fabric easier to fit with fewer sewing seams. Woven velour is usually considered a more durable nap than knitted velour and is mainly used for interior products or outerwear that require excellent durability. Woven velour is nearly always a bottom-weight fabric.

Knitted velour is most often used in women's apparel, tops and bottoms, robes and sleepwear, toys, and sometimes towels. Both weft-knit and warp-knit velour are produced. Warp knits provide a more stable, less flexible fabric that is commonly used in loungewear and toys. Weft knits, often with spandex added, are used in fashion apparel, such as matching velour jackets and pants, tops, and sweaters.

Woven velour is common in interior design and is used to cover sofas, chairs, and drapes. In apparel, outerwear coats and jackets sometimes use velour. Often this velour has been finished for stain resistance. Velour intended for interior design is always produced to a high-quality standard, so the pile surface is quite durable.

Nap direction is important in any velour, so always consider this point when planning the design. Fabrics can be quite varied in color and print.

Panne crinkle velour
All cut-pile knits are velour, not velvet. Only woven fabrics are produced in the velvet production method. This fabric is correctly named panne velour, although the industry will name it panne velvet. This sample has a "crushed" or crinkled finish.

Burnout velour pattern
This velour has been printed with acid to burn out the pile, leaving the knit base visible. This is a common fabric used for women's tops and dresses. This burnout velour design is blended with spandex for comfort stretch.

Velour for interior design use
This tricot knit velour is produced to be very durable as a sofa or chair fabric. Sometimes designers use this fabric for jackets and coats. The plush surface is produced to be retained throughout the life of the product.

Facts and figures

Distinctive features

- Luxurious appearance.
- Soft, deep-cut pile of face and unnapped back.
- Bulky fabric that always feels soft.

Strengths

- Cut pile face does not pill.
- Knit velour is easily available and easy to fit on the body.
- Woven velour is very similar to velvet but more durable than velveteen or velvet.

Weaknesses

- Must consider direction of nap when creating design and cutting fabric.
- Woven velour is especially bulky to sew. May require a walking foot.
- Knit velour must be sewn with a flexible chain stitch, not a single needle stitch.

Usual fiber content

- 100 percent polyester microfiber or regular polyester fiber.
- 100 percent cotton or cotton/polyester blend with spandex.

Velour gloves

Knitted velour is often used for accessories because its pile is shorter than velvet's and has stretchability thanks to its knitted construction. The many seams in these gloves require a fabric construction that will not easily pull apart, and a tricot velour knit fabric is highly recommended.

Enlargement

Velvet

Velvet is considered one of the most luxurious fabrics. Its soft, deep, plush cut-pile surface is uniquely produced on a special loom.

This deep gray velvet absorbs and reflect light in the folds of the fabric. The rayon and silk blend is a soft and luxuriou fabric with a beautiful drape

The depth or length of the cut pile is approximately the same for all velvets. Velvet is always a woven fabric, although many knitted fabrics are incorrectly called velvet.

Velvet is used for evening jackets and coats, blazers, dresses (both long and short), lingerie and loungewear, and evening blouses and skirts. Simple lines for the design are usually required because sewing such a deep-cut pile fabric is more complicated than sewing a shorter cut-pile velveteen (see page 102).

Nap direction is very important, as with any napped fabric. Nap-up direction is especially recommended for velvet because the color change in nap-down direction is quite noticeable in such deep, luxurious cut-pile fabric.

The quality of the velvet fabric is based on the type of fiber used to produce the fabric. Velvet often uses two different fibers: one fiber for the ground fabric and another fiber for the deep-cut pile. Still, the most luxurious velvet—silk velvet—is now commonly blended with rayon for a soft, drapey effect. A less expensive fiber is often used for the ground cloth, such as polyester or even nylon, and the more expensive, softer fiber is used for the cut pile, such as rayon or silk.

Two-color velvet
Iridescent velvet is a good design choice. Ground fabric color is different than the cut pile, showing two colors.

Crushed velvet
The surface of velvet can be intentionally crushed using a fabric finish. The result is more reflection of light from the napped surface, lightening the fabric color and increasing the surface shine.

Velvet burnout
This sample shows a burnout print on a velvet fabric. It is one method of introducing pattern onto the fabric without crushing the surface.

Facts and figures
Distinctive features
- Deep cut pile using soft-fiber yarn.
- Always very soft hand.
- Almost always excellent drape.

Strengths
- Cut-pile face gives a luxurious soft hand to the garment.
- Back side does not have a nap, which makes for easier construction.
- Simple designs create beautiful garments.

Weaknesses
- Must consider direction of nap when creating design and cutting fabric.
- Cannot press seams easily—nap will be crushed.
- Cannot sit in velvet garment for long periods—nap will be crushed from body weight.

Usual fiber content
- 100 percent silk.
- Silk/rayon blends.
- Silk or rayon cut pile, combined with polyester or nylon ground fabric.

Velvet coat and velvet skirt
Velvet is an elegant fabric. This long, sweeping coat (left) uses deep brown velvet to express luxury. The shredded hemline on the skirt (far left) is an interesting use of such an elegant fabric. Designers have the option of using elegant fabrics in unusual ways if they wish.

Medium-weight sweater knits

Sweater knits are almost always a type of weft single knitting, although sometimes they include weft double knits. The size and texture of the yarn and tightness of the knit construction will determine the weight and texture of the knit.

Sweaters can be pullovers with zip or button fronts, and shaped or less shaped, depending on the designer's vision. Dresses and skirts are often produced in addition to the tops mentioned here. Yarn selection is by far the most important part of the design process in sweater knitting.

Color is the next most important design element to sweater knits, and the samples here are meant to show the variety possible when combining colors to achieve surface effects. In almost all designs, yarns are dyed before knitting. There are some instances where the designer will choose to garment-dye a finished sweater knit. This is completely the designer's choice and will not be discussed here.

Stripes, isolated color shapes, and tweed designs are the most common design elements used in medium-weight sweater knits. All elements are achieved by placing dyed yarn in specific locations in the design.

This medium-weight wool sweater kni[t] is a jacquard diamond design in a[?] single-knit fabric. The low-spun[?] woolen yarns create a warm fabric[?]

Intarsia design
This sweater knit uses separate yarns introduced into the middle of the fabric. The process is called intarsia knitting.

Border design
This sweater was designed to include a border. Traditional patterns used in various cultures are sometimes introduced as a design element in sweater knits.

Tweed effect
Tweed effects can be achieved by using a multicolored yarn that has flecks of color spun into it. The result is an all-over multicolored effect that resembles woven tweed fabrics.

Facts and figures

Distinctive features
- Nearly always single- or double-knit weft knits, using knit and purl stitches in a variety of surface designs.
- Nearly always uses colored yarns to create pattern and design interest.

Strengths
- Wonderful surface interest through color.
- Nonseasonal fabric, dependent on the yarn fiber content and colors chosen.
- Extremely versatile fabric through yarn and color placement.

Weaknesses
- Surface snagging is always a problem.
- If using flat yardage, fabric easily stretches during the cutting and sewing process.
- Fitting garment can be difficult—using fewer seams is best.

Usual fiber content
There is no limit to the fiber content.
Spun yarns:
- 100 percent cotton and cotton/polyester blends.
- Rayon, acrylic, or polyester fiber blends.
- 100 percent wool or wool blends.

Multifilament yarns:
- 100 percent polyester and polyester/rayon blends.
- 100 percent silk and silk blends.

Men's pullover
This design uses a colored border to give interest to the sweater. This sweater could have been knitted as shaped pieces on a computerized flatbed, or knitted as flat yardage and cut and sewn into a garment. The cut-and-sewn method is a less expensive production option.

Heavyweight sweater knits

Heavyweight sweater knits are intended for jackets or coats. The yarns used are bulky, and the fabric is usually knitted more tightly to keep air from moving easily through its surface to provide better warmth.

Most sweater-knit jackets use fiber that will resist moisture, such as unfinished wool (which still has lanolin for water resistance) or nonabsorbent fiber. Some heavyweight sweater knits are designed as long coats, either knee-length or floor length. However, the weight of the garment can often lead to the fabric stretching or "growing."

Some heavy sweater knits are produced from flat yardage, cut and sewn, and are lined for additional warmth. Such garments are less likely to stretch or "grow" because the lining and sewn seams add stability. The weight of the knit is an important consideration because of the fabric stability problem. Weft knitting is especially prone to stretching out of shape, and heavy garments increase this problem.

Cable stitches and flat knit stitches are usually used. The fabric texture is usually limited to the texture of the yarn, since the fabric is often bulky and heavy. Adding additional surface texture is unnecessary and makes the fabric more likely to snag. Color is always the designer's choice, although tweed yarns are often a favorite. Manufactured fibers, such as acrylic or polyester, are much lighter weight than wool.

Bulky, long cables
This stitching pattern uses a wool and acrylic fiber blend that creates a very warm fabric.

Puffy stitching pattern
This stitch pattern, which looks like popcorn, is used in addition to other stitches to create bulk and texture. The bulky stitches create warmth with less weight. A lining fabric is recommended if using as a jacket.

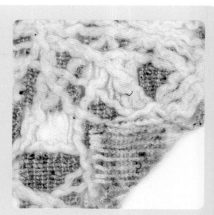

Raschel warp knit
Warp knits, especially raschel knits, can be used to produce bulky yet less stretchy fabrics than weft knits of the same bulk and weight.

Facts and figures

Distinctive features
- Very bulky fabric, often using wool or wool-blend fiber content.
- Nearly always uses colored yarns to create pattern and design interest.

Strengths
- Beautiful texture and color variety through fiber and yarn choice.
- Good alternative to a traditional coat or jacket.
- Knitted fabric is always more drapey than a woven fabric.

Weaknesses
- Surface snagging is always a problem.
- If using flat yardage, fabric easily stretches during the cutting and sewing process.
- Fitting garments can be difficult—using fewer seams is best.

Usual fiber content
Almost always spun yarns:
- Acrylic or polyester fiber blends.
- 100 percent wool or wool blends.
- Mohair/wool blends.

Women's bulky-knit garments
The bulky yarns knitted into loosely stitched fabrics create voluminous garments that can become trims or entire garments. These designs are examples of how the sweater silhouettes can vary.

Ornamentation

Designers often use simple fabrics and then apply decorative elements to the design using cut fabric or other trimming details that will add visual texture and interest to the garment.

Ornamentation is an accent to the design, providing focus, texture, or contrast. In some instances, ornamentation can produce new fabrics, for example, using a simple netting as the base, onto which is attached copious amounts of trim.

Adding embellishments to the garment design can focus or divert visual attention. Experiment with fabric as ornament to extend its role as the designer's medium. Ornamentation can be divided into three major categories:

1. Contrasting fabric: This is cut for edging, borders, collars, and cuffs. Often the same fabric, in contrasting colors, is used. Alternatively, a different fabric, specifically selected for contrast, is applied to the fabric. In this category, fabric uses color, texture, and shape to define ornamentation. Appropriate fabrics selected for ornamentation should consider the garment silhouette. For example:

- Structured fabrics will add definition to the silhouette.
- Fluid fabrics will add softness and sensuality to the silhouette.
- Expansion fabrics will enlarge or expand the garment silhouette.
- Compression fabrics will reduce or minimize the garment silhouette.

Embellished blouse
Narrow satin ribbon has been applied to this sheer chiffon blouse to add pattern and lustrous texture. Exposed shoulder pads, using another contrasting fabric, emphasize the shoulders.

2. Narrow yardage: This is produced either as ribbon or other more complex textures and is applied on top of the garment design as edging. Narrow ornamentation can be:

- ribbon/piping
- passementerie
- novelty narrow trimmings
- narrow closure trimmings
- lace edging

These beautiful narrow yardages provide color and define edges through the application of contrasting, very narrow braided, woven, or knitted fabrics to the design in linear or shaped images. In addition to the narrow yardage, other more opulent pieces can be applied, such as a fringe, patches, or tassels. Designing specific patterns of trim application can create highly decorative arrangements that enhance the design vision.

3. Embroidery: Using a variety of special embroidery threads, machine-produced embroidery imitates hand-produced embroidery. Both in all-over yardage, by using embroidered designs and more detailed, complex embroidered graphic designs that are created digitally for focused application, the designer intends on embellishing the fabric surface with texture and color to help communicate the design message. Machine embroidery is now computerized, and there is software to assist the designer in creating very detailed stitched images. An understanding of threads will help the designer to select the appropriate embroidery thread for the fabric.

Hand-sewn sequins
Oversized sequins, hand-embroidered on this simple stretch-jersey top, add attractive detail to this ensemble.

Ornamentation
Silver colored zippers, placed horizontally on this coat front, and coordinating silver loops attached to tape at the sides, are both functional and decorative. Faux fur shoulder patches alter the silhouette of the coat and provide contrast to the main coat fabric.

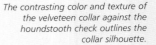

The contrasting color and texture of the velveteen collar against the houndstooth check outlines the collar silhouette.

Contrast fabric shapes

Design elements that include color or texture contrast create visual impact on a garment. While the designer may rely on silhouette and sewn seam details for the quality of the design, contrast fabric used as ornamentation often identifies a designer's style.

Contrasting fabric, when used in pattern pieces such as the collar or cuffs, can create an identity, such as school uniforms or work-related uniforms. The contrasting velveteen collar shown above, for example, identifies a Chesterfield coat. Three types of contrast fabric shapes are used as ornamentation:

Appliqué: A fabric shape that is applied to the surface of the fabric. It is the designer's job to select the image and the fabric from which to form the image. There are no limitations. However, there are practical considerations when selecting a fabric for appliqué:
- What is the texture of the finished image?
- To what kind of fabric surface is the appliqué being attached? Knit or woven? Flat or textured?

- By what method is the appliqué to be attached to the fabric surface? Stitching only? Fusing? Embroidery?
- Knitted fabric surfaces used as the base cloth for the appliqué should be backed with a fusible interlining to stabilize the base cloth surface while the appliqué is attached. Using very lightweight fabrics as a base cloth is not recommended.

Collars and cuffs: Contrasting fabric for collars and cuffs creates immediate visual impact within the usual construction of the garment. Selecting the contrasting fabric is important with regard to texture and color, as well as maintenance issues such as comfort, shrinkage, abrasion resistance, and color loss. Testing fabrics is highly recommended.

Other shapes: Epaulets, tabs, waistbands, bound buttonholes, and yokes are all parts of a garment that can be identified for contrast fabrics. Adding contrast in smaller parts of the garment can provide interest to an otherwise classic design, such as the military uniform using contrast fabrics to distinguish honor and rank.

Appliqué
Fabric shapes can be sewn onto the base fabric. In this example, the appliqué number "5" is sewn onto netting embroidered with sequins. The edges of the netting remain loose.

White collar and button tab
This knit shirt uses woven white broadcloth for a contrasting collar and button tab. However, the colorfastness of the dark red knit fabric must be considered. This white collar and tab are stained with red color that bled off the dark red shirt.

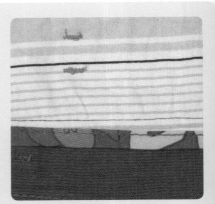

Contrasting waistband
Printed fabric was selected for the waistband inside facing of this skirt, and the same print was also used for the pocket trim. Contrasting thread colors are also used, either as bar tacks or topstitching.

Facts and figures

Ornamentation performance and garment care

- Color may crock onto lighter-color fabric during wearing.
- Abrasion resistance may be different than main fabric.
- May shrink at a different rate to the main fabric.
- Color may bleed onto a lighter-color fabric during care.
- Differences in heat resistance may cause fabric deterioration during pressing or drying.

Usual fiber content

- Fiber content is important when considering what contrasting fabric to use on a design. For example, colorfastness issues, such as dry and wet crocking and bleeding, must be considered. Since most contrast fabrics involve light and dark colors, the designer must thoroughly understand whether color loss will be an issue for the design. Different rates of shrinkage, due to fiber content or fabric construction, must also be considered when selecting a contrasting fabric. Abrasion resistance, particularly with high-contrast fabric trims, should also be considered.

Women's suit with satin

A lustrous satin collar, jacket lapel, and pocket flaps give this suit a dressy appearance. The shiny texture of the satin contrasts with the matte surface of the suiting fabric.

Contrasting fabric: creating lines and outlines with fabric

Creating lines using fabric requires an understanding of how fabric can be manipulated to act as line rather than surface. The first step is to reshape the fabric into lines by cutting it into strips, then to cut along the bias grain line to prevent yarns from raveling, and, most importantly, to allow the fabric strips to be flexible.

Fabric binding is always cut on the bias for maximum flexibility in order to sew in curved or straight lines. Matching or contrasting fabrics are used, depending on the designer's concept.

Folded bias-cut fabric binding
Bias-cut strips can be folded different ways for ease of sewing application. The folding of the strips is now automated and is rarely done by hand pressing. The folding style will help to determine how the bias cut fabric will be used:

- **Single or center-folded:** raw edges can be sewn into seams, sometimes as unfilled piping (see "Piping," below).
- **Double-folded:** top-stitched on top of fabric surface.
- **Tri-folded:** covering raw fabric edges, called "binding."

Using bias strips of fabric to create a line allows for easy placement along the curves to outline shapes as well as straight edges. The designer can choose the same fabric as the garment body for outlining, perhaps using a contrasting color, or use a different fabric with a different texture, such as a lustrous satin trim on a textured crêpe surface. The selection criteria for contrast fabric must take into account color loss, shrinkage, and abrasion resistance when placing contrasting fabrics next to one another.

Types of contrasting linear ornamentation

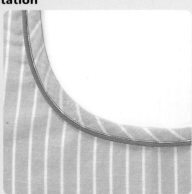

Piping
Piping is bias-cut strips sewn over a round cord "filler" to provide shape, or they can be sewn without filler (called "unfilled" piping). The piping is then sewn into a seam to define an "edge" of the design or outline an element of the garment silhouette. Piping, both filled and unfilled, can be purchased ready-made, or custom piping can be produced to specification at a trimming supplier who has the specialized sewing equipment. Piping is now an automated process. It is almost never produced by hand. Piping always has a seam allowance so that the piping can be sewn into a seam, leaving only the rounded edge exposed.

Cording
Bias fabric strips are sewn around a cord "filler," the same filler as used in piping. In cording, there is no seam allowance edge. The cording is completely covered by the fabric with no raw edges exposed. Cording is used as drawstrings, sewn as linear designs on the fabric surface, or any other application the designer envisages.

Facts and figures
Distinctive features
- Always narrow and linear.
- Used to finish garment edges, define silhouettes, or create linear images.
- Can be the same fabric as the garment, or contrasting color and texture.

Ornamentation performance and garment care
- The same performance and care issues for contrast fabric shapes (see page 196) apply to this type of ornamentation. Any new fabric added to the main design should be tested for performance and care concerns.

Usual fiber content
- Any fiber content or blends will work for a linear bias fabric trim, except loosely woven or knitted fabrics. Tightly woven or knitted fabrics are best because they will be the most stable when cutting into bias grain strips.

Garments with linear edgings

Contrast piping is usually filled with a narrow string to provide a rounded edge, called "filled" piping. The coat shown here uses "unfilled" piping, which creates a sharp, folded-flat edge. The blouse uses contrasting ric-rac (see page 205), topstitched on the edge of the ruffles, shoulder, and cuffs. Contrast color binding defines the features of these garments.

2 in (5 cm)
twill tape

1 in (2.5 cm)
twill tape

¾ in (.
twill t

  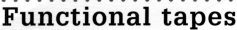

Functional tapes

There are four types of fabric tape that are regularly used in garment construction. These tapes function to finish fabric edges, reinforce or stabilize seams, and add detail to points of entry in a garment.

Designers have also taken these same functional tapes and created inexpensive ornamental details. There are several tapes to consider when deciding on ornamentation. Each is produced for its function and can be adapted to whatever new ideas a designer envisions.

Twill tape

Twill tape is tightly woven, usually a herringbone twill pattern, and is available in several widths from 0.25 in (1.25 cm) to 3 in (7.5 cm). This tape is flat and can be used to finish straight-grain edges as a button placket, waistbands, or reinforcement backing. It is usually 100 percent cotton and, if purchased in a natural color, should always be shrink-tested before use. It is also available in colors and can provide contrast trim for knitted tops. Twill tape can also function as a more visible stay tape to finish knit-top neckline seams to prevent necklines from stretching out of shape.

Buttonhole ribbon (1)
In extremely delicate fabrics—both fine-gauge knits and very lightweight fabrics—premade buttonholes on tightly woven ribbon can help support buttonholes for a closure. Buttonhole ribbon is made from tightly woven ribbed or square weaves.

Herringbone twill tape (2)
This reverse twill tape serves the same function as the twill tapes shown above. The more decorative herringbone weave provides the same stability as the other twill tapes shown here.

Seam binding (3)
Produced as a balanced plain weave, seam binding is used to finish raw edges on seams or the edge of a hemline. It is lightweight, usually using multifilament yarns, and will not add weight to the final garment. It can also be used decoratively (see right).

Stay tape (4 and 5)
Stay tape helps provide stability where seams may stretch out of shape, such as at shoulder, armhole, and neckline seams. Stretching seams is a problem especially on knit fabrics, and many designers will specify stay tape in their designs.

Seam binding
Seam binding is a plain weave ribbon that is used to cover the raw edge of a skirt, pant, or jacket hem. It is attached to the raw edge of the hem and then is blind-stitched (i.e., it doesn't show on the face side of the fabric) to the back side of the fabric. However, seam binding, because of its light weight and low cost, is also used to create interesting three-dimensional shapes by gathering it together.

| 1 | 2 | 3 | 4 | 5 |

Facts and figures
Distinctive features
- Always narrow and linear.
- Functional and ornamental.
- Can be undyed for use in garment dyeing or dyed for contrasting colors.

Ornamentation performance and garment care
- Functional tape must be tested for shrinkage during washing and pressing. Often a functional tape is used to finish the fabric edges. Improper shrinkage testing of the tape may cause puckering and loss of design appeal.

Usual fiber content
- 100 percent cotton—best for garment dye (test for shrinkage).
- Cotton/polyester fiber blends—best for shrinkage control.

Twill tape button placket
The twill tape on this rugby shirt is top-stitched on the front placket opening, with buttonholes sewn through the twill tape, which is a more stable fabric than the knitted shirt fabric.

Webbing
Narrow tape that is woven for strength and durability, webbing is used for belts, and on reinforcement straps for bags, backpacks, and other outdoor gear. Fiber content includes nylon, polyester (moisture-resistant), and cotton. Spandex fiber is added for elastic webbing, which is especially important in suspenders and belts.

Decorative ribbon: satin and velvet

Both satin and velvet ribbons use the same weave as in fabric except it is produced as ribbon, with both edges finished as selvages to prevent the yarns from raveling. Satin ribbon is lustrous and smooth, and velvet ribbon is a luxurious, deep, cut-pile surface.

The designer uses ribbon for neckline and cuff trimming, and lacings for closures and decorative bows. Satin and velvet ribbons are available in many widths and colors, including metallic. Almost all satin and velvet ribbons are dyed solid colors, and almost all are produced using polyester fiber for resilience.

There are two types of satin ribbons: double-face satin, which means the satin weave is on both sides of the ribbon, and single-face satin, which has a satin face side and a dull back side. Double-face satin is more expensive than single face satin. All satin ribbons are very shiny, so the designer usually selects a satin ribbon for a dressier trimming.

Satin ribbon's (yellow) fine, smooth surface provides an ideal surface on which to print images. Double-face satin ribbon (blue) is used for dressy garments and occasions that require shine on both sides of the fabric.

Facts and figures

Distinctive features

- Smooth and very lustrous.
- Flexible but sometimes a crisp hand.
- Finished edges without hem.

Ornamentation performance and garment care

- Color may crock onto lighter color fabric during wearing.
- Abrasion resistance may be different for main fabric; especially with satin and velvet surfaces.
- May shrink at a different rate from the main fabric.
- Color may bleed onto lighter-colored fabric during care.
- Differences in heat resistance may cause deterioration during pressing or drying.

Usual fiber content

- 100 percent polyester is the most common fiber content.
- 100 percent silk.
- 100 percent rayon or polyester/rayon blend.

¼ in (6 mm) ribbon
¼ in (6 mm) wide satin ribbon is often used as lacing for garment closures or threaded into casings for creating fabric gathers, as shown in this image.

Velvet ribbon
Velvet ribbon is always one-sided, its nap is on only one side of the ribbon. Its cut-pile surface can be easily crushed; this is most noticeable in wide widths.

Velvet ribbon lacing
Narrow velvet ribbon is often used as lacing for garment closures or threaded into casings for creating fabric gathers, as shown in this image.

![icon]

Decorative ribbon: grosgrain and taffeta

Grosgrain (pronounced "growgrain") ribbon has a distinctive cross-grain ribbed texture. An unbalanced ribbed plain weave, all grosgrain ribbon is produced with finished selvage edges to prevent raveling and to stiffen the ribbon. Taffeta is also produced as a ribbed plain weave ribbon.

The pronounced ribs on grosgrain ribbon helps provide a stiffness without a special finish. Grosgrain is available in many widths. Here are two wide-width ribbons.

The ribbons are reversible—both sides are ribbed—and come in a variety of widths, colors, and patterns. Stripes and printed images on grosgrain ribbon have made it a popular trimming
A very rigid weave, wide grosgrain ribbon can serve as a band on a man's hat, backing for belts, and sometimes facings for jackets and waistbands. The designer has many options when using this ribbon because it is durable, has a very crisp hand, generally comes in dyefast colors (if polyester fiber content), and is easily available. Taffeta is the lightweight version of grosgrain but is now considered a vintage ribbon. Grosgrain ribbon is also a colorful trimming for handbags, hats, collars and cuffs, shirt plackets, and more.

Facts and figures

Distinctive features
- Cross-grain ribbed texture; crisp edges.
- Maintains stiffness due to ribbed texture.

Ornamentation performance and garment care
- Color may crock onto lighter fabric during wearing.
- Abrasion resistance may be different for main fabric.
- Rigid, ribbed structure holds its shape.
- May shrink at a different rate from the main fabric.
- Color may bleed onto lighter fabric.
- Heat resistance differences between ribbon and main fabric may cause design deterioration during pressing or drying.

Usual fiber content
- 100 percent polyester (usually dyefast).
- 100 percent silk.
- 100 percent rayon.

Printed grosgrain
Grosgrain ribbons can be more decorative when printed or woven in color patterns. This yellow grosgrain ribbon is printed with white spots.

Taffeta ribbon
Taffeta ribbon has a less pronounced rib than grosgrain ribbon. It is lightweight and is often used as bows or other soft trims. The green ribbon in this example uses a picot edge (tiny loops) as a design detail.

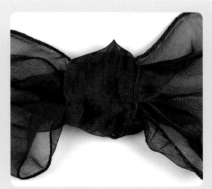

Wired organza ribbon
This stiff organza ribbon is woven with tiny wires in each selvage. These wires help the ribbon to remain in a shape; excellent for bows and other shaped trim details on a garment. Ribbon of any fabric can be wired.

Decorative ribbon: jacquard ribbon

Ribbons produced using the jacquard weave are some of the most beautiful available. The patterns woven into the ribbon can be intricate curved designs that use many colors of yarn or simplified designs that use just two or three colors.

Jacquard ribbons are produced in narrow widths, usually ½ in (1.25 cm) and up to 3 in (9.5 cm). The ribbon is produced with a crisp hand, so this stiffness sometimes limits the type of fabric on which the ribbon can be used. For example, chiffon fabric (see page 136) is usually too soft and lightweight to support a jacquard ribbon unless the ribbon is used as a cuff, waistband, or collar.

The design on the jacquard ribbon will determine its use. When sourcing jacquard ribbon, request the image on the ribbon, such as "animals," "floral," etc., and also specify the predominant colors. There is plenty of jacquard ribbon inventory available worldwide. Also specify the fiber content. There is no limit on fiber content, although much of the ribbon available is 100 percent polyester because it is relatively shrink-resistant and colorfast. Vintage jacquard ribbons are sometimes available, so always ask.

These jacquard ribbons use sophisticated looms that create computer-aided designs. These two ribbons have beautiful designs imitating a Japanese obi belt and a floral striped wallpaper.

Facts and figures

Distinctive features

- Curved images woven into the ribbon.
- Usually light texture.
- Crisp hand and sometimes bulky.
- Most often multiple colors, although monochromatic is also popular.

Ornamentation performance and garment care

- Metallic yarns used in woven-in designs are easily snagged.
- Abrasion resistance should be tested.
- Ribbon may bleed colors onto fabric or vice versa—especially denim fabrics.
- Ribbon may shrink and cause puckering if not wash-tested first.

Usual fiber content

- Any fiber content is acceptable.

Narrow jacquard ribbons (1, 2, and 3)
The various designs on these jacquard ribbons can be used on children's or adults' clothing.

Intricate jacquard ribbons (4 and 5)
These intricate ribbons are woven with metallic yarns and can be used instead of jewelry.

Tapestry ribbon (6)
The look of a hand-woven tapestry design is apparent in this ribbon.

Plant image woven ribbon (7)
Some jacquard ribbons are intended for interior design products, but they can also be used for apparel. This ribbon design, depicting the gingko leaf, has many design applications.

1	2	3	4	5	6	7

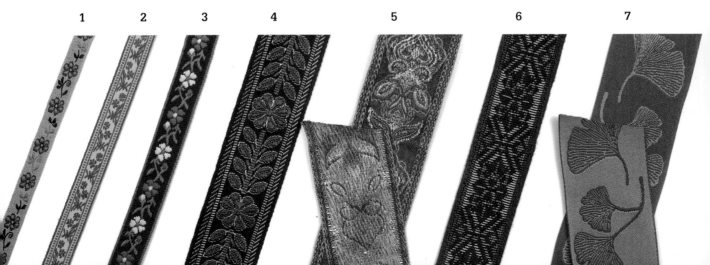

Decorative ribbon: dobby design

Like jacquard ribbon, dobby ribbons are woven-in designs, creating various geometric shapes using a combination of weaves. The results are often one- or two-color designs, and the ribbon tends to have varying textures and edges.

D obby weave ribbon can vary widely in weight and hand because the intention is to create texture and not to create an image in the ribbon.

One of the most interesting uses of the dobby weave ribbon is to combine different yarns into a ribbon, such as combining metallic yarns with shiny multifilament yarns to produce a textured, shiny, metallic ribbon. Many of the dobby woven yarns will have texture as a result of the type of yarn selected in the weaving process.

Dobby ribbons are usually available in narrower widths when compared to jacquard ribbons. The fiber content and complexity of the yarns used will be determined by the type of fabric the ribbon will be used on and how the ribbon will be used. Colorfastness and shrinkage issues should also be considered.

These two highly textured ribbons resemble geometric designs. Though they may also be identified as a jacquard weave, the geometric shapes in the ribbons resemble a dobby weave.

Facts and figures

Distinctive features
- Interesting textures can be achieved by combining different types of yarns.
- Crisp edges, although can be softer than jacquard ribbon.
- Can be lightweight or bulky, depending on the yarns used.

Ornamentation performance and garment care
- Ric-rac trim should be carefully sewn to prevent the zigzag shape from "folding over."
- Dobby ribbons are generally tighter weaves, so they are more abrasion-resistant than jacquard ribbons.
- Test ribbon for shrinkage, compared to main fabric, to avoid garment puckering.
- Test for color bleeding in laundry or dry cleaning.

Usual fiber content
- Can be any fiber content.

Dobby metallic ribbon (1)
This combination weave dobby ribbon shows the texture of the satin and plain ribbed weaves together.

Multicolored and novelty ric-rac (2, 3, and 4)
There are three types of ric-rac shown here: elastic ric-rac (yarn-dyed colors); yarn-dyed pattern (navy and white); and edging that can be sewn into seams (white).

Solid-color ric-rac (5 and 6)
Ric-rac is reversible; the same surface on both sides. It comes in a variety of sizes. Two sizes are shown here.

1   2   3   4   5   6

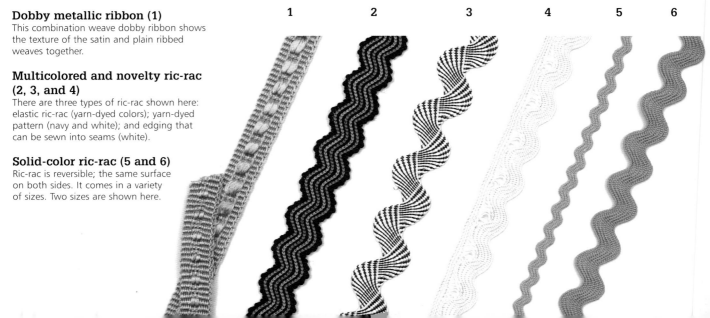

These examples of lustrous "gol[d]
cording, fringe, and a medallion imita[te]
the fine gold metallic threa[d]
traditionally used to ado[rn]
tailored jacket[s]

Passementerie trim

Passementerie trim products are defined as luxurious trimming details that add opulence, status, and elegance to a garment design. The passementerie look is rooted in historic costume from the military or from the Middle East and South Asia, whose cultures have embraced heavily textured trimmings that can be applied to the design.

Passementerie trim is distinguished by the use of lustrous, bulky yarns to create heavily textured braids, fringe, medallions, and buttons. The look is luxurious, sometimes with metallic trim, and is applied to communicate wealth and status.

Passementerie trims can be narrow yardage (such as fringe, braid, soutache, piping, or cording) or small trim items (such as hand-knotted buttons, medallions/patches, or tassels). Metallic yarns are often a feature of passementerie trims, although equally important are lustrous silk or rayon yarns. The design of these trims is intended to add weight, luxury, and appearance of wealth to the design. Therefore, when selecting passementerie trim, the goal of the designer is to feature the trim in the design.

Passementerie trims are used on suits, coats, eveningwear, and cocktail dresses. This type of trim is rarely used for more casual clothing or for work attire. Many of the passementerie trims available are discovered in interior design suppliers, so be sure to look there when searching for these trims.

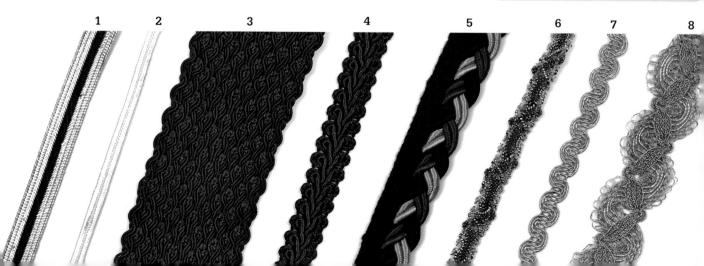

1   2   3   4   5   6   7   8

Fringe
These fringes are used on uniforms or elegant gowns. Gold or black are the preferred passementerie colors, as fringe was always used to show luxury and opulence.

9   **10**

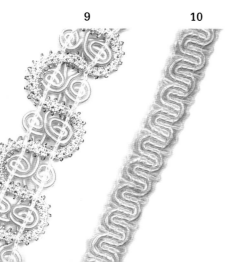

Military-style jacket
There are several gimp braids, soutache, and also piping on this jacket. These passementerie trims can be combined in a variety of ways to add opulent design details.

Braid, soutache, and gimp
There are many styles of these narrow passementerie trims, but they always feature shine, luster, bulk, and weight to communicate wealth and opulence. From left to right: soutache (flat braid, 1 and 2); braid (diagonally woven pattern, 3 and 4); piping (5); gimp (very curved, embroidered-look, 6, 7, 8, 9, and 10).

"Frogs"
Hand-knotted closures, called "frogs," are used like buttons. The braided edging used in this sample was used to finish raw edges.

Fringe

Fringe trimming is available in narrow yardage, sold by the yard. It is applied to the edge of a garment to add movement, and is sometimes added to the body of a garment for the same purpose.

The designer can use fringe to soften a silhouette or add texture and energetic movement. Fringe can also be custom-made using fabric as well as contrasting materials, as shown in the photos here.

Fringe is available in a variety of materials, and each material will express a certain design idea. For example, fringes are produced from beads, metallic yarn, silk and rayon yarns, and leather and suede. They can be casual or dressy in feel. When selecting a fringe, it must be understood that because of the fringe construction, it is not a durable trim. What is important to test on the design is how the fringe drapes on the body, and whether it is appropriate to sit on the fringe. Colorfastness should always be tested.

Fringe is produced from a variety of materials. The goal of most fringe is to finish the edge of a garment, lengthening it and softening the silhouette

Suede fringe
Suede fringe has often been used on apparel in the American West since the 19th century. Notice the different widths of the fringe: the narrower-cut fringe will drape better than the wider-cut fringe.

Chain-mail fringe
This chain-link metal has been designed to function like fringe, softening the edge of a garment while actually using metal.

Feather fringe
This fringe is combined with beads that help reduce the volume of the feathers.

Beaded fringe
This highly decorative beaded fringe can be sewn to a garment or bag using the tape it is already attached to.

Facts and figures
Distinctive features
- Fringe is always parallel to the body.
- Many narrow slivers of material closely joined together on a top band.
- Always shows movement when worn.

Ornamentation performance and garment care
- Fringe is almost never washable; some may not even be dry-cleanable. The dry-cleaning chemicals may damage or destroy the trim. Always test care applications before selecting a decorative fringe. Consider a detachable feature designed into the garment so the trim can be removed before care is applied to the garment.

Usual fiber content
- 100 percent silk and silk blends.
- 100 percent rayon and rayon blends.
- Cotton blends.
- Leather or suede.

Fringed dress
This fringe has been sewn to an underdress that is barely visible. Energy is generated as the fringe swings with the body movement.

Narrow novelty trims

Narrow trimmings are usually machine-produced ribbon-like trims that are designed to add embellished detail to a simply designed garment. The designer can select premade narrow trim or custom-design a narrow trim to be applied to the garment.

The variety of narrow trimmings is quite diverse, spanning all types of fiber content, yarn combinations, materials (such as feathers, beads, and sequins), and contrasting fabrics.

Narrow trims are often added to outline a garment silhouette, for stitched-on embellishment, or to expand the silhouette. The style and function of the garment design will determine the type of narrow trimming to be applied.

Selecting the trim will depend on the fiber content, weight, and texture of the fabric. Some narrow trims are elastic, but most trims are non-stretch, so it is important to determine whether the trim should expand with the body or remain a fixed length. Durability of the trim is dependent on the materials used to produce the trim. Therefore, durability testing, especially to abrasion resistance, is essential.

Narrow sequin trim
Premade sequin trim allows a designer to apply luxurious amounts of sequins without hand-sewing them one by one. These examples use actual sequins or metallic yarn to look like sequins.

Rhinestones and pearls
These chains of pearls or rhinestones can be anchored to a garment in continuous, linear designs.

Pearl edging
Pearls sewn onto single-fold fabric bias tape can be used as an edging or to help add detail to this fabric flower center.

Facts and figures

Distinctive features

- Narrow width and can be sewn onto a fabric surface.
- Surface texture of narrow trim is distinguished by the material used.
- Usually slightly stiff hand.

Ornamentation performance and garment care

- The great variety of this category of trim requires careful planning to avoid unhappy consumers, whose beautiful garment no longer retains the trimming you selected. Always test for abrasion resistance, colorfastness, and behavior during laundering or dry cleaning.

Usual fiber content

- 100 percent silk and silk blends.
- 100 percent rayon and rayon blends.
- Cotton blends.
- Leather or suede.

Sequined trim

The shiny trim on this well-fitted dress is applied to an elastic mesh dress fabric. Trimming yardage is often applied on the surface of a lightweight basic fabric, to create an entirely new fabric.

Narrow closure trims

Narrow trim, with various methods of garment closure attached to the narrow yardage, is a common method for easy application of a method to keep the garment closed. For example, instead of applying individual snaps to garment edges, the designer can purchase premade "snap tapes" that have both snap sides built in at a premeasured spacing.

The application of this type of closure trim can be a functional embellishment to the garment design. Tightly woven and durable twill tape is most often used for the application of the closure trim.

These premade narrow closure trims are offered in different tape and closure colors. Some are dyed/colored to be one color or are intentional contrasting colors. The designer should be aware of these premade closure trims and utilize them in interesting ways. For example, hook-and-eye closure trim was originally intended for undergarments but is sometimes used for fashion camisoles and knit tops.

Fiber content of the narrow tape is limited to fibers that are dyefast and preshrunk, or it can be used when dyeing finished garments.

Snaps attached to twill tape at regular intervals provide a simple way to attach both ring and stud cap snaps to a garment without specialized equipment

Plastic ring-snap tape
These colored plastic snaps are dyed and fastened to predyed twill tape that can be sewn onto a garment. The snaps will not be visible from the outside of the garment.

Hook-and-eye trim
Metal hooks and eyes can be sewn at regular intervals into a narrow trim that is specially designed for this purpose. Originally used in undergarments, hook-and-eye trim is frequently selected to embellish fashion garment closures.

Hook-and-loop tape
Hook-and-loop tape provides instant closure by placing a soft "looped" surface against a stiff "hooked" surface. It can be sewn onto fabric as yardage or in smaller sections and is used for shoes, accessories, and jackets. It is very stiff, although there is now a softer finish available. A recyclable polyester version is available in Japan.

Facts and figures
Distinctive features
- Regularly spaced pre-attached closure units, such as snaps or hook and eyes.
- Narrow tape is woven twill tape.
- Closure unit is separated so there are two narrow tapes, one for each half of the closure unit.
- The width of the narrow tape is approximately ½–1¼ in (12–32 mm).

Ornamentation performance and garment care
- Closure tape should always be tested for shrinkage compatibility, to be sure that the tape will shrink at the same rate as the main fabric. Failure to do this testing is one of the most common errors a designer makes and results in a garment closure that is puckered and unsightly.

Usual fiber content
- 100 percent cotton.
- 100 percent polyester.
- Cotton/polyester blends.

Zippers
Zippers are another method of closing and opening a garment. The prominent silver zippers on this skirt act as design elements, highlighting the pockets and center front line, but also have practical purposes: the pockets have effective closures and the center front zipper could be used to expand the silhouette of the skirt if opened.

Lace edging and appliqués

Lace edging is premade narrow trim lace. It is often produced like lace fabric, except the result is very narrow. Lace edging can be embellished using embroidery or beading, or by shirring the edging into ruffles.

Some lace edgings are produced to match the lace fabric, so if coordinating a lace pattern design with lace edging is important, be sure to mention it to the lace supplier. However, most lace edgings are intended to be used as embellishment on a contrasting fabric as a silhouette extension, for softening edges, or to expand the silhouette.

There is wide variation of lace edging, depending on the method of construction and the fiber/yarn selection. Metallic yarn can be added during lace production, which gives the lace a more opulent surface. Lace trim is added to casual garments, work attire for women, and especially dressy and occasion garments for both men and women.

Some lace edgings contain spandex. However, most lace edgings are rigid trims, produced using polyester, nylon, silk, cotton, linen, or rayon. Some lace edgings can be used in garment dyeing, but be sure to test for shrinking and abrasion resistance.

Intricately detailed lace can be produced in a variety of widths and designs for edge placement at hemlines, cuffs, necklines, and shoulders. These laces are specifically designed to decorate fabric surfaces and add small amounts of expensive embellishment to the design.

Venice lace edging
Venice lace edging has a heavier, less delicate appearance than other types of lace. This lace appears embroidered, though it is produced as yardage. Applying Venice lace adds a feeling of opulence to the design.

Cluny lace edgings (1 and 2)
Cluny lace is a type of bobbin lace. It produces coarse texture, using cotton or spun polyester yarns. This lace is often used for casual designs or less formal apparel.

Raschel lace edging (3 and 4)
Delicate raschel lace edgings are best used for lingerie or lightweight dresses and tops. Example 4 example includes a premade satin ribbon stitched behind a lace edging.

Lace banding (5)
Lace banding (sometimes called galloon) is typically finished on both edges and is often scalloped. It is sometimes produced to match lace yardage or appliqués. Nearly all lace can be produced as banding. The example shown here is metallic gold Cluny banded lace.

| 1 | 2 | 3 | 4 | 5 |

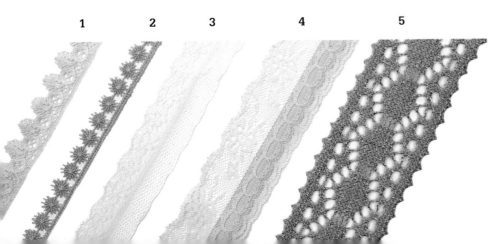

Matching lace edging fabric in dresses

The lace edgings shown in these photos are elegant, complex borders of lace with scalloped (curved) edges. These are often used for the finished end of the design, such as the hem on the white dress or the asymmetrical neckline on the black dress.

Facts and figures

Distinctive features

- Always resembles lace fabric only on narrow bands.
- Usually the lacy design edge is not intended to be sewn.
- Can be scalloped on both edges.
- Lace pattern can be textured or flat, depending on the yarn used and the type of lace.

Ornamentation performance and garment care

- The frail, open designs of lace trim make it easy to snag and break yarns in the lace design. Choose appropriate placement of the lace edging to minimize abrasion that may seriously damage the look of the garment design during wearing.

Usual fiber content

- 100 percent silk.
- 100 percent polyester.
- Cotton/polyester blends.
- Rayon/linen blends.
- 100 percent nylon.
- Combined with metallic yarn.

Lace appliqués

Lace appliqués can be designed as a single motif or in pairs, providing focused, elaborate ornamentation. Usually produced as Venice lace, they are applied to the fabric surface. They provide a much less expensive decoration than labor-intensive hand embroidery. Lace appliqués are often further embellished with beads, sequins, or rhinestones.

Embroidery

Embroidery is the application of patterns of thread or yarn to create interesting textures and designs. Embroidery designs have historically been applied by hand, but since the introduction of embroidery machinery, hand-sewn embroidery is less available. If one could afford to pay for hand-embroidered fabrics, the ability to pay for such time-consuming work would demonstrate wealth and status. Embroidery has historically been used to signify status, class, gender, and wealth.

With the introduction of machine-produced embroidered fabric and garments, the significance of the embroidered product is not so clear. The designer can select embroidery as a design element or as a focal point. Embroidery is now applied by specialized embroidery machines at high speed on fabric, individual pattern pieces, or on finished garments. Computer software has developed new types of embroidery that were not available before. Photographic images sewn as embroidery is one example of new computer-aided embroidery technology.

Embroidery can now be applied to most fabric surfaces if the fabric is properly held in place by a backing behind the fabric as the embroidered image is sewn. Still a sewing process, thread tension and fabric puckering are always problems to be resolved. Fiber content of the fabric to be embroidered should be "stable," meaning the fabric will not shrink or wrinkle badly.

Embroidered images
The embroidered images on this fabric match the fringe trim and printed dot fabric. These embroidered designs were selected by the designer to enhance the concept.

Embroidery threads

The thread selected for sewing embroidery is extremely important to the images produced. There are many thread choices, and the high-speed embroidery machines often require especially smooth and strong thread.

Multifilament threads such as rayon or polyester are most frequently used for sewing embroidery. Silk embroidery thread is very expensive, so rayon thread is generally used instead.

In selecting the appropriate thread for embroidery, a key point is to visualize the finished image. For lustrous finished images, rayon thread is used most frequently. The rayon thread colors are clear and bright, accentuated with high sheen. Multifilament polyester fiber is a less expensive choice and often has less shine, and the colors are less clear and bright than rayon thread. Threads that appear metallic add luxury to the image.

Facts and figures
Distinctive features
- Always a smooth surface after stitching.
- Stitching density is close together to avoid surface fabric from showing through the embroidered image.

Ornamentation performance and garment care
- All embroidery is subject to abrasion damage. The yarns that create the embroidered image are easily snagged, pulled, and broken. Always consider how your design will be maintained using this beautiful but fragile ornamental application.

Usual fiber content
- 100 percent silk.
- 100 percent polyester.
- 100 percent rayon.
- 100 percent nylon.
- Combined with metallic yarn.

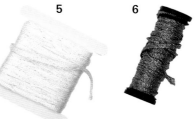

5   6

1   2   3   4

7   8   9   10   11   12

Metallic and space-dyed threads (1–6)
Unusually colored embroidery threads will enhance the embroidered image. These metallic and irregularly dyed (spaced-dyed) threads provide shine and variegated color to the image.

Mercerized cotton threads (7–9)
Mercerized cotton threads produce lustrous and deeply colored designs. This type of spun thread is rarely used in machine embroidery production.

Rayon and silk threads (10–12)
Silk or rayon embroidery threads have a similar lustrous appearance but rayon is less expensive. Silk is stronger and less likely to lose color, while the rayon will be less dyefast and weaker than silk.

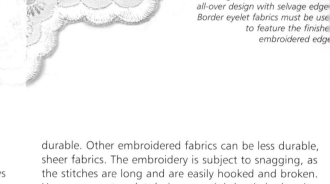

Eyelet fabric (Broderie Anglaise) can be produced as a border design as shown here, or as a all-over design with selvage edge. Border eyelet fabrics must be used to feature the finished embroidered edge.

All-over embroidered fabrics

Top-weight woven fabrics that have an embroidered design are figured, textured fabrics. The embroidery is a type of finish added to the fabric after the fabric is dyed but before it is made into garments or even cut into a pattern.

Fabrics used for all-over embroidery are tightly woven, non-textured surfaces. An example of an all-over embroidered fabric is eyelet. The embroidered images used in eyelets always call for holes to be punched in the fabric, whose raw edges are then finished with the embroidery. The eyelet design is nearly always floral-themed.

All-over embroidered fabric is used for babies' and children's clothing, lingerie, pajamas, blouses, dresses, and products for the home. Traditionally, eyelet is considered a fabric that is easy to care for, so the embroidery thread must be washable, dyefast, and durable. Other embroidered fabrics can be less durable, sheer fabrics. The embroidery is subject to snagging, as the stitches are long and are easily hooked and broken. However, most eyelet designs are tightly stitched and the fabrics do not shrink, so the snagging problem is not a serious one.

All-over embroidered fabrics can be any color, and the embroidery thread selected can be shiny, less shiny, or dull. Eyelet fabrics using lustrous rayon embroidery thread is more expensive than those that use polyester thread.

Embroidered chiffon
Embroidered chiffon is often used for evening dresses. A simple fabric takes on new luxury with an embroidered surface. This combination rayon and metallic yarn embroidery thread adds the look of jewelry to this fabric.

Embroidered plaid broadcloth
The embroidery added to this casual yarn-dyed plaid is a beautiful addition to a lightweight fabric. Embroidery adds little weight and is an ideal embellishment for lightweight apparel. It can be applied to nearly any fabric.

Heavily embroidered voile
This sheer, lightweight fabric takes on weight when it has been embroidered with an all-over stitched design.

Facts and figures

Distinctive features

- Always stitched designs throughout the fabric—sometimes border designs.
- Base cloth is always lightweight, sometimes sheer.
- Fabric sometimes has slight puckering where embroidery has been stitched.

Ornamentation performance and garment care

- Be sure to balance or match the embroidery design in your garment. Also consider the fiber content of the embroidery thread because it may bleed color onto the fabric if a contrasting color is used. Always test embroidered fabric for color loss during care.

Usual fiber content

- 100 percent cotton or cotton/polyester.
- 100 percent rayon or rayon/cotton.
- 100 percent polyester.
- 100 percent silk.

Embroidered chiffon dress

The contrasting white embroidery thread on this sheer chiffon is lined with a lightweight darker color fabric that enhances the color contrast.

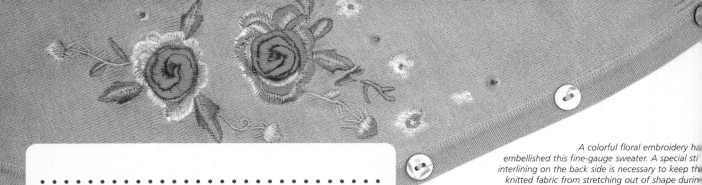

A colorful floral embroidery has embellished this fine-gauge sweater. A special stiff interlining on the back side is necessary to keep the knitted fabric from stretching out of shape during the machine embroidery process.

Garment-specific embroidery

These embroidered designs are located on specific areas of a garment and are usually applied to a specific pattern piece before production. The embroidery is never applied to the fabric before cutting.

Stitching a single embroidered design on a cut pattern piece or finished garment is more problematic than sewing continuous embroidery onto fabric. Different embroidery techniques are required, depending on whether the fabric is a stretchy knit or a rigid woven. Embroidering on knit fabric often requires a rigid interlining fabric backing, placed on the back side of the knit fabric—sometimes fused in place before stitching begins. The knit area to be embroidered is held stationary so the design can be sewn accurately.

Athletic teams stitch their team's logo on tricot knit shirts and pants. Outdoor apparel companies apply the company name onto knit tops and polar fleece jackets. Nearly all knits can be embroidered, as long as the embroidery design is limited to a small area. Because knit fabrics are so popular for casual and athletic tops, many embroidery companies have excellent experience stitching embroidered designs onto knitted fabrics.

Woven fabrics, especially densely woven and bottom-weight fabrics, are embroidered very successfully. If the woven fabric is lightweight or sheer, embroidered images may require a removable layer of tissue paper behind the fabric to assist in accurate stitching.

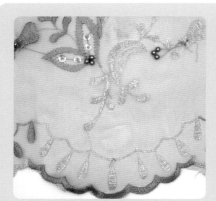

Beaded embroidery on organza
This organza was machine-embroidered using rayon and iridescent metallic threads. The sequins and pearls were sewn on by hand after the embroidery was completed.

Beaded, embroidered handbag
The metallic grid embroidery was machine-applied. The beading was then sewn on by hand, later.

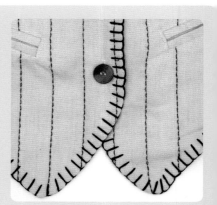

Vest with blanket stitch
The blanket-stitch embroidery on the edges of this vest can be applied via machine as well as by hand.

Distinctive features

- Embroidered image is always focused on a small area—not all over the fabric.
- Always use a backing on the reverse of the fabric to hold the face fabric steady while the embroidery design is being stitched on.

Ornamentation performance and garment care

- Because of the issue of damage through abrasion—common in athletics and other sports activities—embroidery designs used on this type of apparel should use shorter floating yarns to avoid snags wherever possible.

Usual fiber content

- Any fiber content knit can be embroidered, as long as the fabric is compactly knitted.

Embellished dress
This dress uses localized sequin embroidery, bordering each chiffon fabric appliqué. The embroidery could be hand- or machine-applied.

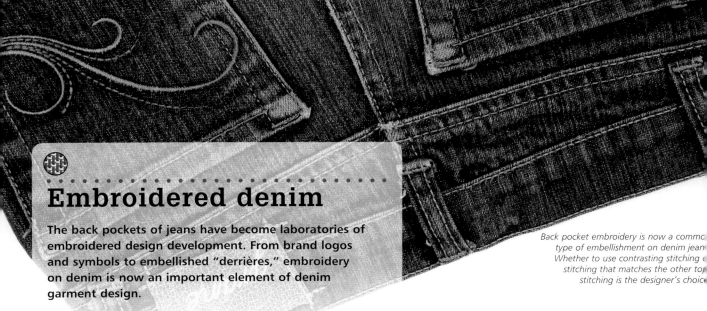

Embroidered denim

The back pockets of jeans have become laboratories of embroidered design development. From brand logos and symbols to embellished "derrières," embroidery on denim is now an important element of denim garment design.

Back pocket embroidery is now a common type of embellishment on denim jeans. Whether to use contrasting stitching or stitching that matches the other top stitching is the designer's choice.

Denim apparel has become an integral part of nearly every person's wardrobe. Denim jeans are a very personal possession, and making them feel more personal makes the wearer feel more unique.

Embroidery on denim began as recognizable stitching lines on the back pockets. Today, sophisticated embroidered designs show images, abstract designs, new stitching patterns, and embellishments of beads, crystals, and studs.

Nearly all jeans are washed after being sewn. Therefore, all embroidery thread must be colorfast and abrasion-resistant. Most embroidery threads used will be polyester or cotton/polyester blends for durability and shrinkage resistance. The embroidery is applied at the pattern piece stage, not to the finished garment.

Since most of the embroidery is sewn by machine, a flat surface is required. After the embroidered design is sewn, the garment is assembled and then washed.

If there is to be further embellishment such as crystals or beading, it is often applied after washing. Metal studs are applied before assembly. Embroidery designs on denim jeans have become an art form, similar to the denim-washing procedure. The application of unique embroidery on denim jeans provides an identity for the designer's company.

Embroidered graphic design
This full-color image adds personality to children's denim. Notice the crystal embellishment trim that accompanies this image.

Denim jeans with crystals
The brilliance of glass crystals adds elegance to this simple pair of jeans. The jeans are washed first to the appropriate wash finish, and then the crystals are fused (heat-set) in place.

Hand embroidery on denim
This hand embroidery on lightweight denim cannot be garment-washed. The denim garment must be washed first, then the embroidery can be applied.

Embroidered coat

The embroidered areas on this denim coat sleeve are appliqués that have been stitched on with embroidered designs, using indigo-colored embroidery threads. The unfinished cut edges of the appliqués add more surface interest.

Expansion

Expanding the design shape requires fabrics that literally stand alone. Unlike fluid fabrics that follow the body's form, expansion fabrics do the opposite. They enlarge the body's form, expand the silhouette, exaggerate, and accentuate.

Fabrics that expand the form

To achieve these qualities in design, fabrics must maintain shapes by themselves, which requires stiff, sometimes thick fabrics that will "stay put" where the designer intends. The human form is masked, reshaped by the way this fabric covers the body, and changes body proportions.

Fabric that creates volume is not easily understood by new designers. Frequently, an expansion fabric begins as a lightweight, drapable fabric and, through a variety of methods, the fabric is transformed into fabrics that add volume to the design. Certain manufactured fiber and fabric finishing techniques have greatly enhanced the designer's ability to experiment with fabrics that can add volume.

The designer's goal in selecting an expansion fabric is to move away from the human form. Exaggerating proportion through fabric requires surfaces that retain a shape after being formed. Frequently, expansion fabrics are very lightweight, using loft (air space between fibers or fabric surfaces) as a key characteristic to expand the design silhouette.

Expansion fabrics are diverse

Designers use expansion fabrics in three ways: to emphasize silhouette, to change proportion, or to accentuate design elements. The designer can participate in the fabric expansion process by selecting particular fabrics.

Pleated capelet and skirt

This drapey fabric has been pleated and the designer has focused the pleating to accentuate the volume in this dress silhouette. The pleated fabric has been used to sculpt a single-layer capelet and expand the skirt volume.

Short, pleated layers
Short layers of sheer, pleated organza keep the silhouette angled with sharp edges, without the need to hem the edges. This fabric was pleated before being sewn as a garment.

How expansion fabrics work

Most expansion fabrics require certain characteristics to sustain the designed shape. They can be knitted, woven, or a massed fiber fabric construction. Those listed below are not one fabric, so remember one or more of these descriptions may apply when manipulating a fabric for expansion.

Stiff hand: A resin is nearly always applied to a lightweight fabric to maintain shape. These resins can be very durable or water-soluble; check carefully which type of stiff finish is on the fabric you choose. Sometimes, monofilament yarns are used in netting, so the fabric can be naturally stiff.

Untextured surface: Except for netting, most expansion fabrics are even surfaces, without much texture before manipulation.

Lightweight: Because expansion fabrics are often manipulated, either by chemical finishes or by heat, the fabric begins as a top-weight fabric, sometimes medium-weight, but never bottom-weight.

Lofty: Fabrics are frequently layered, in a process known as quilting, and the inside fabric filler is the key layer. This inside layer can be very thin or very lofty, creating a thin or thick lightweight fabric.

An expansion fabric will have different forms

Selecting the right expansion fabric depends on the type of silhouette that is envisaged. Since many expansion fabrics are adapted from existing fabrics, it is important for the designer to understand how this transformation happens. Fiber characteristics are key to selecting the right fabric for the design. Manipulation of existing fabrics helps designers create their own new fabric to expand the design silhouette. Watch for examples of how a simple fabric construction can change into a completely different-looking textile by applying a finish.

Fur coat trim
Fur, either freshly harvested, repurposed, or faux, is an important element in garment design. The length of the hair strands will determine the amount of silhouette expansion, as shown by this hooded coat trim.

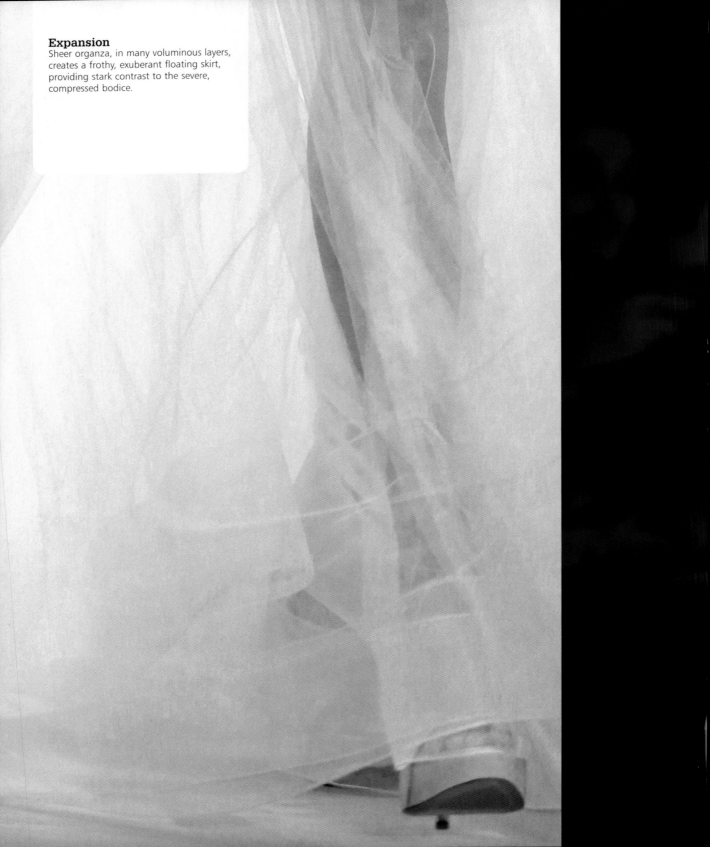

Expansion
Sheer organza, in many voluminous layers,
creates a frothy, exuberant floating skirt,
providing stark contrast to the severe,
compressed bodice.

Netting

Netting is mostly air, not surface. The yarns that are knitted, knotted, or twisted together provide texture, not surface.

Raschel knitting is one of the most common types of netting. The netting surface is shaped by yarns framing a geometric shape (sometimes six-sided, four-sided, or other shapes). The geometric shape will also vary in size depending on the function of the netting fabric.

Netting also varies in hand, but all netting is intended to stand away from the body. Designers will select netting to be an accessory, as in the veil on a woman's hat or wedding headdress. Netting is also used for underskirts to expand the skirt silhouette. Sometimes the garment design itself requires a netting to fulfill the design concept, such as a frilled collar or a fishtail insert that will expand the bottom of a skirt.

Netting hole sizes vary, depending on the design requirement. The large hole size is used on hat veils. The tiny size is used for bridal veils or underskirts. The small to medium sizes can serve as interlining on sheer fabrics or trim. The medium hole size is often used in dance skirts and costumes because most medium-hole netting uses nylon, which has a durable stiff hand with little finishing.

Netting always uses multifilament yarn, although the finishing will determine the degree of "crispness." In some cases, the netting finish is a type of starch that can be moistened and re-formed. Other finishes are chemical and therefore more durable than starch. Finally, the fiber itself may provide the desired hand. Nylon netting is always stiffer than silk fiber. Polyester fiber can be very fine or more coarse, depending on the function of the netting.

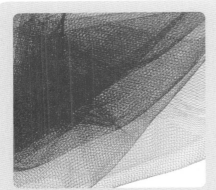

Tulle
Tulle is distinguished by fine yarn size and very small hole size. Silk fiber is often used, especially for wedding veils, although tulle is also an excellent selection for evening gowns. Because of the fine yarn, the hand is much softer than other netting.

Point d'esprit
Point d'esprit is a special netting with larger "flecks" of texture attached to the netting surface. It is used exclusively in millinery veil designs.

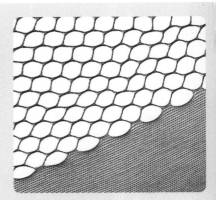

Large-hole netting
This netting is one of many variations on the shape of the hole and the arrangement of the hole sizes. It is up to the designer to choose a netting that fits the style of the design.

Facts and figures

Distinctive features

- Always yarns twisted together, creating geometric "holes" or shapes.
- Always a somewhat stiff hand, although the fiber content and finishing will influence the final hand.

Strengths

- Wonderful surface interest through the size of the yarn and shape of the netting holes.
- Excellent fabric to create silhouette shape with a little added weight.
- Netting can create a mood through the use of veils over the face or by exaggerating parts of the design over the body.
- Does not ravel when cut. Hemming or other edge finishing is not required.

Weaknesses

- Difficult to sew because there is little fabric surface.
- Avoid seams because they will show.

Usual fiber content

- 100 percent polyester.
- 100 percent silk.
- 100 percent nylon.

Evening dress with netting

The overskirt on this exuberant evening dress expands the silhouette with little added weight. The netting acts like a halo above the brocade fabric. The designer can use netting as an accent to the silhouette design.

Organza

Organza is a crisp, sheer fabric that always uses high-twist, multifilament yarns. The result is a lustrous, but not shiny, buoyant fabric that feels "grainy," like fine-grained sandpaper on the fabric surface.

Organza is selected for women's blouses, formal dresses, and trimming details. Because of the crisp hand of organza, it is an excellent choice for exaggerated design details that require changes in silhouette without adding weight. This fabric can be gathered or pleated, and such "layering" of this sheer fabric will add color intensity wherever the fabric layers are shown.

Organza is considered a formal fabric, used for special occasions. Full-skirt silhouettes, bouffant sleeves, and exuberant ruffles make this fabric a designer's choice for their luxurious dresses and blouses.

Originally produced with silk fiber, organza is now most often made using polyester fiber because polyester is less expensive than silk and is easier to care for.

This iridescent polyester organza interlaces green and red yarns to create a brown fabric with red and green highlights. This fabric has a very stiff resin finish.

Facts and figures

Distinctive features

- Lustrous, sometimes "sparkle" surface.
- Sheer fabric.
- Crisp hand.

Strengths

- Crisp hand.
- Sheer appearance.
- Doesn't require interlining.
- Light weight makes it a suitable layering fabric.

Weaknesses

- Crispness and surface texture can be difficult to control in production.
- Raw seam edges must be clean-finished if the seam allowances are visible.

Usual fiber content

- 100 percent polyester.
- 100 percent silk.

Metallic-effect organza
This organza uses metallic yarns in the weft and dyed silk yarns in the warp, resulting in a luxurious metallic effect on colored organza. The stiffness of the metallic yarn supports voluminous apparel designs.

Solid-color organza
The shiny polyester yarns used in this orchid-colored organza make a deeper tone when the sheer fabric is layered.

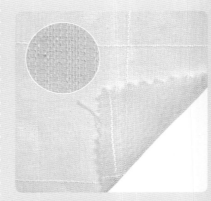

Windowpane organza
Organza is sometimes woven as a dobby design, such as this fabric, a windowpane organza. This is a polyester organza that can be used as window coverings or for women's tops and dresses.

Organdy

Like organza, organdy is a sheer, crisp fabric. Organdy nearly always uses spun yarn and is nearly always cotton fiber or blended cotton and polyester fiber.

Organdy's crisp finish can be starch, which is not permanent and can be removed and restored in the laundry. More durable crisp finishes require chemicals and heat to complete the finishing process. Heat-based chemical finishes are durable in the laundry and do not need to be restored. 100 percent cotton organdy can be finished using this more durable crisp finish, which is recommended. More durable crisp finishes have been developed for organdy, so it is no longer necessary to use a non-durable crisp finish.

Organdy's characteristic crisp hand and cotton fiber's absorbency make this fabric an ideal hot-weather fabric. Summer blouses, shirts, or dresses use cotton organdy. Its crisp hand makes it a favorite fabric for wide-sleeve or full-skirt silhouettes. Organdy is often used for little girls' spring and summer party dresses.

This cotton organdy fabric has been embroidered with contrasting lustrous rayon stripes. The stripes add additional stiffness to this loosely woven sheer fabric.

Facts and figures

Distinctive features
- Sheer fabric.
- Crisp hand.
- Dull surface, spun yarn hand.

Strengths
- Crisp hand.
- Sheer appearance.

Weaknesses
- May crease easily and require pressing.
- Seam slippage may be a concern—keep design unfitted.
- Raw seam edges must be clean-finished.

Usual fiber content
- 100 percent cotton or cotton/staple polyester blend.
- 100 percent staple polyester.

Lustrous organdy
Organdy is known for its stiff hand. This fabric is unusual, using smooth, very shiny multifilament yarns, and the resulting stiff fabric has a very shiny surface.

Organdy color
This sheer fabric intensifies its color in the areas where it is pleated.

Slubbed-yarn organdy
Sheer organdy is frequently used as an overskirt over another deeper-toned fabric. This fabric uses slubbed yarn, which adds texture to its surface.

Crinoline-supported skirt
The skirt of this voluminous dress is held in shape by an underskirt of crinoline and wire/boning.

Crinoline

Crinoline is used to create bouffant skirts and hats. As a balanced plain weave fabric, it is traditionally finished with a very crisp hand, much stiffer than organdy or organza.

Crinoline provides support for other fabrics; it sustains wide skirts or hat brims. It is densely woven but lightweight and should not add much weight to a design.

Crinoline is heavily-sized or stiffened by a variety of methods. Starch is the most common, but other more durable finishes, using chemicals and heat, are now available. Polyester or nylon blends are sometimes used to produce crinoline-type fabric, and their crisp finish is extremely durable and lighter in weight than 100 percent cotton crinoline.

Crinoline can be used to support a garment or can be cut into bias strips to expand a hem. A substitute for bias-cut crinoline is 100 percent nylon braid, produced in 1–2 in (2.5–5 cm) widths.

Nylon braid
This monofilament nylon braid has been sewn to another fabric. Its stiffness extends the design silhouette beyond the softer appearance of the design's main fabric.

Facts and figures

Distinctive features
- Loosely woven, balanced plain weave.
- Very stiff, crisp finish.
- Natural white color.

Strengths
- Very crisp/stiff hand.
- Lightweight fabric.

Weaknesses
- Stiffness may be uncomfortable next to skin. Usually an underskirt is required to keep crinoline away from bare skin.
- Stiff hand is bulky for sewn-in layers.

Usual fiber content
- 100 percent cotton or cotton/polyester blend.
- 100 percent nylon.
- 100 percent polyester.

Buckram

Buckram is the basic building-block of the millinery industry. This loosely woven, gauze-type fabric can be finished with starch or another resin that gives body and weight to the hat design.

Traditionally, starch has been used as the stiffener. It is possible to moisten and reshape buckram with pressurized heat and steam on a hat silhouette form. The buckram becomes the foundation for building the hat, with fabric selected to cover the buckram. The hat will maintain its shape unless it comes into contact with water.

Buckram is nearly always cotton fiber, although polyester and sometimes nylon are blended with cotton in blended spun yarns. Buckram nearly always uses a moisture-sensitive starch or other resin for the stiffening agent because of the need to shape the buckram in the desired hat silhouette. Additional starch is added when the fabric is cut and reshaped with heat and steam.

Facts and figures

Distinctive features
- Loosely woven surface.
- Very stiff hand.
- Stiffness is subject to softening by steam heat.

Strengths
- Very stiff hand.
- Subject to softening and reshaping when exposed to steam heat and pressure.
- Cut edges do not ravel.

Weaknesses
- Cut edges can cause discomfort.
- Non-durable stiffener can cause silhouette to lose shape if exposed to moisture and heat.

Usual fiber content
- 100 percent cotton.
- Cotton/polyester or cotton/nylon blends.

Buckram: before shaping
Buckram is heavily sized for a very stiff hand. It can be woven in different densities, as shown by the white and black samples here.

Buckram: after shaping
The fabric is cut into a shape and placed over a mold, a heavy weight is placed over the mold and fabric, and the entire ensemble undergoes heat, steam, and pressure. Since the resin is

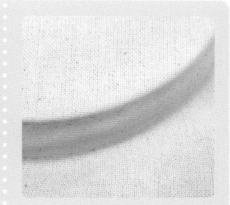

water soluble, the buckram will assume the shape of the mold. Loosely woven buckram is better for shaping.

Textural pleating
This unfitted top uses pleating to emphasize vertical surface texture. The garment will show a "liveliness" to the design as the model walks.

The concept of pleating

Pleating creates an expansive fabric by layering fabric at regular intervals for a "volume" effect or by creating pressed creases in fabric either randomly or at regular intervals. The resultant voluminous effect can expand the silhouette of the design, which is not possible through seaming detail or by any other means.

Pleating effects can be achieved by physically stitching the fabric in specific patterns, through chemical means, and through heat and pressure. How the pleating is accomplished depends on the designer's vision and the fabric selected. Pleated fabrics are never heavier than medium weight and, for the most interesting effects, top weights are recommended.

Pleating a fabric enlivens the fabric, creating movement, space, and loft in what began as a flat, lightweight surface. There are several methods for pleating:

Stitching: Folding and pressing fabric into regular patterns that add expansion to a design. When the wearer isn't moving, the pleats stay closed. When the wearer moves, the pleats expand with the body movement.

There are four main categories of stitched pleats

These categories are changed and manipulated depending on the designer's vision. Sewn pleats will add fit and drape and change the silhouette as the wearer moves and walks. Spacing between the pleats can vary.

Knife pleat

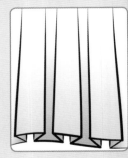

Box pleat

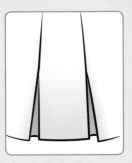

Inverted pleat

Accordion pleat

Chemicals + water + heat: Natural fibers, such as silk or cotton, are finished using a variety of chemicals, heat, and sometimes pressure, to produce the pleating texture. These chemical finishes are usually durable for the life of the garment. However, heat can diminish the texture. The chemicals require water and there may be some chemical waste disposal concerns. Usually, only yardage is pleated using this method.

Heat + pressure: With the introduction of polyester-manufactured fiber, pleating fabrics without chemicals or stitching is now possible. In a technique borrowed from embossing, special pleating paper is used to emboss the pleating pattern on the fabric by using heat and pressure. The variety of pleating designs can be quite diverse, depending on the fabric and design of the pleated image. Only polyester fiber fabrics are used because this fiber is the only one that remains soft after being heated. Therefore, the pleated fabric will retain the original soft hand and drape of the fabric, while taking the new pleated texturing. Pleats produced using this method are durable, except in the presence of high heat. Yardage, cut pattern pieces, or complete sewn garments can all be pleated.

Pleating with pleating paper

During paper pleating, fabric is sandwiched between two pleated paper layers. After paper pleating, the heated fabric cools, and the papers are pulled apart leaving the pleated polyester fabric. Pleating sewn garments is a highly skilled process, and the resulting garments are unique. Pleating papers are recyclable.

Before
The garment is sewn, including the hem, then placed in special pleated paper, rolled, then bundled. The package is placed in an autoclave for pressurized steam and heat to achieve heat setting.

After
The completed skirt, cooled, after several different pleating techniques (pleating on pleating). The texturing can be uniquely changed season after season by the designer.

Hand pleating

Hand pleating does not require pleating paper and must be carried out by skilled hand-pleaters, experienced in creating the same result on multiple garments. By twisting or folding and tying sewn garments through several pleating steps, unique garment designs can be created from a simple silhouette. Many pleating experiments are necessary to develop a signature pleating style.

Beginning
The sewn blouse is being pleated and tied in place for the first heat-setting.

During
The bodice is tightly bundled, ready for heat setting.

Complete
The pleated top, heat-set several times, is now ready for closure details and final trimming.

Pleated silk fiber fabrics

Pleated silk fiber fabrics are some of the most luxurious used in apparel. These beautiful, soft, lustrous silk fabrics—which are very lightweight—are chemically treated to become pleated, while still retaining their original character.

The main point for a designer to understand when selecting a fabric that will add volume to the design is that natural silk fiber can be manipulated into a durably pleated fabric. Pleated silk fabrics are always lightweight. In most cases, the fabric is pleated first and then cut into pattern pieces to be sewn together. However, it is possible to sew the garment first and then chemically treat the sewn garment for the pleated effect.

Lightweight pleated silk fabrics, such as China silk, silk organza, silk georgette, and silk chiffon, are often selected by designers to produce elegant garments. The added pleated volume allows the garment design to expand and contract as the wearer moves. The fabric has new character, which is impossible in non-pleated fabric.

This crinkled silk taffeta has been chemically treated to retain the creases in the fabric. There are also embroidered dots to further enhance the pleated texture.

Facts and figures

Distinctive features
- Textured, creased surface—not a flat surface.
- Usually lustrous surface.
- Fabric is enlivened by the pleating process.

Strengths
- Textured surface.
- Drapes well, but with an expansive surface.
- Resilient.
- Slippage is usually not a problem.

Weaknesses
- Cutting and sewing fabric is difficult to control if pleated as fabric.
- Chemical pleated finish may be neutralized in dry-cleaning chemicals and heat.
- Seams in pleated fabric sometimes cannot be pressed.

Usual fiber content
- 100 percent silk.

Crystal-pleated chiffon
Silk georgette can be pleated with tiny pleats, adding volume to the fabric. This crystal pleating will add volume to the garment design.

Accordion-pleated China silk
This square weave silk fabric retains its luster, adding a crisp hand with the sharply creased pleats.

Pleated suede leather
Another protein material, leather, is sometimes pleated. This sueded lambskin has been chemically treated, like the silk fabrics shown here, to be pleated.

![icons]

Pleated cotton fiber fabrics

Producing a durable pleated cotton fiber fabric requires chemicals and heat. In the past, designers used more traditional pleating designs, such as pleated skirts, bodices, or sleeves. Cotton fabrics are now pleated for different styles of texture, such as crinkling. The resultant "crinkled" fabric has a less defined pleated effect and instead has an all-over wrinkled appearance.

O riginally, pleating and crinkling gave a less durable finish, but now cotton fabric can be chemically treated to retain textures and pleating effects. The hand of the fabric is generally not changed by the chemical pleating process.

Lightweight cotton fabrics are selected for pleating and crinkling. The resultant pleated and crinkled cotton fabrics have a "loft" or volume that makes them suitable for more casual designs. These techniques work well in pleating lightweight cotton jersey, with the benefit of a drapey, knit fabric hand.

Loosely woven cotton voile is transformed into a stiffer hand when pleated with heat and chemicals. This "broomstick-pleated" fabric has also been printed with a leopard-print design, which gives the illusion of more texture on the fabric surface.

Facts and figures

Distinctive features
- Pleated or crinkled surface texture.
- Fabric has volume and is expandable.
- Hand remains soft, although the fabric is less drapey than before finishing.

Strengths
- Fabric accommodates simple designs and expands the silhouette.
- Textured with soft hand.

Weaknesses
- Seams are difficult to press—design with fewer seams.
- Pleating or texture will be diminished if exposed to dry-cleaning chemicals and high heat.
- Loses drapey hand due to pleating texture.

Usual fiber content
- 100 percent cotton.

Crinkle-finish calico
The irregular surface of this square weave, calico cotton fabric is the result of heat and chemicals applied to the fabric while compressed. When released, the calico fabric is durably creased.

Crinkled cotton sheeting
Though not a true pleated fabric, the crushed finish on this cotton sheeting fabric is a popular textured surface that uses the same process as for pleating cotton fabrics.

Pleated cotton voile
This voile was first embroidered and then pleated with chemicals and heat to achieve this texture before sewing into a fabric.

Polyester plain-weave pleated fabrics

Polyester fiber has transformed the world of fabric pleating. By simple heat and pressure, flat, lightweight polyester fabrics can be transformed into luxurious, pleated fabrics that perform better over time than natural-fiber pleated fabrics.

By using only heat and pressure, this thermoplastic fiber retains its soft hand while being transformed into a variety of pleated textures. The pleating process is durable, although it is subject to relaxation if exposed to heat higher than 250°F (121°C).

Produced throughout the world, the concept of heat-setting top-weight fabrics is limited only by the designer's vision. Pleating can be applied to the fabric, to cut pattern pieces, or to a garment that is already sewn. The final pleated garment silhouette is determined before the garment is pleated. The fabric should be no less than 60 percent polyester to be sure the pleating process will be durable. Even natural fiber blends with polyester are acceptable.

This square weave fabric was printed to resemble fabric cut on the bias, then heat-set into accordion pleats.

DESIGN RESPONSIBLY

Polyester fabrics can be pleated without the use of chemicals. Therefore, there are fewer wastewater and emission pollution issues in the pleat finishing process. In addition, polyester fabrics can now be recycled into new high-quality fiber, so there is less concern about garments and fabrics destined for the landfill.

Pleated polyester georgette
This finely pleated fabric resembles silk pleated georgette but provides the same effect for a lower cost and more durable pleated surface.

Pleated taffeta
This 60 percent polyester, 40 percent nylon fabric becomes stiffer after pleating because of the nylon fiber. Only polyester fiber stays soft after being heat-set. Nylon adds crispness to the fabric after pleating.

Pleated lining fabric
This 100 percent polyester fabric performs like a knitted fabric with this unique pleating design. The fabric remains soft after this heat-setting method.

Crêpe and satin crêpe pleated fabrics

The use of thermoplastic fibers, such as polyester and nylon, in heat-set pleating has produced a variety of new textured pleated surfaces.

Designers can add a heat-set pleated texture to a medium-weight fabric, differentiating the garment by the style of the pleated texture. There are pleating masters who design new pleating textures that are exclusive to a design company.

This heat-set pleating procedure allows a designer to use inexpensive fabrics and transform them into signature fabrics. Women's coats and jackets, in water-resistant polyester/nylon fabrics, have advanced the concept of lightweight rainwear with innovative textures and pleating. Women's sportswear companies have transformed simple, inexpensive fabrics into exclusive designs using this heat-set process.

In most cases, polyester multifilament yarns are used, and the fabric retains its soft hand. However, some fabrics include nylon or other fiber blends, and the fabric will retain some stiffness.

This satin-backed crêpe can be pleated and used on either the satin or crêpe side. The high-twist crêpe yarns add drape and weight to the fabric. These qualities are emphasized after pleating, and the fabric retains its soft hand.

Facts and figures

Distinctive features
- Interesting, textured, pleated surface.
- Usually lustrous surface from simple multifilament yarns.
- Hand is often slightly more stiff than original fabric, due to non-polyester fiber blend.

Strengths
- Variety of textures and pleating designs for exclusive appearance.
- Resilient fabric.
- Durable finish unless it exceeds 250°F (121°C).

Weaknesses
- Texture/pleats may relax if exposed to high heat.
- Heat-set hand can be stiff if fiber blend is more than 30 percent nylon.
- Pressing seams can reduce the pleated finish at the seam.

Usual fiber content
- 100 percent polyester.
- Nylon/polyester blends.

Satin crêpe fabric before pleating
100 percent microfiber polyester fiber content gives this fabric a very smooth, drapey hand.

Satin crêpe fabric after pleating
The sharp edges of the new pleating remain soft. The heat-set edges add new linear texture to the fabric.

Twice-pleated satin crêpe
This pleating pattern requires two different pleating designs to be applied separately. The resulting texture is unique to heat-set polyester fabrics.

Stitched pleating

Gabardine, poplin, taffeta, tricot knit

Mechanically pleating by sewing or pressing is the most traditional method for adding expansion to a design. The fabric is layered in regular patterns, with the pleats either pressed or stitched in place.

Pleating mechanically requires a medium-weight fabric. Most lightweight fabrics are too difficult to control to keep the layering of the fabric equally spaced.

Spacing the size of each pleat and the method of holding the pleats in place are design decisions. The main point for the designer, when selecting the appropriate fabric, is to understand fully how a fabric will perform when pleated mechanically.

Almost any medium-weight fabric can be pleated, including jersey knits, double knits, and crêpe fabrics. Fiber content is also not an issue unless the designer intends to heat-set the pleats, which will require approximately 60 percent polyester fiber content for durable pleats without sewing.

This box-pleated skirt is an example of how the spacing of the pleats and the depth of each pleat can be done. There are many variations of spacing and pleating depth.

Bias-cut accordion pleats
Mimicking the bellows of an accordion, this pleating design can retain its pleat volume but is sewn flat into waistbands. Accordion pleats are sometimes edge-stitched to maintain the pleats in wool fabrics.

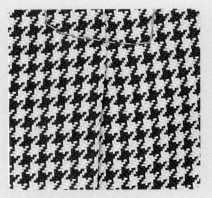

Matched plaid box pleats
This garment uses a plaid pattern that must be matched carefully around the entire skirt. The depth of the pleat must remain the same on all pleats. Note the stitched top of the pleat.

Inverted pleat
An inverted pleat has two creased edges meeting as if a seam. The effect is that no pleat is visible until the body moves. Inverted pleats are often used to expand the circumference of a slim skirt for ease of movement.

Paisley voile knife pleating
This skirt has been pleated in same-sized pleats, all in one direction around the body. This is the definition of knife pleating. This is a 100 percent wool fabric, and the pleats must be carefully maintained to keep the creased edge.

Facts and figures

Distinctive features
• Always adding fabric with layers of fabric to allow the garment to expand.
• Pleats are nearly always parallel to the body.

Strengths
• Functional design method to add expansion to the design.
• When not active, pleats can remain closed and not show fabric volume.
• Pleats can add attractive design details.

Weaknesses
• Pleats can add weight to the garment, since most pleated garments use medium-weight fabrics.
• If stitched pleats, stitching lines must be carefully sewn to avoid pleats opening in an unsightly manner.
• Stitched-down pleats can fit the body poorly.

Usual fiber content
There is no limit to the fiber content.
Spun yarns:
• 100 percent cotton and cotton/polyester blends.
• Rayon, acrylic, or polyester fiber blends.
• 100 percent wool or wool blends.
Multifilament yarns:
• 100 percent polyester and polyester/rayon blends.
• 100 percent silk and silk blends.

Pleated knit skirt
Pleating can be done on knitted fabrics, as shown by this mauve dress. The pleating on the skirt has been cut and pleated before sewing onto the hip seam.

Shirring

Shirring is a sewing method that gathers fabric closely together for the purpose of adding volume to the design. To correctly design a garment with shirring, it is important to select the appropriate top-weight fabric to achieve the expected lightweight gathered fabric volume.

This lightweight gauze fabric has been shirred using elastic thread to create tight gathers in the garment waist that are released over the body to create a full silhouette

Shirring can be achieved by sewing several rows of stitching close together and then pulling the sewing threads to gather the fabric. The result is a densely gathered fabric that creates an expansion of the silhouette at specific design locations, usually over the bodice or arms, or at the waist. Shirring can also be achieved by using elastic sewing thread; this creates the same gathered focal points but allows the fabric to expand with the body. The last method of shirring is a type of machine embroidery that gathers the fabric under the stitching pattern and creates a blouson effect, as in the other shirring methods.

Shirring is used for tops, dresses, robes, and lingerie. It is a designer's choice to use shirring for a certain "blouson" design effect that exaggerates the body proportion. It is always used to avoid closely fitted designs. Top-weight fabrics are always used, in any fiber content.

Printed georgette shirring
Shirring on matte jersey creates additional softness and drape by adding more fabric volume to the design and gathering fabric in focused positions on the dress.

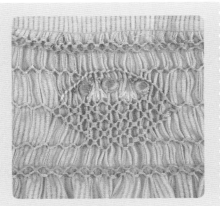

Embroidered shirring
Notice the embroidered stitching design that has been created while simultaneously creating the shirred gathers. This fabric edge has been finished with machine embroidery called "merrow" stitching.

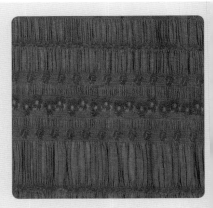

Dobby weave with woven-in shirring
This fabric was produced using spandex-blended yarns to create different tensions in the fabric. When released from the loom, the elastic yarns contract, causing the fabric to "crinkle" in the areas that use nonelastic yarns. The effect can be used in a garment that doesn't use sewn shirring.

Facts and figures

Distinctive features
- Always three or more parallel rows of gathers.
- The gathers expand the silhouette.
- Often uses elastic yarns to allow the fabric to expand with the body.

Strengths
- Shirring stitching patterns add design detail to the design.
- Shirring adds softness to the silhouette and creates a looser-fitting design.
- Shirring can be used on a variety of top-weight fabrics.

Weaknesses
- Garment design is often full, exposing seam allowances, so inside seams may need to be clean-finished.
- Fabrics should be preshrunk if shirring is to be used, to avoid unexpected silhouette changes due to fabric shrinkage.

Usual fiber content
- Any fiber content can be used—spun or multifilament yarns.

Shirred fashion garments
The shirred pockets, bodice, and edging of the orange dress (far left) gather the fabric together to create textured fabric volume. The white off-the-shoulder top (left) uses elastic shirring to hold the top in place and add fullness over the midriff and hips.

Bouclé

When this yarn is used, the resulting fabric texture is so distinguishable that the fabric is usually called a bouclé fabric, rather than the fabric construction name such as a jersey or plain weave.

A bouclé fabric has a looped surface texture. Depending on the concentration of the bouclé yarns in the fabric, the loops will be more or less noticeable. When selecting a fabric with a bouclé surface texture, the amount of loops will determine how bulky the fabric will be. This bulkiness expands the design silhouette, softening and rounding the garment.

Bouclé fabrics can be knitted or woven, although neither fabric will be a complex construction because the looped bouclé yarns can be difficult to manage. A knitted bouclé fabric will be more flexible and drapey, and a woven bouclé fabric will provide structure.

Bouclé fabrics are always medium- to bottom-weight and are used in sweaters, jackets, dresses, and coats. Because of the looped texture, designs concentrating on silhouette and trim details are recommended, rather than complex constructions.

Bouclé yarns add bulk and texture in this suiting fabric.

Facts and figures

Distinctive features
- Always a looped surface texture.
- Usually "hairy," long-textured staple fiber, which is used in looped yarn.
- Bulky fabric appearance.
- Fabric is often different colored fibers in yarns for a multiple-color tweed effect.

Strengths
- Bulky, looped surface texture.
- Softens garment silhouette.
- Looped texture makes the fabric very resilient.

Weaknesses
- Bulky, looped texture is difficult to cut and sew.
- Pressing is difficult due to the bulky volume.
- Fabric adds "weight" to the design, which can be undesirable for some customers.

Usual fiber content
Usual fiber content is always staple fiber in complex spun yarn:
- 100 percent wool or wool blends, especially with mohair fiber.
- 100 percent acrylic or acrylic blends with rayon, wool, and polyester.

Bouclé sweater knit
Bouclé yarns are often used to produce bulky textured knits in warp insertion knits and weft single knits.

Black and white bouclé fabric
The black yarn background of this fabric highlights the looped texture of the contrasting white bouclé yarns.

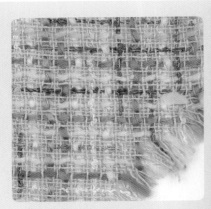

Bouclé woven suiting
The looped yarns are almost always used in combination with other, simpler yarns in woven suiting fabrics. The looped texture adds volume and thickness to a flat structured fabric.

Chenille

Napped fabrics can be created using yarn instead of weave or napped finishing. A chenille yarn is a cut-pile yarn that can be woven or knitted into fabric for a similar napped surface texture as velveteen. Weaving often combines chenille yarn with simpler yarns, in which case the velvety chenille texture is less pronounced.

In knitting, however, where there is almost no tension on the yarn during construction, the fabric can be produced using nearly 100 percent chenille yarn for a luxurious, velveteen-like texture.

Chenille yarns are not durable, with the cut fibers easily pulled out. Woven fabrics produced using chenille yarns must be constructed to withstand abrasion. Knitted fabrics already are susceptible to snagging, so adding delicate chenille yarns will not add further to durability concerns.

Woven chenille fabrics use chenille yarns more sparingly than knits, so the added bulk of the cut-pile yarn is less noticeable. However, the chenille texture is used in interior fabric products, and most knitted accessories and tops create luxurious, velvety surfaces.

Chenille yarn, when knitted into a sweater fabric, creates a soft and velvety textured knit.

Facts and figures

Distinctive features
- Velvety cut-pile appearance.
- Bulky cut pile.
- Soft hand.

Strengths
- Luxurious velvety hand.
- Bulky appearance.
- Resilient if knitted.

Weaknesses
- Chenille yarns are not durable and are susceptible to cut-pile fibers pulling out.
- Bulky fabric can be difficult to cut and sew.
- Pressing may flatten the pile surface.

Usual fiber content
- 100 percent polyester.
- 100 percent rayon.
- 100 percent cotton or cotton/polyester blends.

Chenille yarn
Chenille yarn is a cut pile in yarn form. This example used cotton fiber recycled from fabric waste. The fiber was precolored from the dyed cut fabric.

Chenille rug
The chenille yarn in this area rug adds a velvety touch. Sometimes lightweight area rugs such as this one become inspiration for fashion jackets and skirts.

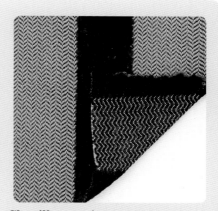

Chenille yarn in a woven herringbone dobby
This interior fabric uses chenille yarns to add texture to the fabric surface. It has been carefully woven in to improve abrasion resistance.

Terry cloth

Terry cloth is designed for maximum moisture absorbency. The looped yarns increase the amount of fiber/yarn surface that is available for absorbing moisture.

Fibers that absorb moisture are generally used, although wicking fibers or nonabsorbent fibers are used for specific functions, or just for creating a beautiful surface.

Terry cloth is bulky, adding volume to the product. Where the function is to absorb as much moisture as possible, such as a towel or beach robe, sometimes less bulk is desired. The looped surface can be on the face and/or back in a woven terry, but the looped surface is only on the face side in a knitted fabric. Limiting the looped surfaces will reduce bulk.

The looped surface can be enhanced for softness by blending with polyester microfiber, rayon fiber, or softener finishes. High-quality cotton fibers, such as Pima or Egyptian long-staple fiber, are often used to produce more luxurious cotton terry cloth. In knitted terry, the fabric is more drapey than woven terry cloth.

Woven terry cloth fabric has a looped pile on both face and back, which adds to the absorbency potential of the fabric.

Facts and figures

Distinctive features
- Looped pile surface (both face and back, if woven).
- Bulky appearance for soft, rounded silhouette.

Strengths
- Very bulky, soft appearance.
- Highly absorbent if using moisture-loving fibers.
- Creates a soft, rounded silhouette.

Weaknesses
- Surface snagging is always a problem.
- Bulky surface makes cutting and sewing difficult.
- Nap direction should be tested.

Usual fiber content
Spun yarns:
- 100 percent cotton.
- Cotton blended with rayon or polyester fiber.

Weft terry knit
Knitted terry is a fabric commonly used for women's tops. This terry is a yarn-dyed stripe, with the colored stripe introduced in the looped pile only into a solid-color knit ground cloth.

Warp terry knit
Knitted terry in a warp-pile knit creates a stable knitted fabric that is very popular for fashion tops. The looped surface uses "thick and thin" irregularly twisted yarn to create irregular loops. The knitted back side shows how it provides the "base" to insert the looped yarns that show on the surface.

Woven terry and velour in one fabric
Some woven terry cloth fabrics are finished with a velvety cut-pile velour side and a looped pile side.

Terry cloth robe

Fluffy, voluminous terry cloth robes like this one are often a featured item in a luxury hotel. What feels better than to nestle into the soft, deep-looped pile of a 100 percent cotton terry cloth robe? An alternative to cotton fiber is bamboo rayon, which creates a softer, more absorbent, and faster drying fabric.

The concept of quilting

Quilting is a traditional method to create warmth by combining three layers of fabric and fiber together. Originally hand-stitched together, quilted fabrics can be machine stitched or even heat-set together.

The purpose of quilting is not only to create something that will keep you warm, but also to expand garment silhouettes. In the apparel industry, quilting has developed into beautifully designed and highly technical fabrics. Quilting creates lofty fabrics that expand the silhouette of the body. There are different design purposes for quilting and different degrees of loft, and the pages that follow will explain this in more detail.

It is important to remember the purpose of each fabric layer when selecting fabrics for a quilted garment. Designers must decide on the type of stitching, thread, and degree of loft required.

Outer layer
This is the side that will be seen the most, so it should reflect the designer's vision. Face fabric is usually top-weight.

Filling
The filling provides the thickness, or loft, of the quilt, so the resilience, thickness, durability of the loft, and care issues should all be considered. It is important to test the filling to see whether the fibers will work their way through the face or back fabric. A high-density lining fabric to prevent fiber or down/feathers from emerging through the fabric face or the backing may be required.

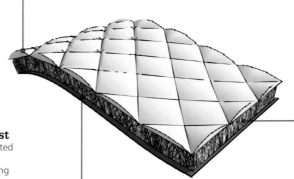

Quilted vest
Creating a quilted fabric always involves stitching an interesting pattern onto the fabric surface. This metallic fabric has been modified by stitching a diamond pattern onto the surface.

Back
The backing is the quilt support and can be quite inexpensive, or it can be a lining fabric if the quilt is intended as a jacket. Comfort, hand, and durability are all considerations for choosing the best backing. Backing is usually top-weight.

Minimum-loft quilting

Quilting a fabric gives the designer great flexibility in creating unique and interesting fabrics specifically for a design.

Minimum-loft quilted fabrics are the least bulky and are most frequently used in fashion jackets and coats. The face can be a patchwork fabric sewn together, or a pattern of sewn stitches on the solid-color face fabric. The function of the quilted fabric will determine what fabric the designer chooses for the face.

The point of quilted fabric is to provide thermal insulation or warmth, which is the function of the filler or batting. Massed polyester fiber is most commonly used for the filler because it does not absorb moisture and dries quickly. Cotton-fiber batting absorbs moisture and therefore is not recommended. Wool fiber can be used, but it has similar problems to cotton batting. The backing can be a lining fabric in either balanced plain weave or tricot knit.

Light polyester fiberfill is used on this diamond stitch patterned quilted fabric.

Facts and figures

Distinctive features
- Three-layer fabric, with an exposed stitching on the face of the quilt.
- Lofty (puffy) texture, outlined by the sewn stitches.
- Sometimes specific sewn stitching designs on the face of the quilt.

Strengths
- Good thermal insulation.
- Subtle lofty appearance.
- Resilient due to filler layer.

Weaknesses
- Bulky, sometimes difficult to cut and sew.
- Pressing seams is difficult, and using few seams in a design is recommended.
- Sewing stitched designs may require matching or balancing the cut pieces.

Usual fiber content
- There is no guidance on fiber content for the face and backing. However, the function of the design, fit, and care instructions should be considered when selecting fabrics.

Channel-quilted fabric
Stitched in parallel rows, channel quilting can be used for minimum- to high-loft quilts, or for garments. Note the low profile of this channel quilting—it would be simple to sew. This quilting uses the same sheeting fabric on both face and back.

Stitched design on a solid color fabric
This sateen fabric could be used for a quilted fashion jacket. Notice the machine-stitched design, which is its main feature. It imitates a hand-stitched *trapunto* effect.

Vintage quilt fabric
The cotton sateen face of this fabric is an ideal fabric for a quilted jacket. Until the 1960s, cotton batting with a gauze backing was used to construct most quilted fabrics.

Medium-loft quilting

Quilted fabrics that have more loft (greater thickness) use different types of fillers. One of the more traditional fillers is down and feathers, usually from ducks or geese.

When used as a filler, down (located closest to the bird's skin) provides the most thermal insulation with the least amount of weight. Down also doesn't have "pins"—the quill-type spine of feathers—so it is less likely to pierce the lining material. Down is the most expensive and loftiest thermal insulation material and can be difficult to launder, so another, less problematic and less expensive fiber has replaced down for efficient thermal insulation: polyester polyfill. Produced for up to 4 in (10 cm) loft, it retains its loft, which is a key point for effective thermal insulation—it is the air spaces in the filler material that keep warm air close to the body.

Again, it is the designer's choice for the face fabric, although most medium-loft quilted fabrics are used for functional thermal insulated jackets and coats. Often the goal is to keep the wearer warm and dry, so water-resistant fabrics are a key functional point. Down, feathers, a combination of down and feathers, or various

The stitching lines are in a contrasting color and provide design detail to this sample. Note the box design of the quilted fabric.

types of massed polyester fiberfill are all good choices for filler. The backing is usually a lightweight fabric that will add little weight and perhaps also shield the wearer from irritating pin feathers or polyester fiber poking through.

Polyester fiberfill
This polyester fiberfill comes in a variety of thicknesses and weights. This example is 1 in (2.5 cm) thick and creates a medium-loft garment. Polyester filler is less expensive than down and feathers and is easier to clean. Being heat-sensitive, it does flatten over time.

Mitered channel quilting
This fabric is channel quilted, which means sewing in parallel lines, spaced apart to allow the filler loft to expand.

Quilted stitch design
This fabric is an example of how a medium-loft quilted fabric keeps the filler from settling to the bottom of the garment. The stitching lines also create an interesting pattern that adds to the overall design of the jacket.

Channel quilting using down/feathers filler
This quilted fabric uses a combination of feathers and down as the filler. The feathers or down are kept sealed in the lining and are then sewn into the jacket.

Facts and figures

Distinctive features

- Filler is thicker, so the stitched patterns are simpler than minimum loft quilts, and the puffiness of the loft is very noticeable.
- Down and feather fillers are often used.
- Often used in outerwear.

Strengths

- Multiple functions combined into a single quilt fabric for more extreme conditions.
- Puffy loft is immediately recognizable for thermal insulation.

Weaknesses

- Cutting and sewing must be carefully thought through to avoid exposing the filler.
- The filler material may poke through the lining material to the discomfort of the wearer, unless it is properly filled.
- Sewing needle holes sometimes allow filler to peak through to the surface.

Usual fiber content

- Face: Usually a moisture-resistant function fabric.
- Filler: Easy maintenance and compacts well.
- Back: Protects the wearer from filler material poking through.

DESIGN RESPONSIBLY

Duck and goose down and feathers are considered a by-product of the poultry industry. They are often used in padding and other forms of thermal insulation. The feathers, down, and "dander," which become airborne if not controlled, can be a significant health hazard if inhaled by workers in a sewing factory that uses down and feathers as thermal insulation. Down and feathers should not be handled in the open air but in a "clean room" where they are controlled via sealed containers. Uncontrolled down/feather management can be extremely toxic to the workers.

Quilted jacket
This quilted jacket uses different thicknesses of quilting, and the quilting is stitched into a chevron pattern across the front of the jacket.

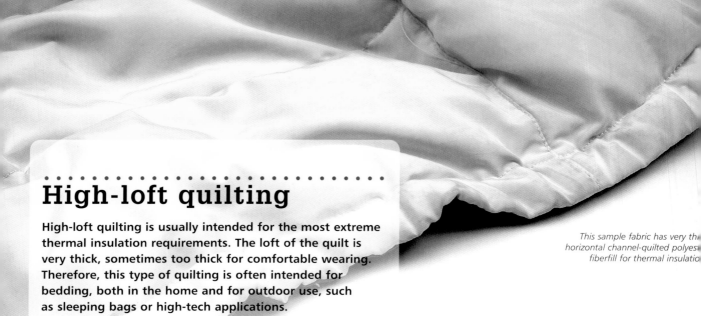

High-loft quilting

High-loft quilting is usually intended for the most extreme thermal insulation requirements. The loft of the quilt is very thick, sometimes too thick for comfortable wearing. Therefore, this type of quilting is often intended for bedding, both in the home and for outdoor use, such as sleeping bags or high-tech applications.

This sample fabric has very th... horizontal channel-quilted polyest... fiberfill for thermal insulatio...

Down, which functions as one of the best thermal insulation fillers, should be used without feathers. Down combined with feathers will reduce the cost of the filler but also reduces the function of the down. Polyester fiberfill, using special polyester fibers that are intended to imitate the down fiber, are also used as filler in such special applications. The goal in high-loft quilts is to provide maximum thermal insulation with minimum weight. Therefore, the high (thick) loft will be filled with air, and the quilt can be compacted into a small space and, when released, will spring back to its high loft immediately.

High-loft products are used in expeditionary items such as sleeping bags and jackets that can withstand extremely cold temperatures. Comforters for beds and even robes can be produced for comfort where there is little exterior heat. Choose face fabrics and filler lining fabrics carefully that will encourage thermal insulation and comfort.

Down-filled fabric
Down-filled fabrics tend to "settle," flattening the quilted appearance. Stitching is designed to minimize settling. Shaking regularly and not storing in a compact place will help keep the down lofty.

Expedition jacket
This jacket, designed for high performance in extreme weather conditions, will insulate the body against extreme cold and wet. The water-resistant/breathable microporous membrane keeps the high-loft fill dry.

Fiberfill fabrics
Fabrics using high-loft polyester fiberfill will maintain their lofty appearance better than down. However, fiberfill is often heavier, though it is also less expensive and easily washable.

Facts and figures

Distinctive features

- Very "puffy," lofty quilted fabric.
- Face fabric is nearly always very lightweight and moisture-resistant.
- Stitching is designed to keep filler in place.

Strengths

- Multiple functions combined into a single quilt fabric for more extreme conditions.
- Puffy loft is immediately recognizable for thermal insulation.

Weaknesses

- Cutting and sewing must be carefully thought through to avoid exposing the filler.
- The filler material may poke through the lining material to the discomfort of the wearer, unless it is properly filled.
- Sewing needle holes sometimes allow filler to poke through to the surface.

Usual fiber content

- Face: Designer's choice, although moisture resistance, light weight, and resiliency are key points.
- Filler: Mostly down and high-tech polyester fiber.
- Back: Designer's choice, with comfort a key factor.

Overstuffed quilted coat

The overstuffed filling of the quilting in this coat is designed to emphasize certain elements of the garment. The custom-stitched quilted effect gives volume and balance to the design.

Fur in apparel

Real fur or faux fur?

The use of fur for apparel has been happening for centuries. Fur is traditionally associated with social standing, be it royalty, leadership, rank, wealth, or another distinction within a social group.

With the rise of the middle class in the late 1800s, fur came within the reach of many more people, and the demand for fur escalated. There are now ranches that raise animals for the purpose of fur fashion apparel.

Animal rights activists have focused on the inhumane treatment of animals for the purpose of fashion clothing and the wasteful use of fur in the fashion industry. Fabrics that imitate real fur seem to be the solution, providing the look of fur without killing a fur-bearing animal.

This section is intended to explain the various types of fur, both real and faux, and to provide an insight into how these textile products can be used. There is no attempt to take sides on the question of "real fur or faux fur?" Instead, it is the designer's choice to select the appropriate product to be used in the design. There are good reasons to use each type of "textile." It is in the designer's hands to provide leadership in selecting appropriate materials.

The legacy of fur

Fur is usually judged for its value on the length and density of the hair, and the depth and purity of its color. Connected to these judgments is affordability. The higher the cost of the fur, the higher the status of the person who possesses the fur. This association of cost and status is undeniable, and although many groups and individuals attempt to provide reasons not to possess high-value fur, this identification with status and wealth is difficult to remove.

The sale of rare and exotic furs, many now from animals that are in danger of extinction—tigers, leopards, panthers, certain species of fox, and others—is now controlled by international law. It is well known that the killing of an endangered fur-bearing animal is not only immoral but also illegal. Yet the attraction of fur, to be made into a coat or other garment, is still undeniable and wearing fur continues to communicate power and wealth.

Faux fur

It is now possible to have a fashion garment that looks like fur without the feeling of guilt that an animal was killed for the whims of fashion and social status. Faux fur can be almost indistinguishable from real fur. The production of faux fur involves acrylic, mod-acrylic, nylon, rayon, and polyester, all of which are manufactured fiber, using oil-based products and resulting in polluting emissions and chemical waste that must be neutralized. Faux fur fibers cannot be recycled or reused easily, as the fur-like fibers are heat-sensitive and not very abrasion-resistant. Therefore, faux fur can contribute to the degradation of the environment.

The designer's choice

The question becomes: "Is fur or fur-like still necessary in the design of fashion apparel, and what is the symbolism of fur or faux fur in a garment?" If inexpensive fur is used in the design of a garment, is the use of such low-cost fur any different than the use of high-cost fur? Is the use of faux fur any better for the environment than the declared inhumanity of killing a fur-bearing animal for fashion apparel?

Real or faux?
The use of real fur or faux fur is a complex issue for designers. This long coat appears to be faux fur... or is it real fur? Who can tell?

Repurposed fur

Repurposing fur, or using fur from existing garments, may be a reasonable compromise compared to killing or "harvesting" fur, or faux fur production that uses non-renewable raw materials and produces unhealthy emissions and chemical waste.

While the demand for fur clothing has changed in the past 30 years, there are significant quantities of fur garments still owned by consumers or available at auction houses and used or vintage clothing stores. Properly stored, fur can have a long wearing life. Some fur garments become surrogate parents in animal shelters, but there are far more fur garments than can be used at the shelters. What should be done with these garments?

Previously worn fur garments, if systematically collected, sorted, and sold to designers for new designs, appropriately labeled and marketed as "repurposed," seems a reasonable approach to keeping existing fur in use, rather than wasting it. Therefore, as a designer selecting fur for a design, consider using existing fur that can be adapted to new clothing.

The mouton collar on this coat could be removed and reused on another garment. Why must fur lose its value simply because it already exists in a garment? Must desirable fur always be new?

Facts and figures

Distinctive features
- Soft hair; short to long hair.
- Fur is distinguished by being from a fur-bearing animal.

Strengths
- Beautiful, soft luxurious hair surface.
- Very warm in cold weather.
- Long lasting if properly stored in a cool, dry place with air circulation.

Weaknesses
- Requires special machinery for cutting skins and sewing garments.
- Expensive when compared to other fabric alternatives.
- May be socially unacceptable.
- One-way nap.

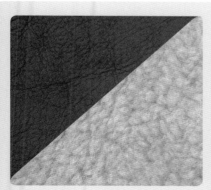

Shearling
Shearling is a sheepskin hide with the fleece still attached. When the long wool fibers are cut (sheared) close to the skin, the result is called shearling. Vintage and used shearling coats, vests, and jackets are readily available.

Fox fur
Fox fur is a long-hair fur. The long guard hairs stand away from the shorter, soft under-fur that gives fox fur a luxurious look and hand. These furs are designed into coats but are most often used as trim for collars, cuffs, and hemlines.

Fine feather trim
Feathers are also used for trim details on garments. The issues of feather use are as complicated as for fur. There are fabric alternatives to feathers, but the appearance and lightweight nature of feathers is unmatched in manufacturing.

This fabric imitates "mouton," a sheared sheepskin. The plush faux "mouton" has been bonded to a polyester microfiber sueded tricot knit

Commonly used faux fur

Faux fur was developed to create a consistent supply of fur-looking fabric that was available by the yard. Instead of shaped skins, faux fur is available in yardage.

The method of production for faux fur for apparel is similar to other napped fabrics, but the nap is longer, and the nap direction is more pronounced than for corduroy or velveteen. The resulting fur-like fabric often produces a similar garment to one made from real fur.

One of the most important elements in apparel design is consistent appearance in fabric. Real fur can only be the shape of the animal, and many fur garments require multiple pelts that must be matched and pieced together. There is often waste due to the inconsistent texture or color of the fur. Using fabric yardage with a consistent appearance makes pattern placement and cutting simpler compared to real fur. Because faux fur is available by the yard, large products, such as bedspreads, full-length coats, and furniture can be produced with more consistent results.

Fake fur can be divided into three main categories:

- **Plush:** This is similar to shearling (shaved sheepskin), mouton (shaved lambskin specially finished for extra softness), or pony. The even pile is thick and a consistent length, about ¼–1in (6–25mm) in length.
- **Medium length:** Imitates fur-bearing animals, such as leopard, zebra, and mink.
- **Long length:** Imitates more luxurious long-hair furs, such as fox, wolf, and lynx.

Designer's tip:
Always cut faux fur with a razor blade on the back of the fabric. Never cut with scissors on the fabric face.

Two-tone faux mink
Adding color helps the pile to look like real fur. For the faux mink, the soft under-fur is one color and the long guard hairs are a different color, as in this sample.

Faux pony
This short, flattened pile is intended to imitate the swirled hair pattern characteristic of pony or cow hair. The black color makes the hair swirl patterns less visible, and the knitted back creates a soft hand, compared to the very stiff hand of pony or cow.

Faux curly lamb
This fabric imitates curly lamb fur. Produced by using spiraling curled yarn that is then sheared, it seems like a better alternative than real curly lamb, which requires unborn or newborn lambs.

Facts and figures

Distinctive features

- Looks very similar to real fur, except with woven or knitted back side.
- Thick pile if medium-to-long length pile.
- Flexible and lightweight compared to real fur.

Strengths

- Variety of naps to imitate different furs.
- Consistent pattern of fur color and nap for easier cut and construction.
- Soft, flexible fabric for easier sewing than fur's hide.
- Easy to use as trim or full garments.

Weaknesses

- Cutting multiple garments requires skill in cutting through the thick pile.
- Very heat-sensitive, so pressing is extremely difficult.
- Usually bulky, so managing sewing is slow.
- Fur color and pattern must match.

Usual fiber content

- 100 percent mod-acrylic, acrylic.
- 100 percent polyester/mod-acrylic blends.
- Mod-acrylic/polyester/nylon/rayon blends.

DESIGN RESPONSIBLY

While the look of faux fur can be quite natural, it is important to remember that it is produced from oil-based fibers or other manufactured fibers that are not environmentally friendly. These fibers produce unhealthy emissions and chemical waste products in fiber production, and none of these fibers are recyclable.

Faux fur collar and jacket

This faux fur collar (above) and "beaver" jacket (right) imitate the real fur they're based on extremely well. It is sometimes difficult to distinguish genuine fur from faux fur.

Exotic faux fur

Because faux fur is produced in a textile mill, it is possible to embellish or extend the look found in natural fur and produce fantasy fur fabric. Designers have discovered that adding unusual colors to a natural-looking faux fur fabric has added a very creative fashion element to the design.

It is not uncommon to find shocking pink or green zebra or tiger faux fur. The results have launched a new genre of apparel for a distinctive fashion look. In faux fur, the term "exotic" doesn't refer to the scarcity of the fur, but instead to the colors and finishing techniques that are used to create a faux fur that could not exist in nature. Faux furs often do not copy nature but help to envision fantasy characters that require a little fur to complete the image.

Exotic furs can be the same type of faux fur categories as mentioned on page 256 for commonly used faux fur: plush, very short and medium pile, and extra-long pile. The key point of exotic faux fur is color and printed image.

This medium-length weft-pile knit faux fur is intended to imitate zebra pattern, but the pink and white colors do not exist in nature.

Facts and figures

Distinctive features
- Always a pile fabric that looks like fur.
- Color and printed image rarely if ever occur in the natural world.
- Soft and flexible.
- Easily available in a variety of piles and colors.

Strengths
- Knitted or woven back provides consistency for the design.
- Colors and printed patterns provide unique appearance, not found in nature.
- Yardage makes cutting and matching easy in production.
- Easy to use as trim as well as in full garments.

Weaknesses
- Fabric is bulky and difficult to cut and sew multiple layers.
- Special expertise is required for appropriate cutting and sewing deep-cut pile napped fabrics.
- Very heat-sensitive, so pressing is extremely difficult.

Usual fiber content
- 100 percent mod-acrylic, acrylic.
- 100 percent polyester/mod-acrylic blends.
- Mod-acrylic/polyester/nylon/rayon blends.

Spotted pattern fur
An exotic printed feline fur in natural colors. This deep-pile fake fur is beautifully soft.

Burgundy crushed surface plush
This tonal burgundy-colored faux fur, imitating mouton, is used for fashion jackets. The color is limited only by how the designer envisages the garment.

Exotic long-hair fur
This orange and black faux fur shows the long, black-tipped guard hairs, imitating fox fur. However, the color is clearly brighter than the natural fur, so the intention is to go beyond nature's colors.

**Purple and
black zebra
faux fur**
Fabulous deep
purple and black are
colors not usually
seen combined in
natural fur. Designers
can imagine nearly
any color they wish
in fake fur.

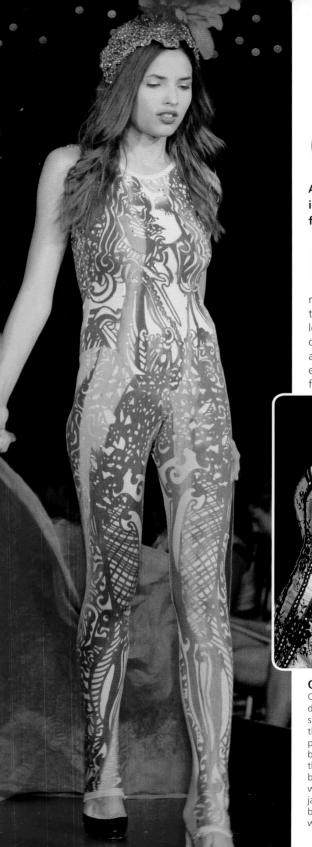

Compression

Achieving the perfect fit for the human form is one of the most important goals in apparel design. Compression describes how fabric helps a garment to fit the human form.

Until the development of elastic fiber and yarns, fit was achieved by elaborate seaming detail and sewing construction. A rigid fabric fits tightly against the body and does not expand or contract with body movement. Now manufactured elastic fibers, yarns, and fabrics have expanded the ability of the designer to create garments that fit the body very well, with less seaming and construction detail. The elastic surface sustains tension that draws the fabric close to the body, expanding and contracting, like breathing, as the body moves. Athletic garments fit the athlete by utilizing engineered elasticity to enhance athletic performance. The type of compression required for the design will determine the type of fabric selected.

The degree of elasticity will be determined by the type and amount of elastic yarns used.

Comfort stretch: 2–5 percent spandex fiber content will provide gentle compression and remain close to the body, expanding and contracting as the body moves. Top-weight and bottom-weight knitted and woven fabrics are commonly available in comfort stretch.

Power stretch: 14–20 percent spandex fiber content will provide "power stretch" for sustained compression that suppresses the body silhouette and supports muscles during athletic performance. Undergarments, athletic garments, and fashion garments intended to showcase the body silhouette all use power stretch fabrics.

Types of compression
The type of elasticity to achieve the desired compression and expansion will vary, depending on the type of fiber, yarn, and fabric selected. There are three types of compression:
- rigid fabrics compressing the body without elasticity.
- ribbed knitted fabrics that conform to the body because of the knitted construction.
- elastic yarns woven or knitted into fabrics that sustain fabric surface tension.

Compression fabrics
Compression fabrics are designed to follow the shape of the body, as in this printed bodysuit, produced from a spandex-blend knitted fabric. Or, they visually compress the body, as in this corset, which uses a strong jacquard weave, supported by extra reinforcement within the design.

With elastic fiber, yarn, and fabric innovations now available, it is important for the designer to stay updated on new elastic innovations and also to understand how to utilize them in design. Many athletic designs have crossed over into everyday consumer apparel, so it is especially important for new designers to stay informed as to how to design with these innovations in mind.

Caution regarding elasticity in fabrics

There are risks when selecting elastic fabrics for designs. First, heat exposure to elastic fabrics will diminish or eliminate the elasticity. Therefore, be sure the design will not be exposed to excessive heat during the production process or in the consumer's hands, as the elasticity will be damaged by heat. Second, comfort stretch fabrics will create a comfortable garment and will not compress the body. Over time, comfort stretch fabrics will exhibit diminished elasticity during the life of the garment. Third, spandex fiber content means the fabric cannot be recycled into new fiber. If a polyester/spandex blend is selected, note that this fiber blend fabric cannot be recycled into new fiber.

Power stretch
Professional dancers require dance costumes that will support their muscle extensions and contractions. Powerful stretch fabrics that allow for this movement are excellent choices for dancewear and activewear.

DESIGN RESPONSIBLY

There are innovations in elastic fibers that address environmental and dyeing issues. Spandex fiber uses oil-based raw materials and is not recyclable. All polyester fibers, though originally produced from petroleum products, are now recyclable into high-quality new fiber, and there are elastic fibers and yarns produced from polyester. These fibers and yarns are increasingly reliable for durable elasticity and can be more easily dyed than spandex fiber.

Compression

The corset-like structured bodice, right, uses a rigid fabric, embellished with black patent studs to compress the bodice and hip areas of the garment, in contrast to the fluid fabric of the skirt-piece. The fitted dress, far right, is also constructed from a rigid fabric, which fits firmly to the figure.

Compression with rigid fabrics

Compressing the body using a rigid fabric has been the traditional method of restricting body silhouette. Strong, bottom-weight, balanced plain weave fabrics have provided designers with the means to compress the body. Corsets, cummerbunds, and waistbands that were intended to reduce the size of the body achieved this goal, but often with great discomfort for the wearer.

The concept of corset design depends on nonelastic fabrics restricting the body to form into the shape of the corset.

Various elastic fabrics now fulfill most of the compression requirements of a design. However, some designers still find rigid bottom-weight fabrics to be their fabric of choice when creating a tight-fitting garment for two reasons:

- The fit does not expand—the fabric holds in the body like a girdle.
- The design silhouette remains as the designer's vision—the fabric will not change as the body moves.

Fit is one of the primary reasons that rigid fabrics are used. There are consumer markets that demand only rigid fabrics for a proper fit because they like the way a rigid fabric holds their body in. Elastic fabrics allow expansion and, for some consumers, expansion means that the body will become wider—an undesirable quality, regardless of wearing comfort. However, because there is no elasticity in the fabric, an extremely strong fabric is required, so most top-weight and medium-weight fabrics are not strong enough to withstand the constant pulling tension. Therefore, bottom-weight fabrics in plain weaves and twill weaves in cotton and cotton blends are the only fabrics that can withstand this tension. Wool fiber is too elastic, and manufactured fibers are uncomfortable next to the body.

Pant yoke
The rigid woven fabric in this pant yoke fits closely to the upper hip, and the stretchable jersey knit fabric below the piping provides a contrast. Combining a compression fabric with a drapey fabric is a common design tool for creating a silhouette.

Denim jeans
Rigid denim is often used to achieve a desired fit. Without elasticity, the wearer is confined to the fit of the jeans. Some designers only use rigid denim because their customers have a feeling of accomplishment if they can fit into their favorite jeans.

Silk jacquard for cummerbund
Originally a tight-fitting accessory, cummerbunds use elaborately woven jacquards, often silk fiber, to show off a man's waist. This medium-weight rigid silk jacquard fabric is still used in ladies' corsets and men's cummerbunds.

Facts and figures

Distinctive features

- Compression with rigid fabrics.
- Closely woven fabric that is strong against pulling.
- Little surface texture that will reduce strength.
- Always cotton or linen fiber content.

Strengths

- Easily available fabric at reasonable prices.
- Easy to cut and sew, using many seaming details.
- Absorbent fiber content.

Weaknesses

- If washed, the fabric can shrink, ruining the garment's tight fit.
- The fabric surface and seams can cause chafing discomfort on the skin.
- Can become bulky depending on the seaming.

Usual fiber content

- 100 percent cotton and cotton/polyester blends.
- 100 percent linen and linen blends.
- 100 percent silk.
- 100 percent polyester.

Corset

Compressing the body for a fixed silhouette is the goal when using rigid fabrics. The wearer's comfort is beside the point, and the envisaged silhouette is the designer's and the wearer's goal.

Ribbed knits

Elasticity

Ribbed knit fabrics are weft double-knit construction, using knit and purl stitches in regular alternating rows that produce cross-grain elasticity.

All ribbed knits produce raised rows of knit stitches and low rows of purl stitches called "ribs," hence the name "ribbed knits." There are many varieties of ribbed knits, all produced by different row patterns of knit and purl stitches. As with all knits, size and texture of yarn will determine the surface texture of the fabric, and the density of the fabric is determined by the closeness of the knitting stitches.

There are two ways to describe a ribbed knit fabric:

Counting rows: 2 x 2 ribbed knit is defined as two rows of knit stitches followed by two rows of purl stitches in a repeating

pattern. 3 x 1 ribbed knit is three rows of knit stitches followed by one row of purl stitches.

Naming fabric: Certain patterns of ribbed knits are recognized as a fabric. Some fabric names for different ribbed fabrics are "poor boy" or "shaker" knits.

Products that use ribbed knits take advantage of the elastic quality of the knit construction. Socks are a good example of how the elastic rib fabric will grip the leg to hold up the sock. Ribbed knits also are selected for a design that is close-fitting to the body. Dresses, pullover sweaters, cardigans, and accessories such as gloves, hats, and scarves, all use ribbed knits.

Ribbed knits come in many varieties, but all have the same characteristic elasticity. Designers use the elastic ribbed knit in both the body of the garment as well as the edges, for fit and to create the desired silhouette.

Shaker knit
The shaker knit uses a larger yarn size, often spun wool yarn, knitted in a compact 1 x 1 ribbed knit. The fabric has good thermal insulation and usually fits close to the body.

Fine-gauge knit
This soft ribbed knit uses 64 percent bamboo rayon and 36 percent PLA (corn fiber). The fabric is very drapey and not very resilient, so the design should use the ribbed texture for surface interest and not for elasticity in fit.

Metallic ribbed knit
This 2 x 1 ribbed knit (two knit wales and one purl wale on the face of the knit) includes metallic monofilament yarn and spun wool yarn. The tight knit and the natural elasticity of the wool yarn make this fabric fit close to the body.

Facts and figures

Distinctive features
- Always rows of knit stitches and purl stitches in repeating alternating pattern to create "ribs" of stitches that sit "high" and "low" in the knit fabric.
- Elastic characteristic: the more ribbing and texture, the more elasticity.

Strengths
- Easily available fabric at reasonable prices.
- Elastic characteristic is a design feature for a garment.
- Available in a wide variety of textures and prices.
- Easily produced.

Weaknesses
- Easily snagged.
- Requires special sewing machine to sew "stretchable" stitching lines.
- Sometimes bulky fabric because of the ribbed texture.

Usual fiber content
- Rayon fiber is often blended to add softness.
- 100 percent cotton and cotton blends.
- 100 percent wool and wool blends.
- 100 percent acrylic and acrylic blends.
- 100 percent polyester and polyester blends.

Sweater with ribbed sections
This sweater shows that a garment with ribbing can fit very closely to the body or have a more relaxed fit. Here, only the bottom portion of the sweater and the cuffs are ribbed, causing these parts of the garment to fit closely to the body and determine the silhouette.

Elastic ribbed knit banding

Ribbed knit banding is designed to finish the openings of a garment to keep them close to the body or to provide trim design detailing. The designer will often specify using ribbed knit trim at necklines, cuffs, and garment bottoms to keep them closed.

Because this trim has very good elasticity without using spandex, it can provide functional elasticity that doesn't diminish on exposure to heat.

Designers can specify to use the same color yarn as was used to produce the garment fabric to ensure exact color matching of trim and fabric. However, knit trim can also be contrasting in color. Knitted trim is produced two ways:

- Knit fabric is first produced in tubes and then cut into bands of fabric.
- Knit bands that are knitted into specific widths and lengths.

Medium-weight ribbed banding functions by fitting snugly to the body even though the body of the garment design does not

Knit band made in a specific length and width.

Ribbed knit fabric "tube" cut into narrow bands for collars, cuffs, waistbands, and edging.

Either method of producing knit trim is acceptable. The type of design and method of construction will determine which type of knit banding will be produced. Polo shirts specify separate knitted collars, so these are always knitted separately. Banding at necklines, sleeve cuffs, plackets, and shirt bottoms can be cut from fabric.

Fine-gauge T-shirt
The knitted trim on this T-shirt uses the same yarn as was used to create the T-shirt, so the trim matches. Note the way the folded knit trim expands at the seamline and contracts at the folded edge so the trims will remain flat against the body.

Ribbed knit collar and cuff
This polo shirt is designed with a ribbed knit collar trim and sleeve cuffs that match the shirt fabric. The ribbed knit construction allows the collar to roll easily and the cuffs to stretch and return to their original shape.

Ribbed knit sleeve
This 4 x 1 ribbed sleeve is from a jacket designed to have close-fitting sleeves and knit banding at the bottom of the jacket to keep it closed around the hips.

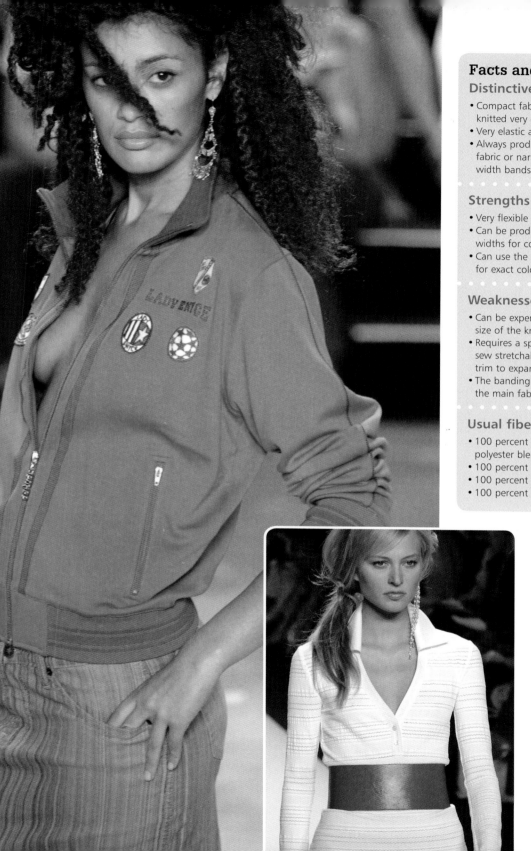

Facts and figures

Distinctive features

- Compact fabric, nearly always 1 x 1 rib knitted very compactly.
- Very elastic and stable fabric.
- Always produced in narrow width fabric or narrow, specific length and width bands.

Strengths

- Very flexible and elastic.
- Can be produced in specific lengths and widths for collars, cuffs, and plackets.
- Can use the same yarn as knitted fabric for exact color match.

Weaknesses

- Can be expensive because of the small size of the knit trim.
- Requires a special sewing machine to sew stretchable stitches to allow the trim to expand at the seams.
- The banding yarn color may not match the main fabric.

Usual fiber content

- 100 percent cotton or cotton/polyester blend.
- 100 percent wool or wool blend
- 100 percent acrylic or acrylic blend.
- 100 percent rayon or rayon blend.

Using ribbed knit banding in garments

The knit banding in both of these designs is used to finish edges of the garment, but in different ways. The blue jacket uses contrasting red and blue knit banding to add design detail at the bottom and sleeve cuffs, with a matching blue collar. The white top uses matching neck banding and a knit collar to complete the design.

Comfort stretch: top weights

Stretch fabrics in top weights have transformed how designers create their garments. The issue of a garment fitting the body is now simpler because the fabric can expand and contract as the body moves.

A small amount of spandex fiber has been combined with polyester in this athletic mesh warp knit. The knit construction keeps the fabric stretchable, and the spandex adds a little more elasticity for comfort.

Comfort stretch makes precise fitting problems less important, as the wearer is now familiar with and wants comfort stretch fabrics. Elastic yarns are now sophisticated in their construction, allowing for finer elastic yarns that do not feel like nonabsorbent manufactured fiber. Yarns now combine the absorbency comfort of a natural fiber with the functional characteristic of an elastic fiber.

Very lightweight fabrics can now be elastic, using high-twist mechanical elastic yarns or textured multifilament mechanical elastic yarns, or complex elastic yarns using spandex monofilament fiber combined with other fiber and yarns. Other lightweight fabrics can be elastic using bare, shiny, monofilament spandex yarn, knitted into the back side of a jersey that will not be noticeable to the wearer or to the eye.

Most top-weight fabrics are one-way (one grain line stretching only) stretch, usually cross-grain stretch. The elastic yarns are sometimes bulky compared to the nonelastic yarns also being used, so in top-weight fabrics, bulky yarns are mostly undesirable.

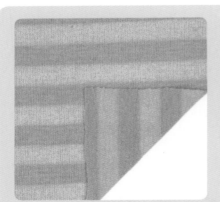

Cotton stretch jersey
Jersey is knitted while a bare elastic monofilament yarn is "laid in" on the back side of the jersey. This is a common way of adding elasticity to a jersey fabric. The elastic yarn is nearly invisible unless the fabric is stretched and the shine of the elastic yarn can be seen.

Stretch broadcloth
Lightweight broadcloth weave fabrics are often used for women's fashion blouses and tops. This yarn-dyed stripe fabric has 2 percent complex, spandex plied yarn in the weft direction, allowing for a slight elasticity. These woven top-weight fabrics are mostly weft-direction stretch only.

Rayon stretch jersey
This fashion weft-knit jersey is 96 percent rayon and 4 percent spandex. The rayon yarn is extremely soft and drapey, and the spandex yarn adds elasticity and wrinkle resistance. This is a yarn-dyed stripe pattern. The black color is a very deep black because rayon absorbs deep color dyes very well.

Facts and figures

Distinctive features

- Fabric has elastic stretch.
- Fabric weave remains easily recognized, although fabric is now elastic.
- Fabric expands and contracts with body movement.

Strengths

- Easily available fabric.
- Easily recognized by elasticity.
- Little change in cutting and sewing compared to rigid woven fabrics.

Weaknesses

- May be more expensive than the non-elastic fabric.
- Very heat-sensitive—elasticity may diminish.
- Fabric may expand during the cutting and sewing process, especially knits.
- Surface of fabric may change due to relaxation of the yarns after laundering.

Usual fiber content

- Cotton or cotton/polyester blend with spandex.
- Blended polyester, rayon, cotton, and spandex.
- Linen blend with spandex.
- Silk blended with spandex.

Stretch jersey knit top

This printed jersey top contains a small amount of spandex, enough for the shirt to hug tightly over the hip while avoiding the soft slouchy drape of a jersey without spandex.

Comfort stretch: casual woven fabrics

Casual comfort stretch woven fabrics are always cotton blend or fabrics that appear to be cotton-fiber blends. Elasticity is achieved by weaving complex elastic yarns into the fabric. These elastic yarns can be woven in the straight grain (called a warp stretch fabric), more commonly in the cross-grain (weft stretch fabric), or in both warp and weft.

How to describe a stretch fabric's ability to stretch:

One-way stretch: Elastic yarns are only in one grain line direction, so the fabric stretches on one grain line. Some textile mills call this fabric two-way stretch because the fabric expands and then contracts.

Two-way stretch: Elastic yarns are woven in both warp and weft directions, so the fabric stretches on both grain lines. Some textile mills call this fabric four-way stretch because the fabric expands and then contracts in both warp and weft.

Stretch cotton chino is a popular fab tailored summer jackets, pants, short skirts. There is only 2 percent spandex cotton fabric, which is enough for a elasticity while adding some w resistance to the

Original fabric shape

One-way stretch   Two-way stretch

Fiber content will always be majority cotton fiber or imitating cotton fiber for a casual hand, and the elastic yarns will hide the shiny, elastic, monofilament spandex fiber or the textured multifilament yarn will not reflect th light. Avoidance of high heat in pressing, garment wash and consumer care are extremely important to preserve t elasticity of the fabric.

Stretch poplin
The elastic yarn is unnoticeable in this weft stretch poplin, and only when the fabric is pulled in the weft direction is the stretch noticeable. The fabric will feel slightly heavier and less drapey than the same rigid fabric. Fiber content is 96 percent cotton and 4 percent spandex.

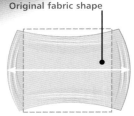

Stretch sateen
This sateen retains its surface luster, although it now contains elastic yarns in the weft direction. Fiber content is 97 percent cotton and 3 percent spandex.

Thick and thin stretch corduroy
This cut-pile weave can also be produced as a comfort stretch fabric. The napped surface remains unchanged, and the spandex yarns are in the base cloth, not the nap. Fiber content is 97 percent cotton and 3 percent spandex.

Facts and figures

Distinctive features
- Usual cotton hand with elasticity.
- The fabric weave remains easily recognized, although the fabric is now elastic.
- The fabric expands and contracts with body movement.

Strengths
- Casual fabric remains absorbent for cooling effect.
- Easily recognized by elasticity.
- Cutting and sewing production remains nearly the same as rigid fabric.

Weaknesses
- Fabric may expand during cutting process.
- Fabric surface texture may change after laundering, especially after garment washing.
- May be more expensive than rigid fabric.
- Very heat-sensitive—elasticity may diminish.

Usual fiber content
- Cotton fiber produced with spandex monofilament fiber.
- Any cotton yarn combined with multifilament, textured, elastic polyester yarn.

Stretch pants
Notice how the fabric stretches over the hip and upper thigh. This smooth appearance is characteristic of a comfort stretch fabric. The silhouette of the pant leg can easily be supported by the slightly elastic fabric.

Comfort stretch: stretch denim

Denim, one of the most popular fabrics used in apparel, is even more popular since elasticity has been added to it. Traditionally a workwear fabric and a favorite for its durability, adding elastic yarn to denim has increased its appeal to a more fashion-based customer.

Stretch denim is now a favorite fabric for jeans because the elasticity allows the wearer to move more comfortably than in rigid denim, yet the jeans still fit closely to the body. An undesirable baggy fit is rarely a problem in jeans for the designer. Almost all denim is a one-way stretch, usually cross-grain in direction.

However, stretch denim has a different hand than rigid denim. The elasticity causes the fabric to "relax," so the surface may have a slightly "bumpy" textured surface compared to rigid denim,

which is very smooth. Some designers dislike this texture, complaining that it makes the wearer feel "fat." However the snug fit of elastic stretch denim nearly always guarantees a satisfied customer. Most prefer a fit that expands with the wearer, and a little bumpy surface texture is a small issue compared to wearing jeans that feel comfortable and yet seem to stay close to the body.

Enlargement

Most comfort-stretch denim fabrics rema. indistinguishable from non-stretch denim This stretch denim fabric, though not ye wash-finished, also has the stiff resin applie for a stiff, yet slightly elastic han

Ring-spun stretch denim
Retro ring-spun denim, produced with elastic yarns in the cross grain, provides more widely accepted denim jeans. The fit in stretch denim is less complicated than in rigid denim jeans. Fiber content is 98 percent cotton and 2 percent spandex.

Lighter-weight denim jeans
Denim jeans can also be produced in lighter-weight fabric, and adding elastic yarn makes them feel heavier than they actually are. Elastic yarns add bulk to the fabric. Fiber content is 98 percent cotton and 2 percent spandex.

Lighter color denim jeans
The stretch in stretch denim can be diminished if the fabric is washed at very hot temperatures for a long time, as is the case with light-blue garment washed jeans. Light blue color denim usually doesn't use spandex blends because of the risk of losing elasticity after the garment washing process.

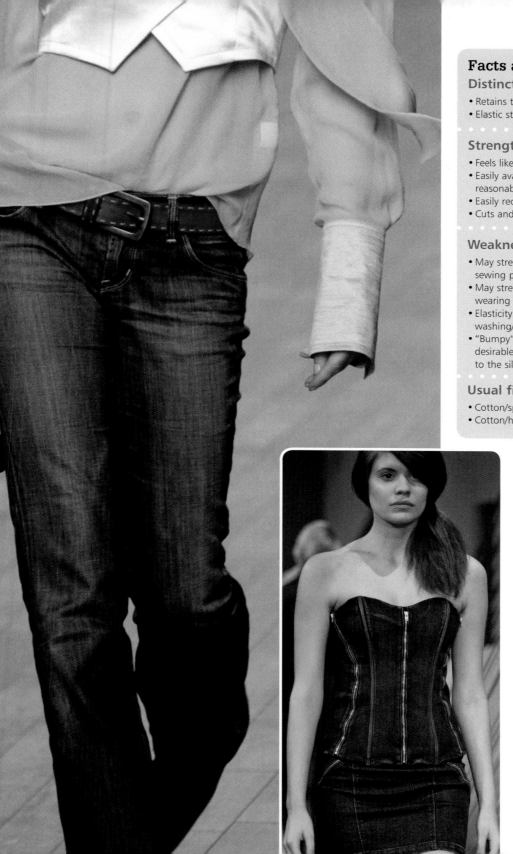

Facts and figures

Distinctive features
- Retains the look and hand of denim.
- Elastic stretch.

Strengths
- Feels like denim.
- Easily available fabric at reasonable prices.
- Easily recognized as denim.
- Cuts and sews the same as rigid denim.

Weaknesses
- May stretch during the cutting/sewing process.
- May stretch out of shape during the wearing process.
- Elasticity may diminish during garment washing/drying or consumer care.
- "Bumpy" surface texture not desirable and sometimes adds bulk to the silhouette.

Usual fiber content
- Cotton/spandex blend.
- Cotton/hemp/spandex blend.

Stretch denim
Stretch denim jeans don't look much different than rigid denim jeans. In this photo, it is possible to recognize stretch denim by the way the wearer can easily move in ways not possible in rigid denim. The way the jeans fit the body looks more elastic compared to rigid denim that will usually have a less snug fit. Stretch denim fabric was selected for the corset and skirt. It is not recommended to use non-stretch denim for corsets because of their very tight fit.

Comfort stretch: stretch suiting

This striped dobby weave is a polyester, rayon, and 2 percent spandex blend, for a comfort stretch in the weft direction only (one-way stretch). The elasticity will not inhibit the tailored construction in a suit.

Elastic fabrics used in suiting have introduced comfort to career and dressy apparel. Adding elastic yarn to traditional suiting fabrics has transformed the suit into a comfortable garment that is more resilient than the rigid fabric, allows the wearer to move more easily, and has less damage to the fabric because of its elastic quality.

The elastic yarns can be placed in both warp and weft directions to create a one- or two-way stretch fabric. Menswear suiting has adopted stretch wool-blend fiber fabrics, creating a new category of suits for the office. Stretch serge, gabardine, and flannel are now available. In women's wear, fabrics for suiting are more diverse, including momie crêpes, satin crêpes, medium-weight double georgette, and dobby weaves, in addition to the more traditional menswear suiting fabrics already described here.

Elastic yarns added to suiting fabrics sometimes add bulk to the fabric, but usually finer yarns are available to balance the use of sometimes bulky, complex, elastic yarns. Lining fabrics, often used in the jackets and skirts of suiting, must consider the elastic behavior of the shell fabric. Therefore, stretch lining fabrics have been developed for use in stretch suits. If stretch lining is not available, extra "ease" must be added into the lining to prevent lining fabrics from tearing as the suiting fabric stretches.

Stretch wool gabardine
Menswear wool gabardine with elastic stretch yarns added provides resilient suits for the workplace that are more comfortable to wear than traditional worsted wool suits. Face and back are the same.

Dobby weave suiting
This interesting novelty weave suiting fabric has stretch for a good fit and resiliency. The twill-weave back side uses absorbent rayon yarns, whereas the plain-weave face uses nylon yarns. There is 6 percent spandex fiber, because this is a two-way stretch fabric (see page 272).

Stretch tropical suiting
Lightweight tropical, used in worsted wool and polyester/rayon blends, is used for suits for hot weather. Adding 2 percent elastic yarns in the weft direction only will add resilience to a suit which, in hot weather clothing, is not always possible.

Facts and figures

Distinctive features
- Elastic fabric that retains the original look of the rigid suiting fabric.
- Easily available in a wide variety of fiber content and fabrics.
- Very resilient.

Strengths
- Easily cut and sewn fabric.
- Resilient, especially for non-resilient fiber content.
- Less drapey hand than original rigid suiting due to elastic yarn.

Weaknesses
- Non-stretch lining fabric may tear or pull out of seams if not properly sewn.
- Fabric may expand during cutting and stretch during sewing.
- Stitching in seams may break due to fabric stretch. Use chain stitches that will stretch with the fabric.

Usual fiber content
- Cotton/spandex or cotton/polyester/spandex blend.
- Polyester/rayon/spandex blend.
- Wool/spandex blend.

Women's suit using stretch fabric
The slim, sculptured look of this suit was achieved by selecting a smooth surface fabric with a comfort spandex yarn in the weft direction. The spandex adds a crispness to the fabric hand when used in a tailored design as shown here.

Comfort stretch: double knits

Double knits, which can be produced in a wide variety of fabrics and garments, have given knit designers a more consistent fabric quality that sustains the garment silhouette.

Because of the knit construction—stitches looped together—the garment could be stretched out of shape when being worn. The addition of elastic yarn into the fabric, almost always laid in on the back side of the double knit, has created more stable garment shapes. Consumers now expect their sweaters and other knit garments to retain the same silhouette as when they were purchased. Adding spandex to double-knit fabrics has increased customer satisfaction with knitted fabrics and encouraged designers to select more knitted fabrics for their apparel.

Double-knit fabrics of all types can be enhanced by adding elastic yarns. Medium-weight double knits are most commonly used, as bottom-weight double knits may be too heavy for the use of bare elastic yarns. Highly textured yarns used in sweater knits often benefit from adding elastic yarns to help retain shape. Bulky, complex yarns often stretch out of shape when worn, so the addition of elastic keeps the sweater's texture in place during and after it has been worn.

Elastic fleece knit

This fleece fabric is elastic and can be used for close-fitting designs. Fleece fabrics are usually bulky and loose fitting, but the addition of spandex changes its character. Fiber content is 97 percent polyester and 3 percent spandex.

Elastic ribbed knit trim

The ribbed collar and side panels on this fleece top, whose function is to keep the garment openings close around the body, work better when elastic yarn is added. The ribbed trim fiber content is 97 percent polyester and 3 percent spandex.

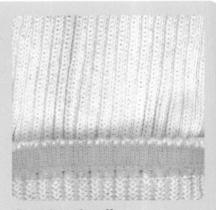

Stretch sock cuff

This sock cuff has laid-in bare elastic yarn on the back side to help keep the sock from slipping down when worn. The spandex yarn in the top of the cuff gently grips the ankle. Fiber content is 98 percent cotton and 2 percent spandex.

Facts and figures

Distinctive features

- The knitted surface remains unchanged with the addition of elastic yarns.
- The fabric retains its original shape during and after wearing.

Strengths

- Easily available fabric.
- Wide range of available elastic, double-knit fabrics.
- Elastic-yarn knit fabric retains shapes more easily.

Weaknesses

- Elastic yarn can be easily broken or damaged by heat and abrasion.
- Fabric often expands when cutting.
- Fabric often stretches when sewing.

Usual fiber content

- Any fiber content can be used.
- Always uses bare elastic spandex yarn laid in on the back of the knitted fabric.
- Alternatively, uses complex elastic yarns to knit the fabric.

Comfort stretch dress and sweater

This medium-weight, comfort stretch, double-knit dress (left) has enough weight to support the white trim on the front and the edging on the skirt. The elasticity of the medium-weight knit fabric fits the body well and adds weight to the silhouette. Adding a little elasticity to the medium-weight sweater weft knit (inset) gives additional resilience and life to the design to "remember" the garment silhouette.

Power stretch: athletic knits

Power-stretch fabrics are always knitted and are usually warp tricot knit fabrics. Tricot knits do not stretch very much in the straight-grain direction, which makes the tricot fabric an ideal fabric for adding high spandex yarns.

Power-stretch fabrics are commonly used in swimwear, which requires powerful compression fabric to retain its elasticity while in the water. Nonabsorbent nylon and polyester are nearly always used for swimwear, combined with 12–14 percent spandex.

Because of the straight-grain stability, the high degree of stretch from the spandex yarns can retain the shape of the garment, especially when the fabric is wet. Swimwear is one of the popular uses of power-stretch tricot knit because the straight-grain direction is more likely to stay in place when the swimsuit fabric becomes heavy with water.

The high content of spandex fiber compresses the fabric against the body, easily conforming to its shape. Seaming details are unnecessary for the fit of the garment. Instead, seams outline the body silhouette, enhanced by interlinings and padding where indicated.

Nonabsorbent fiber is usually selected. Moisture-laden fabric tends to become heavy and uncomfortable, chafing the skin. Wicking polyester fiber may be used for athletic apparel that is not swimwear. For added comfort in compression garments, strategically placed removable soft padding is added.

Fabric for cycling shorts
The power stretch of these pants is the result of at least 14 percent laid-in bare elastic yarn in the back side of the tricot knit. The wicking polyester microfiber is used to keep the athlete dry during competition. Fiber content is 86 percent polyester microfiber and 14 percent spandex.

Fabric for speed-skating
This fabric has a polypropylene/spandex warp-knit backing, bonded to a nonporous film membrane face for minimum wind resistance. The fabric expands on the body as it warms. The high spandex content of the backing fabric and the resilience of the membrane face provide powerful muscle support during the skater's activity.

Seamless pantyhose
These pantyhose are produced using special weft knitting equipment that creates hosiery without seams. The power-stretch yarns provide extreme elasticity and compress the leg to avoid slack in the pantyhose as they are worn. Fiber content is 85 percent nylon and 15 percent spandex.

Facts and figures

Distinctive features

- Smooth, multifilament surface.
- Sometimes lustrous, depending on the type of yarn.
- Fabric possesses extreme expansion and recovery, always compressing the body.

Strengths

- Easily available fabric.
- Provides compression without fabric weight.
- Fits the body with few seams.

Weaknesses

- Cutting fabric requires special handling to avoid expansion during cutting.
- Requires special sewing equipment to allow seams to expand and contract with the garment.
- Expensive compared to comfort stretch fabrics.
- Very heat-sensitive and not abrasion-resistant.

Usual fiber content

- Polyester/spandex blend; at least 18 percent spandex or more.
- Polyester/nylon spandex blend; at least 18 percent spandex or more.

Speed-skating racing fabric
The designer must first consider the athlete's performance when designing a garment with power stretch. One of the key points about power stretch is to allow the muscles to expand, and to support the muscles as they contract to avoid injury.

Power stretch: underwear knits

Underwear knits provide a smooth layer that protects the body from outer garments. Before the invention of spandex fiber, knitted undergarments relied on elastic waistbands to help the knit retain its shape next to the body. Today, fine spandex yarns create fabrics that have extreme expansion capability and compress the body.

Usually 14–20 percent spandex fiber content is enough to provide the necessary compression to restrict the body yet allow comfort during movement. Bodysuits and girdles (rarely used today) contain this amount of spandex because they are intended to compress large areas of the body. These garments are usually two layers of elastic knit fabric, with the inside layer more elastic than the outside layer to prevent the inner layer from wrinkling under the outer layer. Other, less restrictive undergarments may contain 12–14 percent spandex fiber for shape retention but provide a smooth fabric surface over the body. Some undergarments will use a combination of rigid fabrics for compression and power-stretch fabrics to allow the body to move more easily.

Spandex fiber content is intended to keep underwear garments as minimal as possible. However, some designers use white color for garments rather than skin-tone color. By matching skin tone, undergarments are less noticeable showing through outer garments.

Because its function is to compress the body without adding bulk, underwear power stretch is often lightweight or sheer. This fabric is a type of mesh knit containing 15 percent or more spandex.

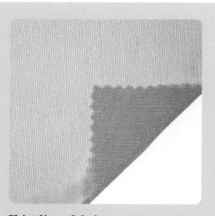

Bodysuit fabric
This bodysuit tricot fabric containing recycled PET polyester and spandex will compress the body silhouette. The polyester used in the fabric has been recycled from plastic bottles. Fiber content is 84 percent recycled polyester PET and 16 percent spandex.

Skirt liner fabric
Skirts require extra smoothing of the body, and tube-shaped skirt liners will compress the hips and thighs in an elastic "slip" garment. Fabric fiber content is 84 percent polyester and 16 percent spandex.

Sports bra fabric
Sports bra fabrics require comfort, absorbency, and compression. Women in athletics need specific fabrics to accommodate the female anatomy in competitive sports. Fiber content is 55 percent cotton, 33 percent polyester, and 12 percent spandex.

Facts and figures

Distinctive features

- Smooth, closely knit fabric surface.
- Somewhat lustrous surface, depending on the type of yarn used.
- Extreme elasticity and fast recovery.
- Elasticity compresses the body.

Strengths

- Smooth, comfortable fabric surface next to the body.
- Often wicking polyester fiber moves body moisture to the surface.
- Easy to sew with proper sewing equipment.

Weaknesses

- Requires specialized sewing equipment to allow sewn seams to stretch with the fabric.
- Fabric sometimes stretches when sewn.
- Fabric snags or damages easily when putting on such restrictive garments.

Usual fiber content

Usual fiber content (always using spandex content as noted above):

- Cotton/spandex blends.
- Wicking microfiber polyester/ spandex blends.
- Nylon/polyester/spandex blends.

Dress and tights

This dress and tights demonstrates the body-hugging function of power-stretch fabrics. This designer combined fabrics normally considered underwear fabrics for this body-shaped silhouette.

Power stretch: elastic power mesh

Power mesh is a raschel knit fabric produced to create breathable comfort while providing powerful elasticity and compression. Invented to accommodate underwear that requires the garment to retain shape and stay in place on the body, power mesh provides an important solution for specialized undergarments and body-conforming fashion designs.

This raschel knit is a type of mesh that is used in small amounts to add focused compression to part of an undergarment, or a garment design that requires compression in certain areas. This fabric is quite stiff and heavy and should be used sparingly.

Power mesh can be used in small pattern pieces to draw in the silhouette of the design. It is used in panels in combination with other fabrics to create the desired silhouette. Spandex fiber content is usually 18–25 percent. The raschel warp-knit process allows multifilament microfiber polyester or nylon yarns to be knitted with the spandex yarns for very lightweight and breathable fabric while compressing the body. Because spandex is often difficult to dye, power mesh is available in neutral colors, such as white, beige, and black.

Power mesh inserts
This athletic pants design uses power mesh as a design element as well as a functional element. The narrow stripes of power mesh not only allow air to circulate but also add strong elasticity to the pants.

Corset using power mesh fabric
Corsets and bustiers using only rigid woven fabrics are uncomfortable to wear. Adding power mesh inserts to the bodice will allow expansion for a more comfortable fit.

Men's travel briefs
This power mesh brief is designed for quick, dry laundering when traveling. The open mesh fabric is cool for hot climates and the fit is less restrictive due to the function of the garment.

Facts and figures

Distinctive features

- Netting appearance for airflow.
- Very elastic and constrictive.
- Crisp hand.

Strengths

- Comfortable fabric because of open netting construction.
- Easily recognized.
- Elastic compression but very lightweight.
- Simple to cut.

Weaknesses

- Requires specialized sewing equipment to stabilize seams and prevent seams from pulling apart.
- Very expensive fabric.
- May expand during sewing process.

Usual fiber content

- Multifilament polyester microfiber/ spandex blends.
- Multifilament nylon/polyester/ spandex blends.

DESIGN RESPONSIBLY

At this time, only spandex fiber is used for such powerful elastic fabrics. However, spandex, an oil-based fiber, is not recyclable. It is recommended to keep searching for polyester-based elastic fiber that will be recyclable into new elastic fiber.

Corset

This corset uses power mesh between the boning inserts to compress the design to the body. Lace appliqués, which must also be elastic, are sewn over the corset shell.

Power stretch: narrow elastic bands

There are three types of narrow elastic, produced for edgings, waistbands, and leg or arm openings. Their purpose is to provide elastic expansion and compression in focused locations on the garment.

This elastic waistband yardage can [be] produced as flat yardage or with drawstring already knitted into the ban[d]

Braided elastic is produced in sizes ranging from 1/8 in to 2 in (3 mm to 25 mm), and is used in waistline, neckline, leg, and sleeve casings. It often uses polyester yarns combined with rubber or spandex; if the sewing needle pierces the rubber yarn, the elasticity is diminished. Round elastic cording and piping are also produced by braided construction. Braided elastic narrows when stretched.

Knit elastic is produced for a wide variety of uses and is designed for specific products such as gloves, socks, face-mask straps, waistbands, and suspenders. Weight, thickness, and tension are adapted for products that have a specific function.

Woven elastic is identified by the windowpane effect of right-angle yarns interlacing together. It is available in a wide variety of widths and patterns. Woven elastic bands keep waistbands flat instead of "rolling" over. When stretched, woven elastic does not narrow. Cotton yarns are often used with spandex and polyester to create a comfortable waistband. Suspenders are commonly produced from woven elastic. This type of narrow elastic is the most expensive of the three methods of production.

Elastic thread for shirring
Elastic thread is usually produced by braiding around rubber yarn. The encased rubber yarn will stretch easily, and the braided polyester thread around it will expand and contract as the rubber yarn expands and contracts. Elastic thread is used for shirring.

Mesh elastic banding
Mesh elastic bands are used in lighter-weight fabrics. They are intended to "roll" less than knitted elastic bands. Though more lightweight than knitted elastic bands, they are stiffer and so are sometimes preferred for waistbands to keep elastic bands from folding over.

Ruffle-edge knitted elastic bands
Sometimes knitted elastics are designed with fancy edging, like this ruffle-edged elastic ribbon. Ladies' underwear is the most popular category for this type of elastic. Another type of "ribbon" elastic will include a "terry" side, which helps cushion and grip the skin, especially when used for straps.

Facts and figures

Distinctive features
- Produced on a narrow machine for narrow yardage with finished edges.
- Compressed elastic stretch with excellent recovery.
- Narrow fabrics are finished with very crisp hand.

Strengths
- Easily available narrow elastic yardage at reasonable prices.
- Can be easily sewn into garment.
- Can be easily cut and sewn into garment casing.

Weaknesses
- Stitching needle can diminish elasticity of rubber yarn.
- Elasticity is diminished by excessive exposure to heat.
- Knitted elastic can easily fold over (roll) in waistband casings.
- All but woven elastic narrows in width when stretched.

Usual fiber content
- Cotton/polyester/spandex or rubber blend.
- Polyester/spandex or rubber blend.

Woven elastic suspenders
Woven elastic suspenders maintain their width when stretched. Suspenders are usually elastic bands that can expand and contract as the design requires. In addition, they can become a design element, using color and hardware to accessorize the garment. Jacquard designs are frequently woven into the fabric.

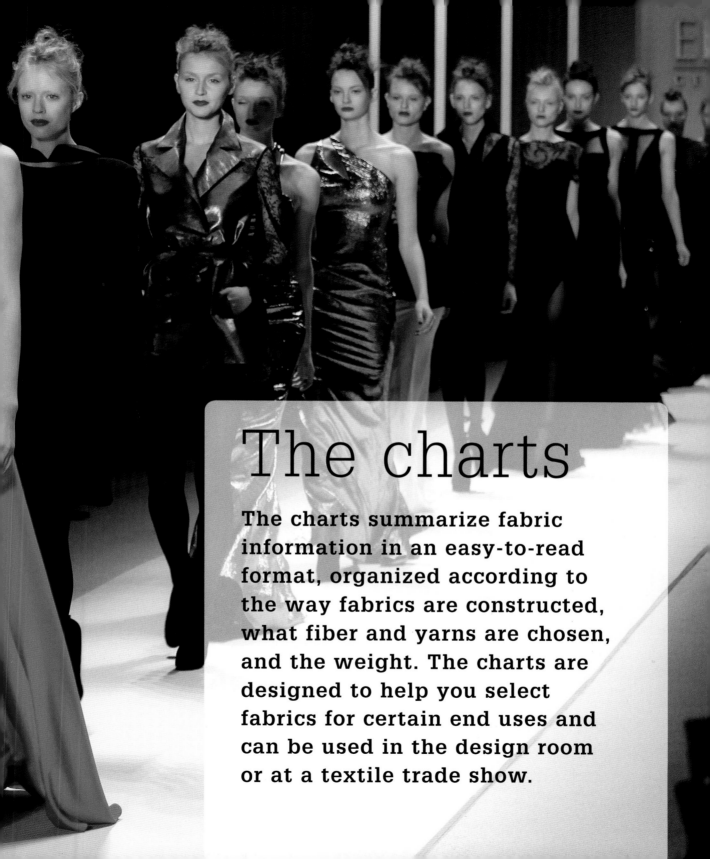

The charts

The charts summarize fabric information in an easy-to-read format, organized according to the way fabrics are constructed, what fiber and yarns are chosen, and the weight. The charts are designed to help you select fabrics for certain end uses and can be used in the design room or at a textile trade show.

Introduction to the charts

The purpose of these charts is to summarize fabric information in the way that textile mills produce fabric. By organizing the information according to the way fabrics are constructed, what fiber and yarns are chosen, and the weight of the fabric, designers can go to specific mills that produce certain types of fabrics.

Mills are specialists in weaving or knitting, using specific fibers and yarns. Machinery is adapted to the fiber/yarn characteristics to efficiently produce the fabrics that the designer has selected. The charts are organized according to the following fabric construction methods:

- **Weaving**
- **Knitting**
- **Massing fiber (non-woven)**
- **Lace making**

Knitting fabrics is governed by the type of yarn used and the tightness of the stitch. Nearly half of all fabrics used today are knit construction, yet the weaving process is more complex in terms of fabric names and type of construction. That is why the charts for weaving contain more information than the knitting ones. The amount of information is not related to the importance of the textile. The fabric names listed in the charts are color-coded to match the five sections of this directory:

Pages 52–131	Structure
Pages 132–191	Fluidity
Pages 192–223	Ornamentation
Pages 224–259	Expansion
Pages 260–287	Compression

Where a fabric is listed in the charts, a page reference number, directing you to where the fabric appears in the textile directory is also included, so you can move easily between the chart and the visual information.

These charts also guide the designer to select fabrics that are traditionally used for certain products or end uses. Designers frequently challenge the way fabrics are used in their designs, so the end uses listed in these charts are guidelines only. The charts can be very helpful in the design room or at a textile trade show. Consider how you can use this information easily and quickly to select fabrics and communicate with suppliers.

Balanced plain weave (square weave)

Weave name	Usual fibers used	Usual yarns used	Fabric names	Usual fabric weight
Balanced plain weave	Cotton staple	Simple spun	Lawn (p.56) Batiste (p.56)	Top weight
			Organdy (p.231)	Top weight
			Madras (p.62)	Top weight
			Gingham (pp.62–63) Chambray (p.57) Calico (p.57)	Top weight
			Muslin (p.81) Sheeting (p.80)	Top or bottom weight
			Flannelette (p.77)	Medium weight
			Crinoline (p.232) Buckram (p.233)	Heavyweight
	Cotton, wool, or rayon staple		Homespun (p.84)	Medium weight
	Cotton staple	High-twist	Voile (p.138) Gauze (p.139)	Top weight
	Flax staple	Simple spun slub yarn	Linen/Crash (p.78)	Top or bottom weight
	Wool rayon staple	Simple spun	Challis (p.148)	Top to medium weight
	Wool staple	Simple spun	Flannel (p.76)	Bottom weight
	Polyester/rayon filament or silk filament	Multifilament	Lining (pp.140–141)	Top weight
			Chiffon (p.136)	Top weight
			China silk (p.140)	Top weight
		Micro-multifilament	High-density fabrics (pp.58–59)	Top or medium weight
		Textured high-twist	Georgette (p.137)	Top weight

Cotton lawn

Printed chiffon

Printed challis

Note: Elastic fabrics using complex elastic yarns can be produced in nearly all woven/knitted fabrics. Check with your fabric supplier.
Note: Faux suede can be produced in woven/knitted/massed-fiber fabrics.

Advantages	Disadvantages	Usual finishing	End use	Chapter
• Sheer/drapable	• Weak fabric—pulls apart at seams • Shrinks easily	• Softener	Tops, dresses	
• Sheer/crisp hand	• Wrinkles easily • Uncomfortable	• Light resin	Blouses	
• Plaids	• Shrinks easily	• Softener	Shirts, blouses, shorts	
• Inexpensive • Easily available • Tailors well	• Colors can bleed • Shrinks easily	• All: preshrunk, softener	Shirts, dresses, skirts	
• Tailors well	• Shrinks easily	• Light resin	Design, pants, skirts, dresses, tops, jackets	
• Tailors well	• Shrinks easily	• Brushed	Sleepwear, babywear	
• Holds shapes well	• Water may ruin stiff finish	• Heavy resin	Millinery, design details, hemlines	
• Holds shapes well • Tailors well	• Unrefined appearance • Lightweights less abrasion resistant	• Fulling/preshrunk	Jackets, blazers, suits	
• Excellent drape • Sheer/soft hand	• Poor tailoring • Weak fabric—pulls apart at seams • Shrinks easily	• Softener	Tops, dresses, skirts	
• Crisp hand • Tailors well • Excellent texture	• Wrinkles easily • Seams wear out	• Beetling	Shirts, blouses, jackets, pants, skirts, suits	
• Drapes/tailors well	• Ray wrinkles easily • Seams may pull apart	• Fulling/preshrunk	Tops, skirts, dresses	
• Tailors well • Soft hand	• May pill • Somewhat bulky	• Fulling/preshrunk	Suits, jackets, dresses, slacks	
• Smooth, lustrous	• Pulls apart at seams	• Preshrunk	Inside linings	
• Sheer, drapable	• Pulls apart at seams	• Softener	Blouses, dresses	
• Smooth, lustrous	• Pulls apart at seams	• Sizing	Linings, tops, dresses	
• Smooth, drapable • Water-resistant	• Expensive, static buildup	• Water-resistant finish	Outerwear, outdoor clothing	
• Sheer, drapable • Resilient	• Shrinks when wet, if rayon	• Softener, if needed	Blouses, dresses	

Unbalanced plain weave (ribbed or unbalanced plain weave)

Weave name	Usual fibers used	Usual yarns used	Fabric names	Usual fabric weight
Unbalanced plain weave	Cotton, rayon, or polyester staple and silk, rayon, or polyester filament	Spun or multifilament	Broadcloth (p.60)	Top weight
		Spun or multifilament	Poplin (p.61)	Top to medium weight
	Silk, polyester, or nylon filament	Multifilament	Taffeta (pp.70–71)	Medium weight
		Plied multifilament	Faille/Bengaline (p.72)	Medium weight
		Plied spun or multifilament	Ottoman (p.95)	Bottom weight
	Silk, polyester, or rayon filament	High-twist multifilament	Crêpe de Chine (p.144–145)	Top weight
	Silk filament	Irregular multifilament	Dupioni (p.73)	Top to medium weight
		Slubbed yarn multifilament	Shantung (p.73)	Top to medium weight

Nylon/cotton poplin

Cotton broadcloth

Ottoman

Reversible crêpe de Chine

Advantages	Disadvantages	Usual finishing	End use	Chapter
• Crisp hand • Tailors well • Fine ribbed texture	• Easily confused with less expensive square weaves • Wrinkles easily	• Softener or resin for crispness	Tailored shirts/dresses	●
• Crisp hand • Tailors well • Fine ribbed texture	• Wrinkles easily • Ribbed surface subject to abrasion	• Softener or resin for crispness • Water-resistant finish if needed	Tops, skirts, casual pants, jackets, dresses, outdoor apparel	●
• Ribbed texture • Lustrous • Crisp hand	• Fabric makes noise • Wrinkles easily	• Water-resistant finish if needed	Evening dresses, suits	●
• Pronounced rib surface • Tailors well • Holds shape well	• Ribs may require matching • Wrinkles easily	• Softener	Suits, dresses, dressy pants, jackets	●
• Tailors well • Very pronounced ribbed surface	• Wrinkles easily • Fair abrasion resistance	• Water-resistant finish if needed	Furniture, coats, suits	●
• Excellent drape • Lustrous • Doesn't slip	• Poor tailoring • Moves easily in sewing	• Softener	Shirts, blouses, dresses	●
• Textured, lustrous • Tailors well	• Doesn't drape well • Poor durability	• Sizing	Blouses, tops, dresses, skirts	●
• Textured, lustrous • Tailors well	• Doesn't drape well • Poor durability	• Sizing	Tops, dresses, skirts, jackets	●

Striped taffeta

Multicolored shantung

Crêpe de Chine

Textured weave (dobby weave)

Weave name	Usual fibers used	Usual yarns used	Fabric names	Usual fabric weight
Textured weave	Cotton, flax, polyester, or rayon staple	Simple spun	Leno (pp.68–69)	Top weight
	Cotton, nylon, or polyester staple	Simple spun	Ripstop (p.94)	Top to medium weight
	Nylon or polyester filament	Multifilament		
	Rayon, polyester, or nylon filament	Crêpe twist multifilament	Momie crêpe (p.176)	Top to medium weight
	Cotton staple rayon, polyester, silk	High-twist spun and high-twist multifilament	Crepeon (pp.146–147)	Top to medium weight

Cotton ripstop

Jacquard weave

Weave name	Usual fibers used	Usual yarns used	Fabric names	Usual fabric weight
Jacquard (pile weave/ looped pile)	Silk, polyester, or rayon acetate filament	Multifilament and high-twist multifilament	Brocade (pp.100–101)	Top to medium weight
	Any staple or filament fiber	Spun or multifilament	Tapestry Damask (pp.100–101)	Medium or bottom weight

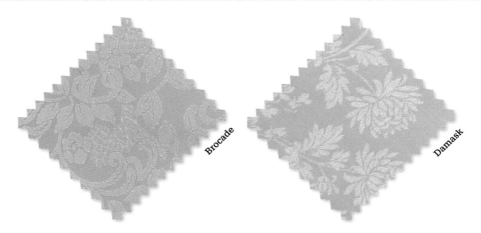

Brocade

Damask

Advantages	Disadvantages	Usual finishing	End use	Chapter
• Woven lacy appearance	• Expensive	• Softener	Shirts, tops, dresses	●
• Square box texture • Very abrasion-resistant • Very strong	• Texture limits design • Fabrics tend to have a stiff hand	• Water-resistant finish if needed • Cire if polyester	Outdoor products, jackets, pants, shorts	●
• Even-textured surface • Texture variety	• Snags easily • May shrink	• Softener	Suiting, jackets, blouses	●
• Textured surface • Resilient • Good drape	• May shrink • Difficult to press seams	• Softener	Tops, skirts, dresses	●

Advantages	Disadvantages	Usual finishing	End use	Chapter
• Beautiful woven-in designs	• Limited supply	• Softener	Blouses, dresses, lingerie	●
• Beautiful woven-in designs	• Expensive • Limited supply	• Softener • Stain-resistant	Furniture, drapes, tabletop accessories, shoes	●

Tapestry

Pile weave

Weave name	Usual fibers used	Usual yarns used	Fabric names	Usual fabric weight
Looped pile	Cotton, bamboo rayon, hemp, or polyester staple	Simple spun	Terry cloth (pp.246–247)	Medium to bottom weight
Cut/sheared pile	Cotton, rayon, polyester staple	Simple spun	Corduroy (pp.104–5) Velveteen (p.102–3) Velour (pp.184–185)	Medium to bottom weight
	Modacrylic, acrylic, nylon, rayon, polyester filament and staple	Variable	Faux fur (pp.256–259)	Medium to bottom weight
	Silk, rayon, nylon, polyester filament	Multifilament	Velvet (pp.186–187)	Bottom weight

Basketweave: balanced or unbalanced

Weave name	Usual fibers used	Usual yarns used	Fabric names	Usual fabric weight
Basketweave (can be balanced or unbalanced)	Cotton and polyester staple	Simple spun	Oxford (pp.64–65)	Top weight
	Long staple cotton	Simple spun	Pinpoint Oxford (pp.64–65)	Top weight
	Cotton or wool staple	Simple spun	Hopsacking (p.85)	Medium to bottom weight
	Cotton or hemp/ polyester staple, nylon/polyester filament	Simple spun or simple filament	Sailcloth (pp.82–83)	Medium to bottom weight
			Duck (pp.82–83)	Medium to bottom weight
			Canvas (pp.82–83)	Bottom weight

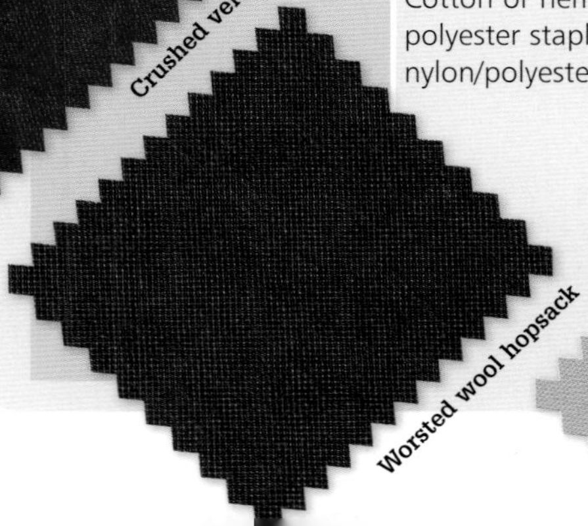

8-wale corduroy

Crushed velvet

Worsted wool hopsack

Sailcloth

Advantages	Disadvantages	Usual finishing	End use	Chapter
• Very absorbent surface • Warm • Loops on face and back sides	• Snags easily • Shrinks easily • Bulky to sew	• Softener	Towels, robes, interiors	●
• Soft, hair-like surface • Soft texture	• One-way napped surface • Bulky appearance	• Sheared/brushed	Furniture, jackets, pants, suits, skirts	● ● ●
• Imitates real fur • Great variety	• Poor abrasion resistance • Heat-sensitive	• Sheared/brushed	Furniture, jackets, coats, bedding	●
• Luxurious soft hand • Lustrous	• One-way napped surface • Cannot be pressed • Nap crushes easily	• Sheared/brushed	Dresses, tops, coats	●

Note: Elastic fabrics using complex elastic yarns can be produced in nearly all woven/knitted fabrics. Check with your fabric supplier.

Note: Faux suede can be produced in woven/knitted/massed-fiber fabrics.

Advantages	Disadvantages	Usual finishing	End use	Chapter
• Fine surface texture	• Shrinks easily	• Softener or light resin	Tailored shirts	●
• Very fine surface texture • Lustrous surface	• Wrinkles easily • Will shrink	• Softener	Tailored shirts	●
• Coarse surface texture • Very durable	• Can be uncomfortable next to skin • Shrinks easily	• Softener	Tailored jackets, suits, and slacks	●
• Very durable • UV-safe if polyester	• Will mildew if cotton • Will shrink	• Water-resistant resins	Outdoor products, light jackets, pants, footwear, accessories	●
• Very durable • UV-safe if polyester • Heavier than sailcloth	• Will mildew if cotton • Will shrink	• Water-resistant resins		●
• Very durable • UV-safe if polyester • Heavier than duck	• Will mildew if cotton • Will shrink	• Water-resistant resins		●

Chambray Oxford

Twill weave

Weave name	Usual fibers used	Usual yarns used	Fabric names	Usual fabric weight
Twill weave 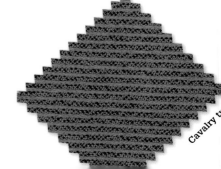	Cotton, hemp, wool, flax, bamboo, rayon	Simple spun	Twill (pp.86–93)	Top weight
	Polyester or PLA staple	Plied spun	Gabardine (p.90)	Medium weight
	Cotton staple only	Simple spun	Chino (p.91)	Medium weight
	Wool staple only	Plied spun	Serge (p.92)	Medium weight
	Cotton, hemp, PLA, flax	Simple spun	Denim (pp.86–89)	Medium to bottom weight
	Cotton or wool staple	Plied spun	Cavalry twill (p.93)	Medium to bottom weight
	Wool staple	Simple spun	Melton (pp.110–111)	Bottom weight
	Silk or polyester filament	Multifilament	Surah (p.149)	Top weight
Twill weave patterns	Staple or filament, any fiber	Variable	Herringbone (p.90)	Any weight
			Houndstooth (p.98)	Any weight
			Glen plaid (pp.62–63)	Any weight

Herringbone gabardine

Pinstriped serge

Cavalry tw

Advantages	Disadvantages	Usual finishing	End use	Chapter
• Fine diagonal surface	• Wrinkles	• Softener	Tailored shirts/blouses	●
• Very fine diagonal surface • Resilient	• Sometimes expensive • Pressing marks show	• Softener	Tailored suits, jackets, pants, coats	●
• Coarse diagonal surface • Drapable	• Pressing marks show • Not very wrinkle-resistant	• Softener • Anti-stain • Anti-wrinkle	Tailored jackets, pants, shorts, skirts	●
• Fine diagonal surface • Resilient	• Sometimes expensive	• Fulling	Tailored suits, jackets, pants	●
• Coarse diagonal surface • Abrasion-resistant	• Shrinks • Cotton dries slowly	• Resin	Tailored jackets, pants, jeans, skirts, shorts	●
• Pronounced diagonal texture	• Relatively expensive	• Resin/softener	Tailored jackets, pants	●
• Very warm • Dense	• Bulky	• Fulling	Coats	●
• Fine diagonal surface	• Wrinkles	• Softener	Ties, blouses	●
• Zigzag appearance	• Sometimes matched	• Variable	Shirts, blouses, jackets, suiting, pants, skirts	●
• Check/plaid	• Sometimes matched	• Variable	Shirts, jackets, suiting, pants, skirts	●
• Plaid	• Sometimes matched	• Variable	Shirts, jackets, suiting, pants, skirts	●

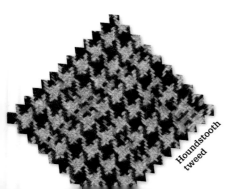
Houndstooth tweed

Satin weave

Weave name	Usual fibers used	Usual yarns used	Fabric names	Usual fabric weight
Satin weave 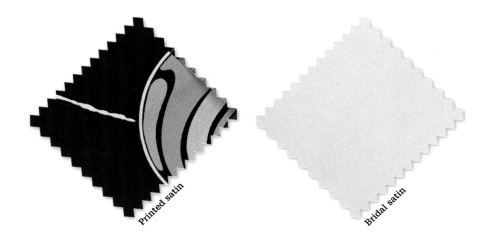	Silk, polyester, acetate, or rayon filament	Simple multifilament	Satin (pp.142–143)	Top to medium weight
		Simple multifilaments with high-twist	Charmeuse (p.142)	Top weight
		High-twist	Crêpe de Chine (pp.144–145)	Top weight
		Simple multifilament	Bridal satin (p.75)	Medium weight
	Cotton, rayon, or polyester staple	Simple spun	Sateen (p.74)	Top to medium weight

Printed satin

Bridal satin

Advantages	Disadvantages	Usual finishing	End use	Chapter
• Shiny/lustrous surface • Presses well	• Snags easily • May wrinkle	• Softener	Blouses, dresses, lingerie	●
• Shiny, lustrous • Excellent drape	• Snags easily • May move during sewing	• Softener	Blouses, dresses, lingerie	●
• Lustrous surface • Resilient	• May snag • Expensive	• Softener	Blouses, lingerie	●
• Lustrous surface • Tailors well • Crisp hand	• Expensive • Pressing marks show	• Softener	Formal dresses, suits	●
• Lustrous surface • Crisp hand	• Pressing marks show • May wrinkle	• Softener	Blouses, dresses, furniture, accessories	●

Polyester crêpe de Chine

Wet-printed sateen

Satin silk charmeuse

Weft knit (circular knitting)

Knit name	Usual fibers used	Usual yarns used	Fabric names	Usual fabric weight
Single knit 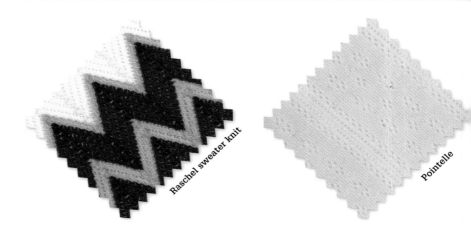	Cotton, polyester, nylon, wool, acrylic, or rayon staple	Simple spun, complex spun	Jersey (pp.150–151)	Top weight
		Simple multifilament, complex multifilament	Sweater knits (pp.154–155, 188–191)	Top, medium, and bottom weight
Single/double knit	All filament fibers and all staple fibers	Simple spun, complex spun		
Double knit	Cotton, polyester, nylon, wool, acrylic, or rayon staple		Interlock (p.152)	Top weight
		Simple spun, complex spun	Ribbed (pp.266–267)	Top and medium weight
	All filament fibers		Pointelle knits (pp.156–157)	Top weight
		Simple multifilament texturized high-twist, complex multifilament	Thermal knits (pp.168–169)	Top and medium weight
			Ponte di Roma (p.112)	Bottom weight
	Silk or polyester filament	High-twist multifilament	Matte jersey (p.153)	Top and medium weight

Wool jersey

Raschel sweater knit

Pointelle

Advantages	Disadvantages	Usual finishing	End use	Chapter
• Lightweight • Even surface • Drapey		• Softener Anti-curl	Non-tailored tops, skirts, dresses, pants	●
• Varied texture • Fine to large gauge • Wide variety • Sometimes knitted as a garment	• Snags easily • Cut edges roll • Easily distorted	• Softener	Sweaters	●
• Rigid knit • Same on face/back • Cut edges don't roll	• Snags easily • Thick fabric for weight	• Softener	Lingerie, lining, backing on bonded fabrics	●
• Elastic • Ribbed texture	• Expensive • Sometimes bulky	• Softener	Cuffs, waistbands, tops, lingerie, dresses	●
• Light, airy designs • Knitted into fabric	• Snags easily • Not easily available	• Softener	Tops, lingerie, sleepwear	●
• Deep texture (high/low) • Cut edges don't roll • Warm fabric	• Snags easily • Loses shape	• Softener	Tops, sleepwear, underwear	●
• Elastic yet rigid • Tailors well	• Expensive • Not easily available	• Softener	Pants, jackets, suits	●
• Lively, drapey • Stable and elastic	• Doesn't tailor well • Snags easily	• Softener	Dresses	●

Polyester matte jersey

Weft pile knit

Knit name	Usual fibers used	Usual yarns used	Fabric names	Usual fabric weight
Looped pile	Cotton, polyester, bamboo rayon, other rayon, or hemp staple	Simple spun, complex spun	French terry (pp.180–181)	Top and medium weight
		Multifilament, complex multifilament	Velour (pp.184–185)	Medium weight
	Silk, polyester, rayon, bamboo rayon, or other rayon filament			
Cut/sheared pile	PET polyester or polyester staple and filament, sometimes blended with acrylic	Spun or multifilament	Polar fleece (pp.182–183)	Medium to bottom weight
	Silk, polyester, rayon, bamboo rayon, or other rayon filament	Multifilament, complex multifilament	Panne velour (pp.184–185)	Medium weight
			Faux fur (pp.256–259)	Medium/heavyweight
Jacquard weft knit	Staple or filament	Variable	Variable	All

Warp knitting (high-speed)

Knit name	Usual fibers used	Usual yarns used	Fabric names	Usual fabric weight
Tricot knit	Filament	Smooth and texturized multifilament	Tricot (pp.160–161)	Top weight
			Mesh (pp.158–159)	Top weight
Raschel knit	Spandex, nylon, or polyester filament	Complex elastic yarns	Elastic power mesh (pp.284–285)	Top weight
	Silk, nylon, or polyester filament	Monofilament, multifilament	Netting (pp.228–229)	Top weight
			Point d'esprit (pp.228–229)	Top weight
			Tulle (pp.228–229)	Top weight
	Polyester staple and filament	Simple spun, multifilament	Mass-market lace (pp.164–165)	Top to medium weight

Advantages	Disadvantages	Usual finishing	End use	Chapter
• Looped surface texture • Drapey	• Loops on face only • Snags easily	• Softener	Tops, dresses, sleepwear	●
• Soft, velvety surface • Drapey	• Sheds fiber • Curls	• Sheared/brushed • Anti-curl	Tops, dresses, loungewear, sleepwear	●
• Soft, lofty textured fabric • Sheared side does not pill too easily • Can be easily recycled	• Brushed inside surface pills easily • Bulky to sew	• Sheared/brushed • Anti-pilling • Softener	Outdoor tops, jackets, jacket liners, robes, and loungewear	●
• Crushed, lustrous surface • Soft, velvety surface	• Irregular surface • Doesn't tailor well	• Sheared/brushed • Crinkled	Tops, dresses, robes, loungewear	●
• Imitates real fur • Bulky but lightweight	• Poor heat resistance	• Sheared/brushed	Coats, bedding, trimming	●
• Variable	• Snags easily	• Variable	Tops, sweaters, dresses, loungewear, sleepwear	● ●

Advantages	Disadvantages	Usual finishing	End use	Chapter
• Smooth • Inexpensive • Rigid in straight grain	• Snags easily	• Softener	Lingerie, lining, underwear, tops, athletic apparel	●
• Air holes in surface	• Snags easily • Difficult to sew	• Softener	Lingerie, lining, underwear, tops, athletic apparel	●
• Very elastic • Resilient	• Expensive • Sometimes too constricting	• Heat-set	Lingerie, underwear, straps, expander inserts	●
• Honeycomb • Easily available	• Breaks easily	• Resins/softener	Millinery, skirts, accessories	●
• Honeycomb with texture	• Breaks easily	• Resins/softener	Millinery	●
• Small holes	• Delicate	• Resins/softener	Millinery, skirts, trim, accessories	●
• Open, airy, imitation lace • Rigid in straight grain • Inexpensive	• Snags easily	• Softener	Tabletop, curtains, lingerie, tops, underwear	●

Warp pile knit

Knit name	Usual fibers used	Usual yarns used	Fabric names	Usual fabric weight
Looped pile	Cotton, polyester, bamboo rayon, other rayon, or hemp staple	Simple spun, complex spun	French terry (pp.180–181)	Medium/heavyweight
	Silk, polyester, rayon, bamboo rayon, or other rayon filament	Multifilament, complex multifilament	Velour (pp.184–185)	Medium/heavyweight
Cut/sheared pile	Silk, polyester, rayon, bamboo rayon, or other rayon filament	Multifilament, complex multifilament	Panne velour (pp.184–185)	Medium weight
			Faux fur (pp.256–259)	Medium/heavyweight

French terry

Panne velour

Faux fur

Jacquard warp knit

Knit name	Usual fibers used	Usual yarns used	Fabric names	Usual fabric weight
Jacquard warp knit	Staple and filament	Variable	Variable	All

Note: Elastic knit fabrics, using laid-in monofilament spandex yarn, or complex elastic yarn, can be produced from nearly all knitted fabrics. Check with your supplier.

Note: Faux suede can be produced in woven/knitted/massed-fiber fabrics.

Advantages	Disadvantages	Usual finishing	End use	Chapter
• Looped surface texture • Drapey	• Loops on face only • Snags easily	• Softener	Tops, dresses, sleepwear	●
• Soft, velvety surface • Drapey	• Sheds fiber • Curls	• Sheared/brushed • Anti-curl	Tops, dresses, loungewear, sleepwear	●
• Crushed, lustrous surface • Soft, velvety surface	• Irregular surface • Doesn't tailor well	• Sheared/brushed • Crinkled	Tops, dresses, robes, loungewear	●
• Imitates real fur • Bulky but lightweight	• Poor heat resistance	• Sheared/brushed	Coats, bedding, trimming	●

Advantages	Disadvantages	Usual finishing	End use	Chapter
Variable	• Snags easily	• Variable	Tops, sweaters, dresses, loungewear, sleepwear	● ●

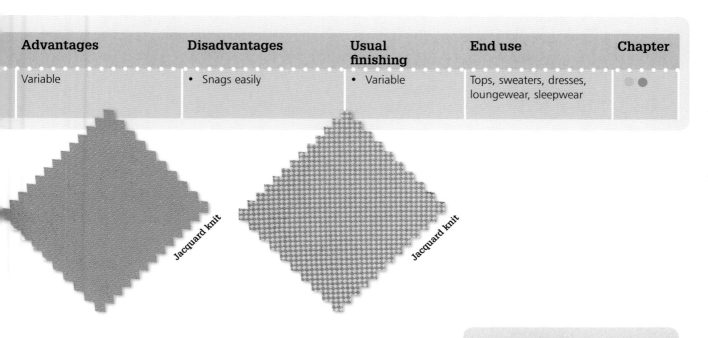

Jacquard knit

Jacquard knit

Fiber to fabric

Fiber massed into fabric	Usual fibers used	Fabrication method	Fabric names	Usual fabric weight
Massed fiber (fiber to fabric)	Wool, rayon, or polyester staple	Felted/needlepunched	Felt (pp.108–109)	Medium weight
	Microfiber or polyester staple/filament	Needlepunched	Faux suede (pp.124–125)	Bottom weight
	Polyester filament	Spunlaced or spunbonded	Interlining (pp.128–131)	Top to medium weight
	Polyester or PET staple		Fiberfill (pp.248–253)	Medium to bottom weight

Spunbonded fiber web

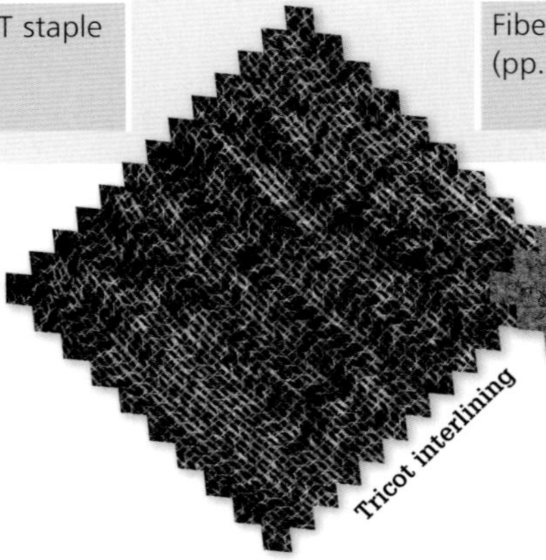

Tricot interlining

Faux suede

Lace (machine-made)

Knit name	Usual fibers used	Yarns used	Fabric names	Usual fabric weight
Bobbin	Silk, rayon filament, wool, acrylic, or cotton staple	Multifilament simple spun	Bobbin Cluny (pp.162–163)	Top to medium weight
Schiffli	Silk or rayon filament, wool staple	Multifilament simple spun	Schiffli (pp.162–163)	Top to medium weight

Note: Faux suede can be produced in woven/knitted/massed-fiber fabrics.

Advantages	Disadvantages	Usual finishing	End use	Chapter
• Moldable	• Poor strength	• Felting	Appliqués, hats, jackets, skirts	●
• Good alternative to leather suede • Strong • Tailors well	• Expensive	• Napping	Coats, jackets, suits, pants	●
• Supports garment structure • Doesn't shrink	• Poor strength • Pills	• Heat-set	Interlining	●
• Adds loft • Thermal insulation	• Difficult to sew	• Heat-set	Thermal filling/stuffing	●

Advantages	Disadvantages	Usual finishing	End use	Chapter
• Allover lace design • Imitates handmade lace	• Limited supply if silk/wool	• Preshrunk • Light resin	Appliqués, edgings, tops, dresses	●
• Embroidered effect • Opulent appearance	• Expensive • Limited supply	• Preshrunk • Light resin	Appliqués, edgings, dresses	●

Bobbin lace

Schiffli lace

Glossary

Abrasion resistance
Does not weaken when rubbed on the surface.

Absorbent
Takes in and holds moisture.

Aesthetic finish
Adding visual appeal or texture to the fabric. Examples are adding luster, brushing, or pleating the fabric surface.

Anti-microbial/bacteria
Does not allow bacteria to grow on the fiber or fabric surface.

Balanced weave
Same number and size of warp and weft yarns within a square inch/cm.

Basketweave
Interlacing of pairs of warp and weft yarns at a 90-degree angle.

Bast fiber
Fiber produced from plant (cellulose) stems. Hemp and flax are bast fibers.

Beetling
Finishing method that will soften and sometimes add luster to the fabric.

Bias grain
The diagonal direction (always at a 45-degree angle between the warp and the weft yarns) across the fabric surface. Creates stretch and drape.

Bicomponent fiber
Blending two or more fibers within a single manufactured fiber. Extruded as a single, blended filament fiber.

Bonded
Putting two fabrics together using a binding agent or heat.

Bottom of fabric
Designated location on the fabric that corresponds to the bottom of the garment.

Bottom-weight fabric
Fabric weight is approximately 9–14+ oz per square yard/meter.

Bouclé yarn
Complex plied yarn with a looped texture.

Bulk fabric production
Textile mills producing fabric for a customer's order.

Chemical (wet) finish
Involves the use of chemicals, water, and heat to apply the finish.

Chenille yarn
Complex yarn that has a cut-pile appearance.

"Closed loop"
A strategy for self-contained production and consumption; creating a means for raw materials and products to be recaptured and collected for future use.

Coated
Application of viscous material to a fabric that is later dried or cured to become a flexible layer on the fabric

Colorfastness
Ability of a colorant to remain on the fiber, yarn, fabric, or garment.

Conducts heat
Does not absorb heat, but moves heat to the surface.

Converter
Textile mill that will convert the greige fabric into dyed, printed, and finished fabric.

Count
The diameter (thickness) of a yarn.

Crocking
Color loss from rubbing action. Can be wet or dry crocking.

Cross-grain
Grain line is parallel to the weft direction or horizontal across the body. This grain line has little "give" when pulled.

Cutting waste
Material left over after the garment has been cut from the fabric.

Density
The number of yarns in warp and weft direction per square inch (cm).

Dobby weave
A combination of weaves to produce small geometric, woven-in designs.

Drape
Ability of a fiber, yarn, or fabric to be flexible and collapse.

Dye
Colorant that will chemically bond to fiber.

Dyeing
Adding color to fiber, yarn, fabric , or garments by immersing them in a dye bath solution.

Elasticity
Ability of a fiber, yarn, fabric, or garment to expand and return to its original shape.

Embossing
Adding surface indentations by applying heat and pressure.

Emissions
Airborne molecules resulting from evaporation or oxidation.

Fabric
Any two-dimensional, flexible surface that can be sewn.

Face of fabric
The outside of the fabric that will be shown in a garment.

Fiber
Small hair-like strands. May be natural or manmade.

Fiber blending
Combination of two or more different fibers in yarn or fabric.

Filament fiber
Fiber that is continuous in length, produced from a spinneret or by an animal such as a spider or silk worm.

Finishing
A process to add aesthetic appeal or function that may change the characteristics of the fiber, yarn, and/fabric or garment.

Fulling
Finishing wool fabrics by shrinking. The finished fabric will be denser and less likely to stretch out of shape.

Functional finish
Adding a new performance characteristic to a fabric, such as water resistance or wrinkle resistance.

Grain line
The orientation of the pattern pieces on the fabric that will best suit the purpose of the garment design. There are three types of grain lines: straight grain, cross-grain, and bias.

Hand
The term used to describe how a fabric feels. For example, the fabric may feel crisp, soft, or stiff.

Heat sensitive
Subject to softening, melting, or shrinking in the presence of heat.

Interlining
Also known as underlining, this type of fabric is added for reinforcement or shape retention. It is placed on the back of the face fabric before garment construction.

Interlock knit
A weft double knit that shows only knit stitches on the face and back.

Jacquard knit
Any knitted pattern—can be a curved or a geometric knitted-in design.

Jacquard weave
Combination of weaves to produce detailed, curved designs woven into the fabric.

Jersey knit
A weft single knit that uses a knit stitch construction on the fabric face and purl knit on the back side.

Jobber
Sales agency that buys small amounts of leftover or defective fabrics from manufacturers, converters, or other sources at low prices and sells locally for the benefit of small designers and manufacturers.

Knit
One or more yarns looped together to create fabric.

Laminating
Bonding (gluing) two fabrics together.

Landfill
Land set aside by cities and other agencies to dispose of garbage and unwanted items.

Leaf fiber
Fiber produced from a leaf. This is a cellulose fiber.

Lining
A separate fabric sewn on the inside of a garment to conceal all raw edges and help it to hang well.

Loft
An amount of air space between fibers creating volume.

Lustrous
Reflects light.

Manipulated fiber
Changing the shape of fiber to change its fiber characteristics.

Manufactured fiber
Fiber that does not occur in nature. Can be regenerated cellulosic fiber or oil-based (synthetic) fiber. Can become staple fiber, though all manufactured fibers are produced as filament fiber first.

Massed fiber fabric
Fabric produced directly from fiber. Fibers are bound together to create a two-dimensional surface.

Matte
Non-lustrous (reflective) surface appearance.

Mechanical (dry) finish
Applied without the use of chemicals or water.

Medium-weight fabric
Fabric that weighs approximately 4.5–8 oz per square yard/meter.

Mercerized
Chemical process applied to cotton yarn or fabric that adds luster and strength, and will improve dyeability.

Microfiber
Extremely fine fiber that does not exist in nature. Only manufactured fiber can be microfiber.

Mildew resistant
Does not allow a type of fungus to grow on fiber or fabric.

Mill waste
Unused fiber, yarn, or fabric that is left at the fiber, yarn, or textile mill.

Monofilament yarn
A single filament fiber is also a yarn. Spandex and metallic fiber are also monofilament yarns.

Multifilament yarn
Combining filament fiber into a yarn.

Nano finishing
The use of extremely small (nano) molecules to apply functional finishes.

Nap direction
The shading that occurs on brushed or cut-pile (sheared) fabrics. The nap will absorb light or reflect light, changing the color of the fabric, depending on the angle of the light.

Natural fiber
Fiber from a non-synthetic source, for example, cotton, flax, silk, or wool.

One-way pattern
A fabric design that can be shown in only one direction.

Performance
Sustained fiber, yarn, or fabric characteristics for the intended use.

Pest resistant
Ability to prevent insects from eating fiber, yarn, fabric, or garment.

PET
Description of raw material used to create low-quality polyester fiber from recycled plastic bottles.

PFD or PFP
Prepared for Dyeing or Prepared for Printing. Fabric has been scoured (cleaned) and bleached.

Piece
A roll of fabric (usually about 50 yds/meters).

Pigment
Colorant that does not chemically bond to fiber or fabric and requires a binding agent plus heat to remain.

Pile
A third dimension of depth (raised surface), usually added by inserting an additional yarn to create this dimension. Can be looped or cut.

Pleating
Arranging or creasing fabric in regular patterns to add volume and/or texture to the fabric surface or garment.

Previously worn
Clothing that has been purchased and worn by the consumer. It is ready for discarding or reuse.

Printing
Colored images applied to the fabric surface.

Progressive shrinkage
Continues to shrink.

Raschel knit
A warp knitting technique that can produce a variety of lacy, open fabric designs.

Recycling textiles or clothing
The collection of textile-related products that can be broken down to its smallest parts to produce yarn from existing fiber or for the purpose of manufacturing new fiber.

Regenerated cellulosic fiber
Manufactured fiber produced from plant-based raw materials. Examples are lyocell, rayon using bamboo, viscose rayon, PLA, and acetate.

Continued ▶

Repurposing textiles or clothing
The collection of textile-related products, either new or previously worn, that can be reused in apparel or other products.

Resiliency
Ability of a fiber, yarn, fabric, or garment to resist crushing/wrinkling.

Sales agency
A company or commercial organization that represents textile suppliers, and markets textiles to designers, manufacturers, and retailers. Includes multinational, national, and local sales companies.

Samples/sample yardage
Small fabric quantity available for immediate shipment. Textile mill produces 50–100 yds/meters as sales samples, so designers can test their designs. Designers can request small swatch samples of 3–5 yds/meters.

Satin weave
Warp yarns float randomly over five or more yarns to create a lustrous or shiny fabric. Can also have weft yarns floating over warp yarns.

Seed fiber
Fiber produced from plant seed. Cotton fiber is a seed fiber produced in the cotton boll (cellulose).

Selvage
The more densely woven edges of a fabric, parallel to the straight grain (warp) direction.

Sheared fabric
Cut pile, usually also brushed. Can be woven or knitted.

Shrinkage
Fiber, yarn, fabric, or garment is reduced in size in the presence of hot water and/or heat.

Slubbed yarn
Yarn that has irregular thicknesses within the yarn.

Sourcing
Researching to find appropriate fiber, yarn, and fabric for garment design and production.

Spinneret
Mechanism used to extrude manufactured filament fiber. Similar in concept to a shower head. Filament fiber shape can be manipulated by changing the spinneret holes.

Spun yarn
Twisting (spinning) staple fibers into yarns.

Staple fiber
Short hair-like strands approximately ½–2½ inches (1.12–6.5 cm) long.

Static buildup
Generates static electricity.

Straight grain
Grain line that is parallel to the warp yarns, or vertical on the body. This grain line is strong, with almost no "give" when pulled.

Strength
Ability of fiber, yarn, or fabric to be pulled until it breaks.

Sun (UV) resistance
Ability of fiber, yarn, fabric, or garment to resist weakening or damage when exposed to sunlight.

Sustainable textile supply chain
Continuous access to fiber, yarn, fabric, and garments for the future, without harm to the environment.

Synthetic (oil-based) fiber
Manufactured fiber produced from petroleum raw materials. Examples are nylon, polyester, spandex, olefin, and acrylic.

Textile mill
These specialize in knitting, weaving, or other types of fabric construction.

Textile supply chain
Sequence of resources used to produce fiber, yarn, fabric, and garments. This includes consuming and discarding apparel.

Textile trade show
Gathering of textile suppliers in one location to promote their fabrics and yarns to garment designers, manufacturers, and retailers.

Texturized
Adding loft to thermoplastic (heat-sensitive) fiber or yarn by application of heat, air movement, or other means.

Thermoplastic
Ability of a fiber, yarn, fabric, or garment to soften (melt) in the presence of heat.

Top of fabric
Designated location of the fabric that corresponds to the top of the garment.

Top-weight fabric
Lightweight fabrics that generally weigh about 1–3.5 oz per square yard/meter.

Tricot
A warp knit that is usually produced at high speed using simple multifilament yarns.

Tweed yarn
Spun yarn that contains flecks of color.

Twill weave
Type of weave where warp yarns float over 2–4 sets of weft yarns at regular intervals to create a diagonal texture on the fabric surface. Weft yarns can also float over warp yarns.

Virgin fiber
Fiber that has not be used in a product before.

Warp
These yarns extend between the front and the back of the loom. The warp grain line, parallel to the warp yarns, is considered the strongest, least flexible grain line.

Warp knit
Knitted fabric created in the warp (straight grain) direction. Does not use knit and purl stitches to create the fabric. Very stable in the straight grain.

Weave
The systematic interlacing of warp and weft threads at 90-degree angles.

Weft
The thread passing from side to side on the loom. Also, the threads along the width of the cloth.

Weft knit
Fabric knitted in the weft (cross grain) direction. Uses only knit and purl stitches to create the fabric. Can be hand or machine produced. Less stable in the straight grain direction than warp knits.

Weight of fabric
Lightness or heaviness of a fabric; will help determine end use.

Wicking
Ability of a fabric to move moisture away from the skin to the outer fabric surface.

Yardage
A quantity for fabric.

Yarn
Continuous strands composed of fiber, either staple or filament fiber.

Yarn mill
Produces spun yarn from staple fiber or multifilament yarns from filament fiber.

Yarn ply
A single strand of yarn. 2-ply yarn contains two plies of yarn.

Yarn twist
The spin given to a yarn to give it strength. The more twist, the stronger the yarn. Twist can also add texture to yarn.

Resources

There are many excellent books on textiles that offer detailed information on the various technical aspects of fabrics. A few are listed here to provide resources for those readers interested in further technical information. The list included here should not limit the reader to these texts, but merely provides a beginning for further investigation and study.

TECHNICAL TEXTILE BOOKS

Bowles, Melanie and Isaac, Ceri
Digital Textile Design
Lawrence King Publishing, 2009

Colussy, M. Kathleen and Greenburg, Steve
Rendering Fashion, Fabric, and Prints with Adobe Illustrator
Prentice Hall, 2007

Hencken Elsasser, Virginia
Textiles: Concepts and Principles
Fairchild Publications, Inc., 2007

Humphries, Mary
Fabric Reference
Prentice Hall, 2007

Kadolph, Sara J. and Langford, Anna L.
Textiles (tenth edition)
Prentice Hall, 2010

FABRIC SWATCH KITS

Humphries, Mary
Fabric Glossary (third edition)
Prentice Hall, 2007

Price, Arthur, Johnson, Ingrid, and Cohen, Allen C.
J.J. Pizzuto's Fabric Science
Fairchild Books, Inc., 2010

The Textile Kit: Pinnacle Edition
Atex Inc., 2010
www.thetextilekit.com

Young, Deborah
Swatch Reference Guide for Fashion Fabrics
Fairchild Books, Inc., 2011

SUSTAINING THE TEXTILE SUPPLY CHAIN

Hethorn, Janet and Ulasewicz, Connie
Sustainable Fashion: Why Now?
Fairchild Books, Inc., 2008

USEFUL WEBSITES

www.bambrotex.com
Bamboo rayon mill in China. (Note: this mill is still using the fiber name "bamboo" instead of "manufactured bamboo rayon.")

www.kenaf-fiber.com
Learn how kenaf has strong potential as a textile fiber source.

www.hemptraders.com
A source for hemp fiber fabrics.

www.naturallyadvanced.com
Learn about Crailar®, a new process that can cottonize hemp fiber quickly.

www.unifi.com
Learn about Repreve®, a fiber produced from plastic bottles, manufactured in the U.S.

www.teijinfiber.com
Learn about Teijin Fiber, Limited's new ECO CIRCLE™ Plantfiber™. A polyester fiber that is plant-based and recyclable.

www2.dupont.com/Sorona/en_US/
Learn about Sorona® triexta PTT fiber, a plant-based polyester fiber that is recyclable.

Index

Credits

Quarto would like to thank the following for supplying images for inclusion in this book:

Bextex, Limited: pp 17, 19tr, 88, 89tl and bl; Corbis: page 103; Fashion Stock: pages 62, 69, 71, 97, 103, 125, 127, 145, 147, 157, 159br, 161, 171, 173, 177, 213, 221, 223, 267, 271, 273, 279; Getty: pages 183, 247; Mark Baugh-Sasaki: page 235; Rex Features: pages 87, 207, 232, 241, 251; Science Photo Library: page 27.

All other images are the copyright of Quarto Publishing plc. While every effort has been made to credit contributors, Quarto would like to apologize should there have been any omissions or errors—and would be pleased to make the appropriate correction for future editions of the book.

Thank you to the following companies for supplying fabrics for this book:

Cloth House
www.clothhouse.com
F. Ciment (pleating) Ltd
www.cimentpleating.co.uk
MacCulloch and Wallace
www.macculloch-wallis.co.uk
The Silk Society
www.thesilksociety.com

AUTHOR'S ACKNOWLEDGMENTS
Sourcing and selecting the hundreds of fabrics photographed for this text involved the help of many individuals and suppliers. Jim Warshell, an experienced senior management executive in the apparel industry and my husband, sourced many of the fabrics. Local businesses, which continue to support the San Francisco/Bay Area fashion industry, also supplied many samples.

Babette, Inc.
Babette and Steven Pinsky
www.babettesf.com
Pleated fabrics.

Turk & Fillmore
Arsalan and Marium Usmani
www.turkandfillmore.com

In2green
www.in2green.com
Lori Slater
Recycled cotton canvas and knitted fabrics.

Paul's Hat Works, since 1918
6128 Geary Boulevard
San Francisco, CA 94121
Olivia Griffith
hatworksbypaul@com
Buckram fabric.

NI Teijin Shoji (USA), Inc.
Polyester fabrics from recycled
ECO CIRCLE ™ polyester fiber.

Sal Beressi Fabrics Company
1504 Bryant Street
San Francisco, CA 94103
Heather Kilpack
Beressi.fabric@gmail.com
Silk fabrics and trimmings.

Sports Basement
1590 Bryant Street
San Francisco, CA 94103
Jon Puver
ipulver@sportwbasement.com
Outdoor apparel.

The New Discount Fabrics
201 11th Street
San Francisco, CA 94013
Linda Blake
415-495-5337
Fabrics and trimmings.

An important source of fabrics and expertise, both for my business and in education has come from my representing NI Teijin Shoji (USA), Inc., whose parent company is based in Japan. I deeply appreciate this global sales agency's willingness to support both my business strategies and educational strategies for the benefit of the future fashion industry and the new low-CO_2 economy.

NI Teijin Shoji (USA), Inc.
ECO CIRCLE ™
www.teijinfiber.com
1412 Broadway, Suite 1100
New York, NY 10018
Mr. S. Nikko, President
Mr. K. Kondo, Deputy
General Manager
212-840-6900
Mr. Y. Hamatsu, Manager
3524 Torrance Boulevard, Suite 105
Torrance, CA 90503
310-792-5700

Japan
Mr. R. Miyatake, Marketing Manager,
Teijin Fibers Limited.
Mr. T. Sugimoto, Manager,
NI Teijin Shoji, Osaka
Thailand
Mr. C. Fujimoto, President
NI Teijin Shoji, Bangkok

Now retired:
Mr. H. Okuda, President (retired)
NI Teijin Shoji (USA), Inc.
Mr. K. Fujiyama, President (retired)
NI Teijin Shoji (USA), Inc.

OTHER PROFESSIONALS
Empire Sales Agency
Seoul, Korea
Mr. Ben Hur
empireag@kornet.net

Bextex, Limited
Beximco Industrial Park
Sarabo, Kashimpur
Gazipur, Bangladesh
Sardar Ahmed Khan
Chief Operating Officer
sardar@beximtex.com
www.bextex.net

Additional photography:
Mark Baugh-Sasaki
Industrialforest@gmail.com
www.industrialforest.com

Teaching designers about fabric in the design room is not too different to teaching in the classroom, so the transition to becoming an educator was smooth. However, academia is very different to private enterprise, so I am thankful for those who supported my work for this book.

Dr. Connie Ulasewicz, Associate Professor, Consumer Family Sciences/ Dietetics Department, Apparel Design and Merchandising, San Francisco State University, San Francisco, USA

Julie Stonehouse, Lead Instructor, Textiles.
Janice Paredes, Department Coordinator, Fashion Design.
David Orris, Department Coordinator, Merchandise Marketing and Merchandise Product Development.
All at The Fashion Institute of Design and Merchandising, San Francisco, USA.

Dr. T. Kimura, Professor
Graduate School of Advanced Fibro-Science, Kyoto Institute of Technology, Kyoto, Japan.

Dr. Youjiang Wang, Professor
School of Polymer, Textile, and Fiber Engineering, Georgia Institute of Technology, Atlanta, USA.

Dr. Margaret Rucker, Professor, Textiles and Clothing, University of California, Davis, USA

Dr. Brian George, Associate Professor, Engineering, Director of Graduate Textile Programs, School of Design and Engineering, University of Philadelphia, Philadelphia, USA. Needle-punched fiberfill web with reused shredded plastic bag.

PERSONAL ACKNOWLEDGMENTS
There were the people who supported my writing effort; each was instrumental in making this book possible.

James B Warshell, my husband, my friend, my coach and mentor, experienced in large-scale apparel design, product development, and retail. He generously donated his own wardrobe collection and made many sourcing trips to find fabric samples.

Jim Tibbs, industry colleague and good friend, experienced in large-scale knit design, product development, and retail.

Linda Sue Baugh, author, editor, and my sister, my counselor in the world of publishing.

Arsalan Usmani, Marium and their new son, former students and now colleagues.

Maria Lamb, US Olympic speed-skating athlete.

The team at Quarto, especially Lindsay Kaubi, a saint and steady hand throughout the writing and editing process and Susi Martin, who coordinated the monumental task of photographing over 800 fabric samples on the correct side and in the straight-grain direction